*From Arm's Length to Hands-On:
The Formative Years of Ontario's
Public Service, 1867–1940*

J.E. HODGETTS

From Arm's Length to Hands-On: The Formative Years of Ontario's Public Service, 1867–1940

A publication of the
Ontario Historical Studies Series
for the Government of Ontario
Published by University of Toronto Press
Toronto Buffalo London

© Her Majesty the Queen in right of the Province of Ontario 1995
Printed in Canada

ISBN 0-8020-0620-5 (cloth)
ISBN 0-8020-7581-9 (paper)

Printed on acid-free paper

Canadian Cataloguing in Publication Data

Hodgetts, J.E., 1917–
  From arm's length to hands-on

  (Ontario historical studies series)
  Includes bibliographical references and index.
  ISBN 0-8020-0620-5 (bound). ISBN 0-8020-7581-9 (pbk.)

  1. Civil service – Ontario – History. 2. Ontario –
  Politics and government – 1867–1905.* 3. Ontario –
  Politics and government – 20th century.* I. Title.
  II. Series.

  JL272.Z1H6 1995   354.713001'009   C94-932186-9

This book has been published with the assistance of funds provided
by the Government of Ontario through the Ministry of Culture,
Tourism and Recreation.

This volume is affectionately dedicated to the memory of Ruth, my constant critic and intellectual energizer throughout half a century.

Contents

The Ontario Historical Studies Series

For many years the principal theme in English-Canadian historical writing has been the emergence and the consolidation of the Canadian nation. This theme has been developed in uneasy awareness of the persistence and importance of regional interests and identities, but because of the central role of Ontario in the growth of Canada, Ontario has not been seen as a region. Almost unconsciously, historians have equated the history of the province with that of the nation and have often depicted the interests of other regions as obstacles to the unity and welfare of Canada.

The creation of the province of Ontario in 1867 was the visible embodiment of a formidable reality, the existence at the core of the new nation of a powerful if disjointed society whose traditions and characteristics differed in many respects from those of the other British North American colonies. The intervening century has not witnessed the assimilation of Ontario to the other regions in Canada; on the contrary it has become a more clearly articulated entity. Within the formal geographical and institutional framework defined so assiduously by Ontario's political leaders, an increasingly intricate web of economic and social interests has been woven and shaped by the dynamic interplay between Toronto and its hinterland. The character of this regional community has been formed in the tension between a rapid adaptation to the processes of modernization and industrialization in modern Western society and a reluctance to modify or discard traditional attitudes and values. Not surprisingly, the Ontario outlook has been, and in some measure still is, a compound of aggressiveness, conservatism, and the conviction that its values should be the model for the rest of Canada.

From the outset the objective of the Board of Trustees of the Ontario Historical Studies Series was to describe and analyse the historical development of Ontario as a distinct region within Canada. The series includes biographies of several premiers, and thematic studies on the growth of the provincial economy, educational institutions, labour, welfare, the Franco-Ontarians, the Native peoples, and the arts.

From Arm's Length to Hands-On is a detailed account of the evolution of the Ontario bureaucracy from 1867 to the Second World War. This period was characterized by slow but steady growth in the number of government departments and autonomous administrative agencies. The establishment of new departments and non-departmental bodies was indicative of the gradual expansion of the role of government in Ontario and the shift from 'arm's-length' relationships in which the central government assisted private and municipal institutions in performing certain tasks to 'hands-on' arrangements in which government provided specific services or regulated the carrying out of certain functions. The resulting growth in the public service and increase in government expenditures focused attention on the recruitment and management of the civil service and the maintenance of accountability in the use of people and the taxpayers' monies. Since the 1940s the role and the costs of government have grown enormously. These developments in turn have led to the proliferation and consolidation of departments, boards, and commissions, and have resulted in renewed efforts to keep the civil service 'civil' and to ensure that funds are expended efficiently and honestly.

J.E. Hodgetts has written a scholarly, thoughtful, and perceptive study of the formation of the administrative state in Ontario. It will be essential reading for those concerned with reshaping the role of government in Ontario and in Canada. We hope that it will encourage others to initiate further critical historical analysis of the issues involved.

The editors and the Board of Trustees are grateful to J.E. Hodgetts for undertaking this task.

Goldwin French
Peter Oliver
Jeanne Beck
J.M.S. Careless, Chairman of the Board of Trustees

Toronto
August 1993

The corporation known as the Ontario Historical Studies Series ceased to exist 31 August 1993. This volume was completed and approved for publication before 31 August 1993.

Preface

This examination of the evolution of Ontario's administrative services is essentially a sequel to my *Pioneer Public Service: An Administrative History of the United Canadas, 1841–1867*. During this period of uneasy legislative union, Upper Canada and Lower Canada were served by a system of administrative departments, largely the inspiration of Lord Sydenham, the first governor of the Province of Canada. That system had evolved so as to accommodate the peculiar dualistic nature of a province where, as Lord Durham had expressed it, two nations warred within the bosom of a single state. Thus, the dualism displayed at the political level by double-barrelled ministries and the concurrent majorities in the legislature required to sustain them was mirrored at the administrative level by dual ministerial headships and segmentation of most departments into separate branches for Canada East and Canada West. This duality even extended after 1849 to the four-year rotation of the capital between Toronto and Quebec City.

In 1867, confederation entailed a dispersal of this administrative apparatus to correspond with the allocation of jurisdictional terrain set out in the British North America Act. Since the new Dominion government was awarded the lion's share of responsibilities, much of the administrative establishment of the former Province of Canada remained in Ottawa to comprise the core of the federal bureaucracy. The five Offices prescribed for the new Province of Ontario by the BNA Act had to be organized and staffed, almost from scratch.

This study focuses on the evolution of the province's public service from its emergence in 1867 to the Second World War period. The election of the Whitney Conservative government in 1905 has been used as a dividing point. During the early period, dominated by Mowat's Liberals, the organization of Offices remained much as the BNA Act had prescribed, with the addition of modest satellite appendages. In meeting the somewhat rudimentary needs of a largely agrarian community, reliance was placed on the pre-confederation heritage of local authorities and the assistance of private clientele and charitable associations. These arrangements encouraged development of what I have termed a facilitative, arm's-length administrative mode that placed minimal demands on the minuscule staff and simple structures of the emergent public service.

The arrival of Whitney in 1905 marked the turning point for this nineteenth-century bureaucracy. Mounting pressures from New Ontario created a need to expand the agencies involved with natural resources. Growing urbanization and industrialization, accompanied by advances in technology affecting communication and transportation, all conspired to expand the province's agenda and affect the public service. The response took the form of an expansion of regulatory and hands-on administrative modes, which was reflected in the consolidation and growth of departments out of the old BNA Act Offices, the creation of new organizational satellites, the growth of staff, and the emergence of central agencies to reform, coordinate, and control in the name of efficiency and accountability. These are the main strands in the maturation of the public service during the second half of the seventy-five-year period closed by the Second World War.

The decision to conclude the story with the outbreak of the Second World War has been dictated by three considerations. First, despite the thinly scattered nature of the evidence and the surprising absence of the general inquiries into the state of the public services which enriched the examination of the pre-Confederation period, enough material surfaced to create problems of time and space, were justice to be done the more contemporary period. Secondly, for the post–Second World War period there is considerably more published information available in reports of comprehensive inquiries into the public service and in the scholarly contributions to the literature of public administration in general.

Finally, closing the story at the outbreak of the Second World War makes a logical cut-off point. The full maturation and modernization of Ontario's bureacracy largely took place during what K.J. Rea describes as 'The Prosperous Years,' from 1939 to 1975. While this study describes the formative period of Ontario's public service, many of the developments on the administrative front foreshadowed problems of organization, staffing, control, and management which were to become ever more recalcitrant after the Second World War as the number of civil servants grew precipitously and their organizational habitats multiplied and assumed ever more varied and complex structural forms. These post-war developments must be left for a separate study on their own. The Epilogue of this study will carry the story forward only with the broadest of brush strokes, in order to reveal how past trends and practices have been perpetuated or distorted as they have been projected into the present.

I am grateful to the Editors and the Board of the Ontario Historical Studies Series for practical support, encouragement, critical assessment, and (considering the length of time this manuscript has been in progress) a patience which passeth understanding. All but the author are absolved from responsibility for interpretations and errors of omission or commission.

From Arm's Length to Hands-On:
The Formative Years of
Ontario's Public Service, 1867-1940

Prologue: A Government Reborn

On the stroke of midnight, Monday, 1 July 1867, the bells of St James Cathedral in Toronto rang in the first day for the new Province of Ontario in the new Dominion of Canada. As befitted the return of the seat of government to Toronto after so long an absence, city council had laid elaborate plans and allocated the munificent sum of one thousand dollars to commemorate the occasion. Ironically, for this national celebration the fireworks required had to be purchased in Buffalo, where the city clerk apparently found the pickings slim because places like Hamilton, Montreal, and London had been shopping before him.[1]

With the church bells still resounding at 4 a.m., a detachment of the 10th Royals hoisted the Union Jack on a new flag-pole at the Drill Shed and a salute of twenty-one guns ensured that the rest of the city would be up and about to join in the celebrations that were to stretch out to late evening. At 6 a.m. Captain Woodhouse of the barque *Lord Nelson* began to roast an immense ox at the foot of Church Street for subsequent distribution to the poor. In the lecture room of the Mechanics' Institute at 9:30 a.m. an interdenominational service to bless the new Dominion was held. In the gathering heat of a clear summer day the citizenry flocked, many by street railway, to the government grounds west of Spadina Avenue where sundry voluntary brigades and the militia greeted the arrival of Major-General Henry William Stisted, C.B. (rumoured to be the first lieutenant-governor) with a *feu de joie* from the infantry and a royal salute from the artillery, followed by mock skirmishes and manoeuvres. At noon the troops were entertained at the nearby residence of their colonel-in-chief, C.S. Gzowski, while the onlookers enjoyed a picnic and festival on the grounds. For others, there were boat excursions to Lewiston, Niagara Falls, Buffalo, and, closer to hand, the Toronto Islands. Under the auspices of the Horticultural Society, the Queen's Park was the site for an evening of dancing under the romantic light of Chinese lanterns and a dazzling display of fireworks. The special effects created by gaslit illumination of the Post Office, the Gas House, and other public buildings were particularly noteworthy. Not to be outdone, the town of Yorkville to the north had its triumphal arches across Bloor Street and at the Yonge Street toll-gate, as well as its own fireworks and illuminated town hall.

As the citizens of Ontario, exhausted and euphoric after the celebrations, repaired to their beds, few would have been giving thought to the need to put in place the governing instruments for the new province. For those few, the requirements laid down by the terms of union in the British North America Act must have weighed heavily. To begin with, not one of the basic elements of provincial government there envisaged – a lieutenant-governor, an Executive Council, and a Legislative Assembly – were in place. Even the modest bureaucratic underpinnings would have to be created *de novo* or else disentangled from the new Dominion's public service and transferred back from Ottawa – to which they had only been sent two years before, with the decision to make that city the capital for the former Province of Canada. One can surmise that both politicians and civil servants must have become inured to the upheavals created by a peripatetic government that since 1848 had rotated between Quebec City and Toronto. It had time to come only briefly to rest in Ottawa before the enlarged federation precipitated a more far-reaching but, in the end, more stable dispensation.[2]

The first move to make good the deficiencies in the new province's governing apparatus came on 8 July when Major-General Stisted was installed as temporary lieutenant-governor. So hastily was this arranged that the *Globe* was able to convey the news only the very morning the ceremony was to take place. Ontarians, hoping to put on a more impressive show than had reportedly occurred on July 1 in Ottawa to inaugurate the new governor general of the Dominion, had arranged a champagne luncheon to follow the colourful swearing-in ceremony. Alas, when the caterer presented himself and his culinary contributions at the door of Osgoode Hall, functionaries turned him away, claiming no knowledge of the event and insisting, in any case, that there was no suitable accommodation. The presiding judges, who had lamented the lack of appropriately festive arrangements at the Ottawa ceremony, were obliged (as the *Globe* reported) 'to take comfort in their dignity instead of champagne and all dispersed in good humour.'

This contretemps surrounding the effort to put in place the first formal element of the provincial government was occasioned by the need for hasty improvisation and set the tone for the subsequent measures taken to install the remaining, outstanding mechanisms of government. After many rumours involving the alleged machinations of Sir John A. Macdonald, on 11 July the new lieutenant-governor charged the Honourable Sandfield Macdonald with the task of assembling an Executive Council. Lacking a legislature and a popular electoral vote to indicate what the political complexion of his cabinet should be, Sandfield Macdonald was to spend the next eleven days cobbling together what the Reformers scornfully characterized as a 'combination cabinet,' made up of Tories and 'renegade' Reformers.

The BNA Act had enumerated five officers who were to compose the Executive Council. Macdonald's problem was not the limitation imposed by the number but the fact that he encountered great difficulty in finding colleagues to fill even this modest roster. Not until 22 July did Macdonald complete his task: apart from himself as premier and attorney general, he was joined by Stephen Richards as commissioner of crown lands; John Carling, the brewer and only non-lawyer of the group, as commissioner of agriculture and public works; M.C. Cameron as provincial secretary; and E.B. Wood as provincial treasurer. So ill-assorted were the members of this team that the *Globe* of that day sourly editorialized: 'It is fortunate that the Government buildings on Front Street are surrounded by a considerable piece of ground, else the neighbours might be disturbed by the deliberations of Council.'

In the event, the *Globe's* gloomy forecast had little opportunity to be fulfilled because the next two months were spent on the election trail rectifying the third deficiency in the reconstitution of the province's governing machinery – an elected Legislative Assembly. Both the new Dominion and Ontario faced the same constitutional requirement to establish and convene legislatures by the end of 1867. The complication was that until 1872 it was possible to stand for election and hold seats simultaneously in both legislatures. The electoral campaign extended through August and September, and the first Dominion parliament was not convened until 6 November. Three of Ontario's Executive Council – Macdonald, Wood, and Carling – won seats in the Dominion parliament. While far from measuring up to the performance of their Quebec counterparts – where all six members of the Executive Council won federal seats – the attendance of the Ontario cabinet members in Ottawa exacerbated the problem of meeting the constitutionally imposed deadline for convening the provincial legislature before the year was out. Thus, the belated summoning of the Dominion House compelled Ontario to countermand no less than three proclamations setting the date for convening the Assembly, finally getting in just under the deadline with the date of Friday, 27 December.[3]

However inconvenient the timing, the postponement enabled the firm of Jacques and Hay to refurbish the Government Buildings on Front Street to the point that at least the chamber was readied for the occasion even if 'the departmental offices [still wore] a demoralized appearance.'[4] Given the hard wear to which these buildings had been subjected since their occupation by the legislature and government of Upper Canada between 1832 and 1841, the contractors faced and, as the years wore on, continued to face a losing battle in seeking to maintain, let alone upgrade, the accommodation. Used variously as the site of the Court of Queen's Bench in 1839, for university and medical purposes in 1846, and as an asylum for the insane between 1848 and 1849, they once again served the needs of government during the four-year periods of rotation between Quebec City and Toronto. In the off years the buildings were used as military barracks. Despite the depredations perpetrated by such diverse users and despite their early characterization as 'a mark of the bad taste of Little York' and the perennial complaint about accommodation so ill-suited to the stature of Canada's 'premier province,' politicians and public servants continued to put up with the fire risks, the inconvenience of stove-heated rooms, gas and oil illumination, and dreadful ventilation until the new Parliament Buildings at Queen's Park became available in 1892–3.[5]

It was in this setting that the minuscule group of civil servants who were to provide the administrative support for the five executive Offices took up their duties. By the end of 1867 the staff at headquarters or, as it was then expressed, at the Seat of Government, inclusive of messengers, office keepers, and firemen, numbered just under fifty. Three of the Offices had to be organized from the ground up because their counterparts remained in Ottawa to form the core of the new federal bureaucracy. Thus, the Offices of the Attorney General, the Provincial Secretary, and the Provincial Treasurer started from scratch, staffed with one or two clerks whose appointments began for the most part on 1 October. The Office of the Commissioner of Agriculture and Public Works was even slower off the ground, its most distinguished senior official, Kivas Tully, only being transferred from the Dominion payroll in mid-1868, to become chief architect. On the agricultural side, for a number of years to come, a lone secretary was able to handle the province's limited involvement with its most important primary industry, while responsibility for immigration matters (shared with the Dominion) required a similarly modest staff at headquarters.

The Office of Commissioner of Crown Lands was not only the largest but was also the first to be installed in the Government Buildings. The transfer from Ottawa was accomplished quite smoothly because of the pre-confederation practice of organizing the major operating departments in separate units for Upper Canada and Lower Canada (Canada West and Canada East). Thus, it was possible to lift virtually the entire Upper Canada component of Crown Lands, both personnel and papers, and transfer it from Ottawa to Toronto.[6] Many of the members had been so long employed in the Upper Canada divisions of the pre-confederation service that, once back in Toronto, they found themselves in familiar surroundings. 'In that mouldering old pile,' one observer in the 1880s remarked, 'whose decayed timbers make it the merest fire trap, [wherein] are stored not only the valuable library of the Ontario Legislature ... but all the title deeds of lands held from the Government in the Province of Ontario.'[7]

Into this fire trap the records of the Crown Lands Department came from Ottawa in early August, followed later in the month by the first contingent of staff. By mid-October the Woods and Forests Branch and Accountant's Branch arrived to swell the staff to some thirty-five members. However, even though Commissioner Stephen Richards, unlike his colleagues, was reportedly at his office daily transacting routine business, the Office's main responsibility for handling land sales had to be held in suspension until the provincial legislature could meet and come to grips with the high-priority issue of policies for land settlement.[8]

Looking back at this headquarters' bureaucracy, and observing how surprisingly long this administrative dispensation endured, one might readily endorse Sir John A. Macdonald's view of the provinces as glorified municipalities. Such a conclusion, however, is justified only if one assumes that the five named Offices and their personnel embraced the sum total of the province's responsibilities. In fact, there were no less than four major areas of activity assigned by the BNA Act to the province for whose administration the act was silent.

To begin with, education found no place in the departmental roster; yet section 93 of the act placed it squarely on the shoulders of the provinces. Moreover, long before confederation, under Egerton Ryerson, the province had been in the forefront of providing elementary education for its youth. The Education Office had been set up and administered quite independently of its Lower Canada counterpart, never having been transferred to Ottawa but remaining in its own building in Toronto under Ryerson and a Council of Public Instruction. Thus, unlike Crown Lands, where the transfer to provincial hands necessitated a wholesale upheaval, the transfer created scarcely a ripple for the Education Office. Indeed, now Ryerson no longer had to travel to Ottawa to make his annual report.[9] Education had to wait until 1876 for its major shakedown and its formal inclusion as a ministerial portfolio alongside the 'Founding Five.'

In addition to education, there were three other areas of responsibility assigned to the province under section 92 of the BNA Act. The first of these derived from subsections 6 and 7 of section 92: the establishment, maintenance, and management of public and reformatory prisons; and hospitals, asylums, charities, and eleemosynary institutions. The original designated portfolios gave no recognition to this area of responsibility. Yet from the outset, under the general heading of 'Public Institutions,' close to one-fifth of the province's expenditures was devoted to an extraordinary variety of hospitals, asylums, gaols, reformatories, orphanages, homes for the aged, and schools for the deaf, the dumb and the blind.[10] J.W. Langmuir, appointed inspector of public institutions in 1868, reported to the lieutenant-governor on his single-handed administration of matters affecting the human condition in the province. In due course, his one-man inspectorate was to demand the attention of thousands of civil servants employed by departments responsible for custodial and correctional services, social welfare, and public health.

The second area that loomed large on the list of provincial responsibilities but initially appeared to have no corresponding administrative sponsor was that of municipal institutions (section 92, subsection 8). The well-entrenched tradition of local self-government, dating back to the Baldwin Act of 1849 as applied to Upper Canada, would explain this apparent administrative oversight. The provincial headquarters could remain as small as it was only because of this heritage of organized local governing bodies with their own array of local officials.

While the Office of Provincial Secretary maintained from the outset a loose surveillance that involved the collection and collation of statistical reports from the municipalities, the province did not come to exercise the significant powers vested in it as the 'senior' government through any of these original Offices. Beginning in 1906, it would be two non-departmental agencies, Ontario Hydro and the Ontario Municipal Board, that would carry the banner of provincial centralization.

The third major provincial responsibility appeared in section 92, subsection 14, the administration of justice – 'the Constitution, Maintenance and Organization of Provincial Courts both of Civil and of Criminal Jurisdiction, and including Procedure in Civil Matters in those Courts.' Apart from the actual appointment and payment of the judges of the superior, district, and county courts, which by sections 96 and 100 of the BNA Act was a responsibility of the Dominion government, the whole financial burden of court administration fell on the provinces. Rather like municipal institutions, the judicial administrative apparatus was well entrenched in the province with a strong tradition of self-regulation. Indeed, a number of municipal affairs – especially in 'unorganised territories' – were conducted by officials who, in effect, comprised the dispersed agents of the judicial branch: sheriffs, magistrates, peace officers (i.e., police), and sundry local court officers and registrars.

The Office of Attorney General was primarily responsible for directing and supervising the adminstration of justice. Because of the connection between the administration of local and judicial affairs, the attorney general tended to be at the centre of a significant appointments pool. During the long period of Liberal dominance, the Conservative opposition constantly complained that municipal authority was being undermined by the centralist thrust of the provincial government. In reality what really perturbed the Conservatives was that with each diminution of municipal powers the provincial government's (i.e., Liberals') share of patronage appointments was increased.

In summary, the administrative infrastructure required in 1867 to support the responsibilities imposed by the new constitution on the province was, at the outset, modest, not to say rudimentary. During the first twenty-five years, the ability of the original five Offices to absorb any new responsibilities postponed the need to expand the departmental system. However, the apparent adequacy of that system was deceptive. Contributing to the perception of a lean provincial bureaucracy was the practice of listing as public servants only those employed at the seat of government. If one were to include, for example, the salaried employees in the public institutions, the land agents and surveyors in Crown Lands, the lock-keepers and superintendents of works in Public Works, and provincially appointed officials concerned with the administration of justice, the four dozen or so officials initially employed in the five original Offices swell to something like four hundred.[11]

Yet another reason for the seemingly modest size of the bureaucracy is to be found in the practice – particularly noticeable in the field of agriculture – of relying on the various publicly funded but private societies and associations to perform essentially public tasks.

Finally, making a scarcely perceptible mark on the formal administrative machinery of the province were the two responsibilities for municipal affairs and the administration of justice. Both these areas would gradually register within the provincial bureaucracy as the process of coordination, regulation, and outright assumption of an operating role inexorably supplanted the traditions of local self-government. Similarly, the advent of administrative tribunals began at the outset of the twentieth century to contest the claims of the judiciary to monopolize the determination of rights.

How has the tiny public service incorporated within the five constitutionally ordained Offices multiplied its departmental components five times over and its roster of civil servants grown from a few hundreds to tens of thousands today? How does one account for the proliferation outside the growing departmental system of a myriad boards, commissions, and crown corporations – a complex, fragmented army of administrative camp-followers whose creation is an inseparable part of the story of the province's emergent public service? These are among the questions to be addressed in the pages that follow.

It is a story that must be told against a backdrop of changing societal and economic conditions that have effected alterations in the expectations and needs of citizens towards their government. Technological innovations, especially in the fields of communication and transportation, also profoundly altered the character of a parochial, agrarian community and brought with them not only fresh public demands – as in the fields of public health and safety – but also created new administrative challenges for a public service geared to simpler times.

Fortunately, the same technological innovations that laid new burdens on the state also made available to the public service improved means of coping with them. The overall administrative response to such challenges from a changing environment is characterized here as a gradual maturation process in which the role of government shifts from a facilitative, arm's-length relationship to a direct hands-on involvement.

The consequences for the public service are readily apparent in the emergence of a complex set of institutions, manned by such a formidable work force, that the province's administrative history must also incorporate the search for solutions to problems of securing and maintaining an efficient and effective administrative establishment. And finally, since much power over the lives of citizens has accrued to non-elected administrative officials, it becomes necessary to trace a vital thread in its history: the extent to which the democratically elected representatives of the people have succeeded in preserving control over their appointed servants.

1

To Know Thyself: Early Ontario's Administrative Needs

The exhortation 'physician heal thyself,' when applied to the governance of a community, requires the application of yet another axiom: first 'know thyself.' Amongst those responsible for operating the governmental institutions in the newly minted province of Ontario, one finds widespread acknowledgment of the validity of these ancient adages: before public policy is made and administrative means established, one must discover the facts of the situation. Some of the earliest measures to reach the statute books of both the new Dominion and the province was legislation to provide for commissions of inquiry to be initiated by the executive branch of government.[1] Should the executive fail to respond, the Legislative Assembly was always prepared to create committees of its own.

Despite the brevity of the legislative session (or perhaps because of it), these fact-gathering probes, no matter who the sponsor, were undertaken with remarkable competence. Even the most sophisticated of today's social researchers would have to be impressed with the systematic way in which subject-matter was subdivided among the members of the investigative body, questionnaires formulated, respondents selected, returns compiled, witnesses heard, and orderly conclusions and recommendations expeditiously made.

Far from accumulating dust in the archives – as cynical comment on similar fact-gathering exercises would have it – the reports of these early commissions and legislative committees invariably resulted in governmental responses that included provision for the administrative arrangements for implementing the proposed policy. The collaboration between the executive and the legislature that characterized many of these fact-finding ventures (perhaps attributable to the rather undisciplined state of the party system) undoubtedly accounts for the surprisingly high rate of acceptance of these reports. Moreover, the facts, when they came to be known, spoke so clearly to the needs which had to be addressed that the proposed administrative means emerged as virtually unavoidable conclusions.

This early insistence on knowing one's situation before taking action serves to remind us to be wary of passing judgment on the basis of the superior knowledge that hindsight brings. What follows endeavours to heed this warning by seeking to describe Ontario's early social and economic situation as contemporaries would have viewed it with the information assembled and available to them at the time, rather than through the enriched information base that recent scholarship has produced.[2]

Reliance on Local Government

In 1867, and for a good many years thereafter, the province which the fact-gatherers were to probe occupied only about one-half the terrain it was ultimately to bring within its borders. Not until 1912, when its northeastern border with Quebec was finally determined, did Ontario confirm its full metes and bounds.[3] This settlement, along with earlier ones involving Manitoba and Quebec, only began to impinge on public policy makers around the turn of the century as glowing expectations of the resources from 'New Ontario' began to surface, calling for fresh administrative initiatives from the province. At confederation, however, even the northern reaches of a geographically more constricted province were viewed as 'unorganised districts,' lacking the infrastructure of local governments in the southern and southwestern areas where the bulk of the population of some million and a half congregated.[4] There, a well-rooted system of local authorities continued after confederation to provide the rudimentary services of policing, protection, and regulation which the embryonic administrative apparatus of the province was not yet equipped to provide.[5]

This pre-confederation heritage was reaffirmed by the province in a large municipal act that grew bulkier as advantage was taken of the authority conferred by the BNA Act to make laws in relation to municipal institutions. However, less than a decade after confederation, the evidence produced by successive fact-gathering exercises led to the creation of provincial agencies that were to oversee, regulate, or even supplant the local authorities. Despite the often bitter resistance of the opposition in the Assembly, which viewed these developments as invasions of local autonomy, the trend towards centralization advanced inexorably to become a constant feature of the province's administrative landscape.[6]

Within the thirty-five counties, 394 townships, and 104 cities, towns, and villages that made up the municipal system in 1867, approximately three out of every four persons were designated rural dwellers.[7] Even this proportion of urban residents is exaggerated because of the practice of generously upgrading villages to the status of towns. Not only was Ontario overwhelmingly rural, it was also a province of small communities. Of the ten designated cities, Toronto's residents accounted for one-third of the total of city dwellers – and yet its population was under sixty thousand.

It is clear from these figures that the demands placed on municipal services were relatively limited. The primary burden of provincial liaison with the municipal authorities was assumed in 1872 by the Office of Provincial Secretary and Registrar when it took over from the Dominion's auditor general the task of collecting and compiling municipal statistics. In subsequent years this fixation on fact-gathering led to the creation of separate Bureaus of Industries, of Mines, and of Labour. Such statistical over-kill produced extensive duplication which lingered well into the twentieth century. The Provincial Treasurer's Office was also involved with the municipalities through its handling of the Municipal Loan Fund and the issuance of drainage debentures. In addition, the attorney general's overall responsibility for law and order brought that Office into contact with municipal officials – a contact that was to generate considerable friction in the 1880s and 1890s as licensing and regulatory regimes were tightened and centralized.

Transportation and Communication

In an age before the telephone and the automobile, the new province's responsibility for communication and transportation linkages between small, scattered, communities was limited. The loans made to local companies to build railways were as unrewarding for the province as for the localities that competed so assiduously for the presumed privilege of having their own lines, only to see them suffer frequent failure and bankruptcy.

As for the roads, the province had not yet got back to the business of road-building. This enterprise had been turned over to the local authorities as far back as 1835 and left to the tender mercies of private or municipally sponsored toll companies.[8] Not until the arrival of the automobile and the Good Roads Association in the 1890s was the province to set out on a course that started with an instructor in road making in 1896 and led to a full-blown Department of Highways in 1915.

Ontario's involvement in road-making at first was confined to the elaboration of a colonization roads program that it inherited from its pre-confederation days.[9] This program lavished large sums, scattered widely in small amounts, on an extremely inefficient system of providing transportation linkages, especially for the outlying regions of the province. As attention came to be focused on New Ontario, the program continued to operate there, despite the growing presence of a Highways Branch in Public Works. The fact was that the patronage value of this form of road-building enabled local members of the Assembly to control the dispensation of scattered sums to 'politically deserving' areas and often to enjoy some of the proceeds themselves as purveyors of supplies.[10] In consequence, not much thought was given to mileage constructed for dollars spent, nor for the quality of the work performed by unskilled workers.

With transportation by water the story was different. In pre-confederation times, the Province of Canada had assumed responsibility for the construction and maintenance of canals, locks, bridges, and dams. While the key water route comprising the equivalent of today's St Lawrence Seaway became the responsibility of the new Dominion, Ontario was left with the maintenance and extension of a more localized network as essential to the lumber interests as to the travelling needs of the local populace. Such works constituted half the mandate of the province's commissioner of public works, the other half being the construction and upkeep of the public buildings turned over to the province at confederation and subsequent additions in the form of gaols, asylums, and schools for the blind and the deaf. By the early 1890s the 95 public buildings coming within the commissioner's fold just after confederation had increased to 348 – the most prominent being the new Parliament Buildings at Queen's Park, started in 1887 and occupied in 1892–3.[11]

Immigration

The population of one and a half million showed little of the ethnic mix that has characterized more recent immigration into the province. An historical reliance on the 'old country,' aimed at securing female domestics and male farm labourers, was the orientation of immigration policy.[12] By the terms of the BNA Act, immigration was a matter of shared jurisdiction with the Dominion. Possibly because agriculture was bracketed with immigration in section 95 of the act, the commissioner of agriculture and public works assumed oversight of the province's share of the responsibility. It was to be a troubled partnership, with as many ups and downs in the relationship as there were in the annual intake of immigrants. An agreement reached in 1874 effectively placed the province's recruiting agents abroad under Dominion supervision, while at home some of the half-dozen agents responsible for forwarding immigrants to their final destinations were on the payroll of both governments. A large portion of the not inconsiderable sums spent by the province was devoted to covering the costs of transportation and support of the newcomers once in Canada. Always an irregular business, the early flow of new arrivals peaked at twenty-seven thousand in 1883 and thereafter declined steadily to a low of about four thousand towards the end of the century.

Welfare

A special category of 'juvenile immigrant,' the particular concern of such religious and charitable organizations as Dr Bernardo's Homes, also experienced its largest intakes in the 1870s and 1880s. In 1888 the arrival of over seventeen hundred children represented a high point which, by century's end, had dropped to about one-third of this number. The perceived need to create a special provincial office, the Superintendent of Neglected and Dependent Children, was in part attributable to the accumulated number of such arrivals and their subsequent problems of adjustment. However, the juvenile immigrant was but one element in the growing constituency of the superintendent as the province faced the advancing tide of industrialization and urbanization in the latter years of the nineteenth century. As with so many other problems, the welfare of children now began to fall beyond the administrative competence and the financial resources of the municipalities themselves, let alone the capabilities of the private charitable organizations which had long been looked to as the necessary and sufficient providers of services. Even so, as the evolution of the Superintendent's Office was to reveal, the tradition of relying on the private sector was perpetuated in the peculiar mixture of private and governmental commitment that still finds expression in the Children's Aid Society.

Whenever the province confronted welfare problems such as those affecting the aged, the infirm of mind and body, the orphaned child, or the deserted mother, the resources of a host of voluntary, charitable organizations could be relied on to undertake the lion's share of responsibility. Judging from the size of the church-going population, there was a deep well-spring of religious sentiment upon which this effort could draw. In over four thousand churches, splintered into a bewildering variety of sectarian groups, the four major denominations – Methodist, Presbyterian, Church of England, and Roman Catholic, each claiming more than one-third of a million adherents – preached and practised a doctrine of social outreach that supported a great network of charitable causes and institutions.[13]

Perhaps more importantly, the churches generated an ethos of solid Christian virtues that one finds permeating the rhetoric and motivating the prime movers and administrators of the day. The whole educational system, both in the common schools under that 'Pope of Protestantism,' Egerton Ryerson and up to the church-sponsored institutions of higher learning, was imbued with the principle of instilling Christian values and attitudes. The reports of such officials as the principal of the School for the Deaf, the superintendent of the Toronto Asylum, the inspector of prisons and charities, the superintendent of neglected and dependent children, even the factory inspectors, impress one with the sincerity with which they regularly and prayerfully invoke the name of the deity to forward their respective causes. In their attitudes and behaviour these officials reflected and, indeed, contributed to the creation of a public opinion receptive to the ultimate extension of direct state-run services to supplement and, in more recent times, supplant private action.

The well-entrenched religious institutions and beliefs provided the mainstay for an early welfare safety net and yet still left room for direct administrative involvement of the province. The extent of this involvement in monetary terms – even if it did not register at the time in the large bureaucracy that has become a feature of welfare administration in Ontario today – compels a rethinking of our conceptions of the Victorian laissez-faire state. The reports of J.W. Langmuir, the inspector of public institutions, embraced the province's welfare responsibilities for the first decade and a half after confederation. These, together with the reports of other provincial agents, provide a rather different perspective that helps to explain why such a large portion of the provincial budget was committed to supporting not only the public institutional infrastructure but the private charitable organizations dedicated to the provision of social welfare services.

Education

Another feature of the province's population also required an early administrative response: it was extremely youthful, the average age being just over twenty-three years. Although not unique in this respect (the overall average for the new Dominion was about the same) almost from the moment Lord Sydenham had come to preside over the united Province of Canada in 1841, provision of education for the young had been given high priority. From 1844 onward, promoted with religious zeal by Egerton Ryerson, the superintendent of schools for Upper Canada, the way had been paved for the introduction (in accordance with Christian principles) of free public instruction in 1871. Following confederation, Ryerson continued to preside over his creation for eight more years, having to contend with a student population of over 425,000. His claim of universality for the system stands up quite well when compared with the population of potential school attenders – aged from five to sixteen – listed at the time as 464,000.

In 1871 there were already over one hundred high schools, even though they were a very recent addition to the public schools then numbering over 4,300, and the separate schools, numbering more than 160. This impressive school complex was staffed by over three thousand teachers, males slightly outnumbering females in the early years. Administered by local school boards that also hired their own teachers, the system was extraordinarily dependent on the province's Education Office.[14]

More than financial support, however, was involved in the province's commitment to education. The creation, maintenance, staffing, and supervision of teacher-training institutions – the normal schools – were direct operating responsibilities of the province, as was the slowly expanding corps of school inspectors. In addition, a depository, which became a focus of much criticism for its alleged monopoly over the selection and provision of school textbooks, was another important unit in Ryerson's headquarters. Central control over the curriculum emerged as a consequence of financial dependency, the imposed standardization of teacher training, prescribed texts, and provincial school inspectors. In short, the provincial government's response to the educational needs of its youthful population simply perpetuated the direct hands-on approach that had characterized the pre-confederation system. Thereafter, in administrative terms, the most significant change was the placement of education under the direction of a responsible minister of the crown to whom the permanent head who replaced Ryerson would now report, rather than, as during Ryerson's regime, rendering account to a non-elective Council of Public Instruction.

Superior education was provided by church-supported colleges – Victoria, St Michael's, Trinity, Regiopolis, and Queen's, and by University College in the University of Toronto. The province's commitment was confined to modest grants to the former, which were terminated in 1868. Within a few years after confederation, the Agricultural College at Guelph and a Technical College in Toronto (later to become the School of Practical Science in the University of Toronto) were much more under the direct control of the province, and subjected to public scrutiny by such bodies as the Assembly's Public Accounts Committee.

Agriculture

Reference to the early creation of an agricultural college is a reminder that for such a predominantly rural population agriculture was the major occupation, with heavy emphasis on field crops of oats, wheat, and barley. Most of the secondary manufacturing establishments were engaged in activities supporting the basic industry: agricultural implement works, brick and tile yards, carriage and wagon shops, flour and grist mills, foundries and machine works, saw mills, tanneries, and woollen factories. These enterprises were mostly small, reflecting their parochial base and local market orientation. As late as 1883, for example, incomplete returns from some 5,800 establishments, polled for the first report of the newly created Bureau of Industries, showed that the vast proportion employed fewer than twenty-five persons, while only a handful employed three hundred or more workers.[15]

That this agrarian, localized economy was far from an Arcadian utopia was soon demonstrated by one of those grand fact-gathering expeditions to which earlier reference has been made. Ten years after confederation, the commissioner of agriculture, S.C. Wood, reported that 'Ontario land is being indifferently farmed and even gradually exhausted. Ontario stock is not well developed or cared for. The statistics on the value of farm land and farm buildings are unreliable.' This last criticism is surprising coming as it did from the minister in charge of a department whose sole preoccupation at that time was to collect, compile, and disseminate the data assembled by grant-supported agricultural societies and various associations representing special interests in livestock, dairying, and the like. Nonetheless, Commissioner Wood was moved to recommend the creation of a royal commission whose task it would be to compensate for the deficiencies in data and, from the facts acquired, to come up with proposals for more extensive governmental involvement in this major area of life and livelihood for Ontario's citizens.[16]

Wood's recommendation was acted upon and he himself became chairman of the Ontario Agricultural Commission whose 1881 report is a veritable Domesday Book for the province. The eighteen-member commission was divided into seven subject-matter teams, assignments being made in accordance with the interests and expertise of the members. While essentially performing fact-gathering, the commission also argued for 'an enlargement of the powers and functions of the Bureau [of Agriculture and Arts] ... in order that a more active supervision should be exercised over the application of the public money voted for the encouragement and advancement of agriculture.' As a corollary, the commission recommended that 'the Department of Agriculture should be more clearly identified with the great agricultural interests of the Province than, with its present limited machinery [for years, one secretary!] is possible.'[17]

The immediate administrative response to the commission's recommendations was the creation in 1882 of a Bureau of Industries as a central statistics agency largely devoted, despite its title, to the compilation and dissemination of agricultural statistics. For several years the bureau really *was* the Department of Agriculture.

For a full generation after confederation, fact-gathering remained at the centre of the province's involvement with agriculture. In this respect, the situation had changed little since the 1830s when governments began to make grants to agricultural associations with a view to assisting them in holding fairs, offering prizes and, generally, supporting the dissemination of farming information. The emphasis on education extended beyond matters purely agricultural, as the title Bureau of Agriculture and Arts testified. Under the bureau, Mechanics' Institutes were created to provide adult education programs. To be entitled to receive a provincial grant, all of these bodies had to comply with statutorily imposed organizational and reporting requirements that seem to be extraordinarily demanding. The explanation is to be found in the fact that the annual reports required of all these organizations were treated as if they were formal government documents and, indeed, served for many years in place of a report from the commissioner of agriculture.

This approach to the administration of agricultural affairs will be characterized as *enabling*: provincial support to private interest groups organized at state behest to perform services for their members that will, in due course, be provided more directly by a provincial bureaucracy. While the facts these organizations were obligated to assemble were for the immediate benefit of the concerned organization, when compiled and published by the government they were often put to much broader use – as, for instance, in dissemination abroad for the edification of would-be immigrants.[18]

In only one respect was this early arm's-length administrative pattern modified to incorporate a more hands-on approach, namely through the opening of an Agricultural College in 1874, staffed and paid for by the provincial government. This relatively unadventurous commitment of the province to what was the basic enterprise of its people was to persist until the early 1900s. Even then, the undoubted reflection of the individualism of an agrarian society expressed through this hands-off approach to administration continued to cast its long shadow over administrative responses of more recent times, such as the use of producer-dominated marketing boards.

Public Health

The proclivity for gathering facts was also the moving force behind administrative changes that set the course of public health regulation in the province. A select committee of the provincial Assembly dominated by members who were medical practitioners reported in 1878.[19] Once again, typical of so many of these early inquiries, a carefully prepared questionnaire was sent out to all municipal authorities, medical practitioners, directors of hospitals and other institutions. The answers provided discomforting evidence of the deplorable state of sanitation throughout the province and revealed the inadequacies of a policy that left responsibility for the regulation of public health in the hands of local authorities. The committee's conclusions were pithy and pungent: 'That with the exception of passing by-laws and appointing committees on the public health the Municipal Councils in general have not adopted or exercised any practical means for promoting the public health, or for removing filth, refuse, or other causes of injury.'

The committee's questionnaire elicited bad news on every front. Where, as was universally the case, reliance was placed on wells for a potable water supply, only twenty out of the responding eighty municipalities claimed to have good water; the majority suffered from pollution from the ubiquitous privy. Most places reported no means of drainage while ventilation and drainage of cellars was 'almost universally neglected.' The obvious consequence was a distressing number of cases of typhoid, diphtheria, and even malaria. The committee pleaded for better public education, the proper isolation of victims of contagious diseases, and more access to purer 'lymph' in order to inaugurate what was a relatively new technique of vaccination against the recurrent epidemics that swept the countryside.

In the committee's view, these distressing conditions were 'readily preventable,' and its proposals for action placed high priority on the strengthening of rudimentary municipal agencies and the creation of new provincial administrative authorities. While the committee was divided on some specific measures, it was unanimous in recommending that 'the responsibility should rest with the Legislature and the Government and a Central Committee or Board with local boards and medical officers.' The committee's preference for more centralized supervision was based on the testimony of numerous witnesses that locally appointed officers 'are too subject to local influences to act efficiently.'

Just as the recommendations of the agricultural inquiry had brought about the creation of a Bureau of Industries in 1882, so in the same year a Provincial Board of Health, recommended by the select committee, came into being. In both cases, but particularly with public health, the administrative response signalled the centralizing, hands-on mode of the future. The permissiveness, neglect, or sheer inability of local authorities to meet the challenges posed by a rapidly developing and urbanizing community would increasingly call for province-wide administrative responses. Interestingly for an inquiry dominated by members of the medical profession, the committee's conclusions and proposals for action give no suggestion that it may have launched a leviathan that would be viewed nearly a century later as a threat to the self-controlled guild of the medical practitioner. This unquestioning acceptance of the need for strong central government intervention clearly indicates that the deplorable situation revealed by their investigation dictated a solution for which the tiny band of professional health administrators attached to the Board of Health became dedicated missionaries.

Natural Resources

It is appropriate to conclude this rapid tour of the administrative arrangements called for by the state of development in early post-confederation Ontario by examining government's involvement with the land. In sharp contrast to the enabling approach we have seen the province adopt towards agriculture, is the hands-on administration of the land itself and of its most important crop, the forests.[20] The staff of the commissioner of crown lands was the first to be put in place, even though it represented more than half of the tiny headquarters establishment that began to be built up in Toronto in the fall of 1867. This rapid organizational response was possible because, apart from the ordnance lands that were left to the new Dominion and a small fisheries branch that also remained in Ottawa, the rest of the department was a complete hold-over from the Province of Canada.

When Ontario's legislature approved a Free Grant and Homesteads Act as one of its first actions in 1868, Crown Lands was ready to resume its familiar role as the province's real estate agency through its Free Grants and Land Sales Branch. A Surveys and Patents Branch also stood ready to continue the headquarters' function of registering and recording land transactions and supervising the field agents who conducted surveys. The fact that the colonization roads program was located in this branch reveals the close connection between settlement (that is, colonization) and the development of the so-called unorganized territories.

A Woods and Forests Branch represented the other major functional responsibility of Crown Lands. This responsibility would continue to contribute to an internecine struggle between the interests of the settlers – represented by the surveys and lands branches – and the often quite contradictory interests of the lumbermen – represented by the woods and forest section of the department.[21] In the performance of its multifarious tasks, Crown Lands churned out the most significant annual financial contribution to the provincial treasury, at times even exceeding the province's other major source of revenue, the subsidy from the Dominion that was part of the confederation settlement.[22] Not surprisingly, the largest division in Crown Lands was the Accounts Branch.

The continuity of the Crown Lands Department with its pre-confederation past was accompanied by a much more elaborate structure than any of the other early post-confederation departments. Such organizational complexity reflected not only its importance as *the* revenue department but also its unusual (for the times) hands-on involvement with the surveying, sale, and settlement of the province's prime asset, the land. It was equally involved in the licensing of the land's most lucrative crop, its forests and their timber products. The hands-on nature of the tasks performed by Crown Lands also accounts for its large staff of field agents to conduct surveys, handle land sales, measure timber cut, or supervise construction of colonization roads.

This sense of sprawl and of direct contact with a clientele out in the field was to become even more conspicuous as other treasures of the land and its waters yielded to developers towards the close of the century. Beginning with mining in the 1890s and, once jurisdictional disputes were settled towards the end of the century, moving into the fisheries, the department's already wide embrace was further extended. Once again, fact-finding inquiries were set afoot for forestry, mining, and game and fisheries.[23] The administrative fallout in nearly all instances came home to burden the Department of Crown Lands.

Tracing the course of the province's commitments to the land and its resources has carried the story well beyond the immediate concerns of the early post-confederation period. Nevertheless, the forward look reveals an administrative feature of the Crown Lands Department that was to linger well into the present century; from the outset, it was by far the largest and most complex of all government departments. These features have been ascribed to the hands-on nature of its work, a characteristic that the Education Office also shared but which did not show up in the original establishment until after its formal addition to the departmental roster in 1876. Among the BNA Offices, however, only Public Works showed some of the same features associated with the hands-on administrative mode, particularly when, in the early 1900s, it absorbed an incipient highways department. In contrast, all the other original BNA Offices started out very small and remained relatively simple in structure – a feature which derived from the manner in which their administrative mandates were fulfilled.

2
Early Administrative Modes

In the two decades immediately following confederation, Ontario's administrative response to the perceived needs of its citizens would appear to conform to the prevalent philosophy that advocated limited government. A budget in which expenditures on what was then termed 'civil government' represented less than 10 per cent of the total provincial outlay and a headquarters staff that initially counted about four dozen persons would seem to confirm this perception of the Victorian state. However, such a conclusion must be tempered by noting that the civil government component of the budget excluded expenditures on such items as agriculture, immigration, settlement roads, public health and welfare institutions, even law and order. All of these were separated from the civil government component, which embraced just the highly visible part of the administrative iceberg at the seat of government in Toronto.

Nonetheless, it is true that the size of the civil service was very small; a generous estimate, including even the seasonal employees in the field, would have been somewhere about four hundred during the early seventies.[1] Accustomed as we are to measuring the extent of governmental involvement by the size of the bureaucracy required to deliver its programs, it is easy to view this tiny staff of the early years as yet another confirmation of the potency of the classical philosophy. Yet here again, this conclusion needs to be reconsidered in the light of what will hereafter be referred to as the particular *administrative mode* by which governments seek to cope with the perceived needs of the time.

Broadly speaking, when governments seek to respond to the collective needs of their communities, they have a choice of three administrative modes. The first and least intrusive mode is that of *enabling* various private organizations to provide services deemed of value to the entire populace. Secondly, governments may opt for a more coercive *regula-*

tory administrative mode as a means of ensuring that the elusive public interest for which they hold themselves responsible is, in fact, being served by private sector providers of goods and services. Thirdly, governments may themselves assume a direct *operational* role – a hands-on administrative mode – to provide such public goods and services.

The successful implementation of each of these administrative modes relies on administrative *instruments* which are specific to the particular mode. In turn, the choice of instrument determines not only how large and sophisticated the public service will be but also what sort of tasks and consequent qualifications will be required of its personnel.

In Ontario the findings and recommendations of early inquiries, along with the pre-confederation heritage of institutions, favoured the emergence and application of all three administrative modes and their accompanying instruments. However, for the first three decades it is clear that the hands-on mode had limited use, whereas the enabling and regulatory modes were the most pervasive. Tracing the impact of these preferences provides a suitable means of coming to grips with the organizational contours, the administrative tasks, and the working ethos of Ontario's early public service.

The Enabling Administrative Mode

The primary instruments for implementing the indirect, enabling administrative mode involved the allocation of funds to designated recipients to be used for clearly specified purposes. The conditional nature of the granting instrument usually required a reporting responsibility on the part of the recipients and, on the government's part, an auditing function to ensure that the recipients had complied with predetermined requirements. Because the delivery system necessary to provide the service was not generally part of the government's own establishment, staff requirements were minimal – enough to satisfy even the most ardent contemporary exponent of a leaner bureaucracy. One might even speculate that lurking within current proposals for 'privatization' is the basic philosophical outlook that influenced early Ontario's reliance on the enabling role of government, encouraging as it did the avoidance of the direct hands-on involvement which has come to characterize the contemporary administrative mode for the delivery of so many services.

The success of such a mode depended, of course, on the existence of non-governmental organized groups capable of using the public funds placed at their disposal to provide the services or programs which otherwise would have to be provided by a governmental bureaucracy. This condition was most clearly met in dealing with agriculture. There, the enabling mode was deployed so completely that the government's commitment in terms of personnel was limited for the better part of a decade to one full-time secretary of agriculture and arts, George Buckland.

From pre-confederation days, the government had conceived of its role in agriculture as primarily concerned with education, including the dissemination of information that would improve the productivity of the various branches of agriculture. This educational service had been provided by enlisting a hierarchy of county, district, and township agricultural and horticultural associations and societies, each of which had to be incorporated according to elaborate provisions contained in provincial statutes in order to receive a modest grant.[2]

Despite the opening in 1874 of an agricultural college and the creation in 1882 of a Bureau of Industries, the essence of the Department of Agriculture's tasks was still described in the early 1890s as 'the general supervision of all societies and associations in receipt of Legislative grants, receiving from them general reports and financial statements which are carefully examined.'[3] By this period, there were ninety electoral district agricultural societies, 357 township and horticultural societies, seventy-seven local farmers' institutes, as well as associations for dairymen, fruit-growers, sheep-breeders, swine-breeders, poultrymen, bee-keepers, and more.

Even with the supervision of such a numerous and varied assortment of groups and the processing of their reports, a staff of some half-dozen was sufficient to handle the workload with which, for nearly two decades, after confederation, George Buckland had been able to cope single-handedly. Indeed, were it not for the reports from the various grant-supported groups, the commissioner of agriculture would have had virtually nothing to report on his own. By the mid-1890s the Department of Agriculture was undoubtedly the biggest publisher in a public service wedded to the production of paper. Yet the material disseminated (in some cases more than thirteen thousand copies of some association's report) was initially generated by the associations themselves. In this respect and judged merely in quantitative terms, the government received a bountiful return on its modest investment – and all this without the need to create an elaborate bureaucracy.[4]

Although this reliance on the indirect enabling mode was to continue into the new century, Agriculture began to respond to pressures that moved it beyond its original focus on education into areas where the required services could only be provided by a more direct hands-on administrative mode. The repercussions from this shift were quickly seen in the growth of branches and staff at headquarters as well as in the field. The associations hitherto relied upon to generate services to meet their own needs now came to be supervised by counterpart divisions in the department's headquarters, as for fruit-growers and dairymen. Even the educational function became bureaucratized, as an extension branch came to preside over a network of county agricultural representatives who themselves shifted from the status of employees of the municipalities to become provincial employees.

While these transformations of traditional responsibilities were occurring, new concerns for research, for marketing, and for financial assistance began to surface and take organizational root in the department. In short, a veritable organizational explosion occurred in the early decades of the twentieth century, the more dramatic because of the initial reliance on an enabling administrative mode that had placed few demands on either staff or structures.

Agriculture was not the only arena in which the indirect administrative mode flourished in the early post-confederation years, but no other department so completely embraced this approach. Where an element of the enabling mode was visible, as in the areas of public health and social welfare, just as much reliance had to be placed on other more direct modes. However, there was another facet of the arm's-length approach which was displayed in the province's relations with its inherited system of well-organized municipal authorities. Until it began to walk with more confidence, the province was disposed to lean on this inheritance for the provision of such services as the protection of persons and property, schooling, sanitation, and the like. Here again, then, much as in the case of agriculture, the indirect administrative mode proved to be the most appropriate provincial instrument for enabling the municipalities to maintain and improve upon the range of services they had historically provided.

In these circumstances, it is not surprising that Oliver Mowat should have placed high priority throughout his long regime on the consolidation of legislation dealing with municipal institutions, their powers, and their rights of taxation. One of the major obstacles to improvement in municipal administrative capacity was the burden of indebtedness incurred even before confederation because of indiscriminate borrowing from the Municipal Loan Fund. Accordingly, Mowat adroitly arranged for the surplus in the province's coffers (so adventitiously garnered in the early years after confederation) to be distributed to the municipalities to restore their administrative capabilities. Even with this encouragement, however, the time would come when the province would be driven to assume a more hands-on approach, although more than a century would pass before a full-blown Department of Municipal Affairs would be created.[5]

Provincial reliance on the municipalities, viewed as instruments of the indirect administrative mode, had the same minimalist impact on the central government Offices as it had on the commissioner of agriculture. Perhaps the largest burden fell on the most accommodating of those Offices, that of provincial secretary and registrar. However, there was one major difference that was to compel that Office to move more rapidly than did the commissioner of agriculture to rely on other administrative modes. The difference lay in the constitutional subordination of the municipal authorities to the province. In the case of agriculture, the central government was sponsoring and enabling private groups to perform specified functions deemed to be of a public nature; but municipal bodies were public or governmental agents incorporated under their own municipal charters. They operated under a comprehensive provincial enactment that for its range and detail has no counterpart in the statute books and that with the passing years has increased in bulk and complexity.

It is true that within this much more formally structured relationship the concept of the municipality as a subordinate agent of the province has been tempered by the tradition of local self-government. Even so, the constitutional right of the province to treat all local powers as delegated powers subject to its legislative fiat has encouraged a built-in bias towards invoking a more directive administrative mode to supplement or even displace the purely enabling or facilitative mode. The combination of the two modes, though enhancing the province's involvement with the services provided by local authorities, did not necessitate the large expansion of staff and organization that later followed from the outright assumption by the province of municipal responsibilities.

Nevertheless, when enablement-cum-regulation failed to provide the standard of service dictated by changing circumstances (as, for example in the field of public health), the centralizing thrust became increasingly irresistible. The reason a central provincial department to cope with the hands-on operating role took so long to appear may be attributed partly to the fact that the services provided at the municipal level constituted such a smorgasbord that nearly all the provincial departments had some involvement. Moreover, in the first decade of the twentieth century, provincial intervention came not through a conventional department but by a regulatory commission (the Ontario Railway and Municipal Board) and a provincial corporate entity (the Ontario Hydro-Electric Commission).

The Regulatory Administrative Mode

Although the arm's-length enabling administrative mode found its purest expression in Agriculture, even here an element of a second major mode – the regulatory administrative mode – had to be invoked. This particular mode comes equipped with several instruments, each of which carries a different degree of coerciveness. Thus, in the case of Agriculture, the regulatory mode was invoked by the reporting requirements imposed on the recipients of grants and by the auditing or monitoring duties imposed on the department. The constant references to the recalcitrance of those required to report – not only in the agricultural field but in such other statistics-gathering enterprises as were set up for mining and industrial/labour matters – suggest that the early reliance on the carrot of grants needed to be supplemented by stronger regulatory instruments.

The Auditing Instrument. The somewhat stronger leverage provided by the regulatory instrument of auditing never seems to have been much used by the tiny headquarters staff of Agriculture during the period of its reliance on the enabling administrative mode. However, in the other area of provincial-municipal relations, where the arm's-length mode, *faute de mieux*, was invoked and where there was the same problem with the least coercive instrument, reporting, great stress ultimately came to be placed on the more coercive regulatory instrument of the audit. Since the province was slow to bring its own departments and agencies under the healthy control of a central audit office, it is not surprising that a central office for a provincial municipal auditor was not created until 1896. Thereafter, improvements in and standardization of the account books maintained by the municipalities and the use of teams of provincially appointed or approved auditors led to a great reduction in losses from fraud. Combined with the subsequent creation in 1906 of the Ontario Railway and Municipal Board (ORMB), the gathering momentum of involvement by the centre becomes readily apparent.

The Licensing Instrument. The third instrument of the regulatory administrative mode is licensing. Today licensing is regarded as an important coercive regulatory instrument. In early post-confederation times, however, licensing must be viewed more as a device for raising revenue, its impact on the behaviour of the regulated very much a secondary consideration. In the absence of the variety of direct taxes that is available to the provinces today, it is easy to underestimate the significance to the province of the power conferred on it at confederation to raise revenues through licensing (section 92, subsection 9 of the BNA Act).

The overwhelming contribution to the province's coffers, averaging over 40 per cent of the total during the first twenty years, came from the Dominion subsidy. Almost as lucrative, though much less stable, were the contributions from crown lands. Of a lower order, but nevertheless important, were the revenues from licences and law stamps.[6] The Department of Crown Lands was viewed essentially as a revenue department, the commissioner's licensing powers not really being used to regulate the behaviour, for example, of the holders of timber leases.The two largest divisions of the department reflected the revenue bias: the Accounts Branch looked after the returns from land agents and the Woods and Forests Branch took care of timber leases, saw-log fees, and other returns.[7]

When it came to the revenues accruing from licences, the largest portion by far came from the returns from licensing the sale and distribution of liquor. As far back as 1864, legislation inspired by temperance advocate Christopher Dunkin had provided for local licensing boards to regulate the liquor trade. By the mid-1870s what was to become a familiar pattern of centralization began to evolve, with the province taking over the appointment of the local boards and the inspectors of licences.[8]

In no other area has the ambivalence of licensing, perceived either as a means of raising revenue or as a regulator of behaviour, been more apparent. Certainly, from earliest days the effectiveness of the liquor licensing power to govern behaviour has at times been called into question, but never its revenue-raising capabilities. At best, governments have been able to take the high ground by stressing the salutary results of temperance-based (if not total prohibitionist-based) regulation, all the while quietly banking the large revenue so serendipitously forthcoming!

In early times the bias in favour of the revenue-producing potential was reflected in the appointment of a so-called inspector of licensing accounts who operated from the Provincial Secretary's Office and whose main task was to keep the accounts, deduct the expenses of collection, and split the remainder between the province and the municipalities.[9]

The early emphasis on the revenue-raising aspect of the licensing instrument did not give way to the more contemporary view of licensing as an instrument of social and economic control until the rise of the independent agency, beginning with the ORMB in 1906. Distinguishing this new breed of regulatory agency was the conferral of a broader range of discretionary powers. This expansion of authority tends to be associated with a more complete armoury of regulatory instruments that may run the gambit of coercion, from compulsory reporting, auditing or monitoring, to inspection, licensing, and on to the adjudication of rights and even rule-making. In short, the contemporary regulatory administrative mode may invoke the use of instruments and procedures that combine all three classic elements of government – the legislative, judicial, and executive or administrative.

Inspection as Regulatory Instrument. This potent expansion of the regulatory mode into specialized boards with their ambiguous endowment of assorted powers was still very much in the future. During the early post-confederation years inspection was the pre-eminent instrument of regulation. Today inspection is regarded as one of the least coercive intrusions of the state into our daily life. In the early nineteenth century in Britain, however, its introduction was viewed as the first major intrusion of the central government, the only precedent being the much-maligned 'revenooers.' From the critics' point of view, this was the beginning of the growth of a central bureaucracy, all the more insidious because its tentacles reached out to the localities and interfered with the sacred rights of private property. Charles Kingsley's *Water-Babies* is a moving testimony to the strength of the laissez-faire tradition which as late as 1849 could still dominate a debate over a bill to regulate the masters of the tiny chimney-sweeps. The subjects of Kingsley's concern were at that moment probably suffocating in the cramped chimneys of the Houses of Parliament beneath which the debaters contested the right of the state to interfere with private property rights.[10]

The inspectorates created by Ontario during its first thirty or so years seldom met with the same fierce resistance as their British progenitors. Perhaps only the factory inspectors had to face moderately comparable hostility. Was this because the battle had already been won in England? Or had the early reliance of Upper Canadians on government muted the hearty individualism which in England had raised obstacles to the work of the inspectorates? Or was it because for those areas where the individualism associated with the frontier flourished – as for game and fisheries – the regulatory hand of the state rested so lightly?[11] Perhaps all of these factors were at play. In the event, Ontario's early inspectors were a singular breed, virtually lone-wolf impresarios, and without exception inclined to push their regulatory powers well beyond concerns with revenue-raising and revenue protection (as expressed in the licensing instrument) even to the point of a direct hands-on involvement.

The modest one-man *Inspectorate for Insurance Companies*, created by legislation in 1879, provides an illustration of the use of licensing to regulate behaviour rather than primarily as a revenue-raising instrument. In this instance, the discretionary powers conferred on the first incumbent, Inspector J. Howard Hunter (for example, to cancel a licence), were all subject to the approval of the provincial treasurer and required confirmation by order-in-council. Hunter's reports reveal some of the problems of regulating a financial sector whose operating arms have been incorporated and licensed variously under Dominion and/or provincial laws. With the passing years this situation has become so confused that Hunter's early grievances are but moderate forecasts of the persistent problems still experienced with this area of shared jurisdiction.[12]

While Hunter's duties involved licensing (including the licensing of insurance agents), the major aspect of his work appears to have been much more that of a registry office, as evinced by his detailed statistical reports which by law he was obliged to make to the legislature, as well as the added title in the 1890s of registrar of friendly societies. This was one inspectorate that never strayed far from its ministerial fold, for even when it came to rejoice in the title of Department of Insurance in 1912, it never acquired a ministerial head of its own.

A second rather different *Inspectorate for Registry Offices* was occupied by the Honourable Sydney Smith. By his own account, he was the author of the legislation under which he operated. Testifying before the Public Accounts Committee in 1879, Smith contended that he had not only drafted the provincial legislation for Sandfield Macdonald but had devised a similar plan for Ireland, claiming that 'the Ontario system stood second to none in the world.' Some inkling of the inspector's regulatory role is to be found in his response to a question about the adequacy of the legislative base from which he operated. Discounting the need for remedial legislation, he testified: 'I am the legislator, I have unlimited power to amend and correct any errors in any registry office. I cannot alter a conveyance, I cannot alter a deed, but I can put the registration right.' His authority extended even to recommending plans for new registry offices. Smith's testimony wavered between self-congratulation and self-pity as he spoke of the long hours spent in inspecting over fifty offices and the strain imposed on his health and the ruining of his eyesight by the detailed scrutiny he was required to make of so many documents.[13]

Impressive as was this testimony, Smith's account of his inspectoral duties pales by comparison with those of John Langmuir, the first head of the *Inspectorate of Prisons and Charities*.[14] The domain over which Langmuir assumed jurisdiction in 1868 had already been occupied by a board of inspectors for the Province of Canada in 1859. At confederation, in accordance with the allocation of jurisdictions in sections 91 and 92 of the BNA Act, penitentiaries and marine hospitals became Dominion responsibilities, while the lion's share of all other institutions fell to the lone care of Langmuir. Even before confederation, a tangled web of privately owned and controlled, and provincially owned and operated institutions had grown up to meet varied social welfare needs. This was the polyglot domain which Langmuir inherited. He was to shape it into a system that became the source of three of the largest of Ontario's contemporary departments: corrections, social and community services, and the hospitals side of a ministry of health.

We have Langmuir's own description of the workload he sustained virtually single-handedly during his fourteen years in office. Even a bare-bones outline of his manifold responsibilities ten years after he assumed office occupies two densely packed printed pages.

Langmuir's comprehensive mandate extended to two types of institutions. First, there were by 1878 the ten institutions exclusively owned and managed by the province: four asylums for the insane, one asylum for idiots, a school for the deaf and a school for the blind, the central prison in Toronto, and a provincial reformatory in Penetang with another for females in course of construction. The second category contained a more bewildering mix that included thirty-seven county gaols and five district lock-ups under local government management (to Langmuir's regret) but sustained by provincial grants representing roughly one-third their operating costs. In addition, there were twelve hospitals, thirteen houses of refuge, five Magdalen asylums, and nineteen orphanages – all receiving support from the province under the Charity Aid Act, a clear illustration of the enabling administrative mode.

With respect to the first category of institutions, Langmuir's tasks were described not only as inspection but also as 'general supervision and control.' The generality of this latter phrase makes it difficult to grasp the range of tasks and the direct hands-on operating stance which Langmuir adopted towards them. Early on, we find him immersed in the preparation of the sketch of architectural plans for the new lunatic asylum to be erected in London. He must have had something to do with any modifications to existing buildings such as the asylum in Toronto, about whose renovations its superintendent, Joseph Workman, was prone to complain to his superior. In one early sardonic comment, Workman reports on 'the marvellous efficiency of those galvanized excrescences called Griffith Ventilators' which had the unfortunate tendency in big windstorms to vibrate, encouraging the 'patients to join in and almost overtop the hubbub.' In the same report we find the broad hint to Langmuir that before the forthcoming meeting of the American

Association of Medical Superintendents of Insane Hospitals, scheduled to be held in Workman's institution, 'some curative applications may be found for the deep cutaneous disease which now disfigures the ceilings of the new wing verandahs.'[15]

When the erection of a school for the deaf was approved in Belleville, it was Langmuir who accompanied the provincial secretary to the United States to acquire ideas for both the structure of the building and the curriculum to be taught. In prompt order, Langmuir produced the plans for both, along with a detailed prescription for the staffing of the school which then became the basis upon which he conducted his subsequent inspections.

This exercise was but one instance of the fulfilment of his general responsibility for framing the by-laws and regulations governing 'the discipline, management and general economy' of all public institutions and for defining the duties of all officers and employees. Included in these responsibilities was the letting of contracts for supplies and the general supervision of the purchase of goods for the ten publicly owned institutions – a task that also involved a monthly audit of all their accounts.

Langmuir's general supervision and control also extended to the large group of common gaols, even though they remained under municipal auspices. Here again, his inspectoral reach extended not only to the structures themselves but to all matters affecting discipline within the gaols. The need for discipline was accentuated by the low calibre of staff recruited for the gaols, a situation created by the niggardly remuneration offered by the municipal authorities which in the end remained beyond Langmuir's powers to reform.

That he had much reason to press for reform was revealed in 1881 when his inspection of the Belleville gaol turned up a distressing story involving the alleged immoral conduct of female prisoners engaging in 'singing, dancing and unseemly conduct' outside their cells in the presence of male visitors. Langmuir found that the gaoler was indolent, the turnkey had been under the influence of the matron and a frequenter of houses of ill fame, and, as for the matron, 'even before her elopement with a prisoner [she] had given evidence of her entire unfitness.'

Langmuir's response was to confer on the sheriff of the county power to appoint staff and to monitor the application of a detailed dietary regimen of Langmuir's preparation. But despite Langmuir's authority and prestige, he was unable to surmount the barricades set up by the traditional reliance on local authorities and convince the provincial government to assume the complete financial burden, thereby permitting the upgrading of the quality of staff which he had vainly sought.

Perhaps he may have found compensating satisfaction in gaining governmental acceptance of a complete hands-on administrative mode for
the Central Prison in Toronto and for the reformatories.

Hospitals and charitable institutions, being grant-supported rather than
owned and managed by the province, were nevertheless susceptible to
Langmuir's ministrations. Indeed, one of his first assignments – most
appropriate for a man of his business talents – was to examine the
method of providing financial support to the hospitals and benevolent
institutions. Proceeding on the bases of answers to the questions 'What
class is entitled to aid?' and 'To what extent and upon what principles?'
Langmuir produced a schema that was adopted wholesale in the Charity
Aid Act of 1874.[16]

By invoking the enabling administrative mode, Langmuir took a
much more regulatory approach to the recipients of the grants he allocated than was the case in Agriculture. The extent of Langmuir's responsibilities for the private agencies engaged in health and welfare
activities is revealed in his annual report for 1873, described as comprising 'the inspection of, and report upon, every institution receiving
Government aid, from one to four times a year; the audit of their
accounts, and the regulation of their organization and discipline, and I
am, in addition, the official medium of communication between them
and the Government. These institutions now number seventy-seven, the
aggregate expenditure of which is close upon half a millon dollars per
annum, which is subject to audit in this office.'[17]

Langmuir's varied and extensive tasks included the managerial and
judicial discretion arising from his responsibility for the estates of all
lunatics committed to the asylum, 'where committees have not been
appointed by the Court of Chancery.' This trusteeship role paralleled the
power conferred on him to recommend to government the transfer of in-
mates from one institution to another. Given the laxness in the classification system that often led to the confinement of the mentally disturbed or the alcoholic in the common gaols, this was a significant
authority.[18]

Langmuir was prone to complain of the burdens imposed upon him
and, like Sydney Smith, disposed to boast of the great progress made
under his management: 'The Province of Ontario,' he proclaimed in his
report for 1873, 'may challenge the world to show a more liberal and
effective, and yet more economically managed system of Public Institutions, for the care and relief of the mental, physical, and moral defect-
ives of our population.' All this was achieved, he would reiterate, by
himself with the help of 'a secretary, who is also a short-hand writer,
a chief clerk who acts as accountant, an ordinary clerk and a messenger'

– cost complete, $7,350! Despite his increasingly insistent requests for more help, it was not until a year or two before his retirement in 1882 that a second inspector was added.

Langmuir's endeavours clearly reveal that the powers conferred on this solitary official anticipated in a unique way the full maturation of the regulatory administrative mode which in the twentieth century would come to be exercised collectively by independent boards and commissions. The title 'Inspector' did less than justice to the breadth of Langmuir's mandate or to the vigour with which he was prepared to wield the discretionary instruments placed at his disposal. Not only was he performing the regulatory role of inspector but he also took for granted that the making of rules, even the outright direction of particular operations, was somehow subsumed in the inspectoral mandate.

Langmuir stands out as a dedicated administrator and as a policy innovator with firm convictions of where he wanted to go and the boundless energy to pursue his goals and induce the powers that be to accept them. In this respect, then, he was anticipating the direction taken by contemporary regulatory boards which, in exercising the discretionary powers confided to them, in a very real sense are 'legislating' policy as an inseparable part of deploying their regulatory instruments. Nevertheless, for all his stretching of discretionary powers, Langmuir maintained a clear understanding and respect for the concept of personal accountability to ministerial masters who in turn were responsible to the Legislative Assembly. This understanding of the rules of the game undoubtedly accounted for the high rate of success attending the various initiatives which entitle Langmuir to be credited with being the true founder of Ontario's social welfare system.[19]

This account of Langmuir's contributions underscores a point that might otherwise be obscured by focusing only on the response of bureaucracy to changing economic and social conditions and the community's perception of its corresponding needs. There is no question that, historically, this has been a reciprocal relationship. As Langmuir's work so admirably demonstrates, the bureaucracy (here represented by a few dedicated and legally empowered officials) assumes a pro-active stance by educating politicians and their constituents to the need for supporting policy innovations inspired by the officials' reading of the environment in which they operate and which they wish to alter.

In the last quarter of the nineteenth century no other inspectorate could match Langmuir's office for the range of its activities or for the variety of enabling, regulatory, and even operating modes to which the implementation of his generous mandate gave rise. Nevertheless, the inspectorate as an instrument of regulation was much favoured as the province confronted new challenges posed by a community shifting away from its predominantly agrarian roots towards a more diversified, industrial, and commercial economy.

A measure dealing with the protection of children in 1893 might well have been added to the already comprehensive domain marked out for the inspector of prisons and charities. However, perhaps because of the dedicated promotion of this particular cause by J.J. Kelso, the *Office of Superintendent of Neglected and Dependent Children* was given a separate identity. The energy with which it pursued its task came from Kelso, who was to preside for over forty years as superintendent and pilot his tiny office into a major branch of a Department of Public Welfare in 1931.

As in other fields, leaving matters to the local authorities had proved inadequate. Earlier legislation in 1887 placed 'the Protection of Infant Children' entirely in the hands of the municipalities. The 1893 Act for Prevention of Cruelty to and better Protection of Children replaced this earlier legislation and was a long, carefully constructed enactment in view of the new powers conferred on a central authority. Kelso used these powers to initiate the formation of Children's Aid Societies and Visiting Committees at the local level. To this enabling function was added the task which municipal councils had shirked – visiting and inspecting industrial schools, temporary homes and shelters, together with the maintenance of records on children placed in foster homes, a new program borrowed from Australia. A special aspect of Kelso's mandate was the inspection of houses registered for the reception of children. Over the fifteen years since 1878 some ten thousand children had been brought from the old country to Ontario by seven sponsoring agencies.

In a letter directed to the prospective Visiting Committees which Kelso incorporated in his first report for 1893, he deftly summarized the intent of the act under which he operated: 'In the adoption by the Ontario legislature of the Children's Protection Act of 1893, we have what has long been hoped for by philanthropic workers – the union of State aid and private effort for the amelioration of the condition of the neglected and dependent children.' To this end, he concluded, 'the State offers advice and countenance.'[20]

Much like Langmuir before him, Kelso operated virtually as a one-man entrepreneur under the benign but loose embrace of the provincial secretary. Unlike Langmuir, however, he lacked both the statutory authority and the financial leverage to bring the full weight of the province into play in his dealings with the municipalities. Many councils rebelled at shouldering such expenses as those involved in meeting the obligation, imposed on every town or city over ten thousand, to provide a temporary home or shelter for children between the ages of three and fourteen. Despite the later reliance on a more direct hands-on administrative mode, Kelso's vision of the state in partnership with the private, voluntary sector was to remain enshrined in the Children's Aid Societies, dimmed but far from obliterated by the contemporary thrust of bureaucratization.

The *Factory Inspectorate* was also the primary administrative instrument for provincial involvement in another late nineteenth-century arena of social policy – that is, the regulation of conditions in the workplace. Once again, until the province moved in 1887, a familiar pattern asserted itself: factory inspection, where considered at all, had been left to the discretion of local authorities. The early reports of the first three provincial inspectors appointed in 1887 were enough to convince even the most sceptical that the prevailing permissiveness had completely failed to check the appalling use of children in factories or stem the flood of devastating accidents in workplaces of every kind. It would be difficult to find a better policy arena in which to demonstrate how the facts gathered through inspection and adroitly deployed in published reports could lead to the building of an administrative regime capable of ameliorating the harsh conditions stemming from an hitherto unregulated workplace.

No one was more conscious of the power of publicity to promote causes in which they were so clearly emotionally involved than the factory inspectors themselves. Their early reports were used successfully to prove the need to expand their jurisdictions, for example to 'shops and places other than factories.' Largely as a consequence of this extension, explicit statutory provision was made in 1895 for the appointment of a 'female inspector.' The reports submitted by Margaret Carlyle, the first appointee who was to serve for twenty-five years, focused on the long hours and, in particular, the problem of night work for women and girls in factories, bake-shops, and mercantile establishments. In recommending legislative changes to improve the conditions she was finding, she was echoing the reactions of her male colleagues whose reports constantly preached against the evils of child labour – one of the primary reasons for creating the inspectorate in the first place.[21]

A typical Victorian hortatory note is nicely sounded in Miss Carlyle's first report, an interesting mix of the salty and sermonizing: 'There is no reason why the condition of the working girl should not be a useful, honorable and happy one. There is honor in every walk of life ... It is very evident that work in moderation is healthy as well as agreeable to the human body. It is well that human nature should not have the road of life made too easy. Better the necessity of working and enjoying the fruits of our labour than having all our wishes gratified without effort, as it leaves no object for our hopes and desires.'[22] Judging from the serious and single-minded way in which she approached her inspectoral tasks, Miss Carlyle practised what she preached. That it seems to us from this perspective to be a stern set of values should be taken in context: she apparently considered it normal that a workday in cotton, woollen, and knitting mills should start at 6:30 a.m. and go to 6 p.m., with an hour out for 'dinner,' while the urban shop worker should put in between forty-five and fifty-five hours, rather than the sixty hours a week for the factory girl. What drew inspectoral fire were the measures taken by employers to compress mealtimes and so gain the extra hours which they would otherwise lose in giving their employees a half-day off on Saturdays.

Looking back on these early years from over a quarter-century's experience, Chief Inspector James Burke, in 1925, wrote: 'There was a time when owners and employers looked with certain disfavour on those appointed by the Province to enforce the Factory, Shop and Office Building Act ... It took considerable diplomacy to deal with this class of employers ... With few exceptions the day has gone by when the visit of the factory inspector is met with growing opposition. The employer and his employee along with the general public have been enlightened and appreciate practical safeguard reforms.'[23]

There can be no doubt that the early inspectorate's preference for persuasion rather than more coercive measures – 'a readiness to instruct and a dignified manly courtesy' and a willingness to 'leave indurated recalcitrants to the courts,' as one male inspector grandly put it – had much to do with this outcome. In 1904, when still a relatively new recruit to the inspectorate, James Burke nicely captured this attitude: 'Before closing this report,' he wrote, 'I feel it my duty to briefly lay before you certain amendments to the Shops and Factories Acts, that would equalize and facilitate their usefulness as a safeguard to public rights and interests.' Then, in words that encapsulated the very essence of the administrative mode which his inspectorate represented, Burke continued, 'The experience of the operation of legislation proves its strengths, justice, and weakness. Hence it is that we have learned the weak points in the shops and factories, and appeal to you and your Government to have the same corrected.'[24] In these words, Burke captured what was to become a predominant feature of the regulatory mode, namely, that future policy emerges from the experience with day-to-day administration of current policy.[25] The accentuation in more recent times of this phenomenon has led to the characterization of the policy-cum-administration process as part of a seamless web.

The factory inspectorate contributed another element to the administrative process. The inspectorate's efforts to impose safety standards in response to the rapid changes in technology that affected plants and machinery induced a transfusion of new professional blood into the somewhat hardened veins of the early paper-bound bureaucracy. Specialized knowledge of ventilation, hoisting devices, steam boilers, and the mysteries of electricity could only be provided by recruiting persons professionally trained in civil, mechanical, and electrical engineering. After the turn of the century these attributes became so vital to the inspection of the workplace and the health and safety of the workers, that separate boards of inspectors and examiners were created for stationary and hoisting engineers and for steam boiler operators.

What might be termed the professionalization of the province's bureaucracy had begun modestly with the emergence in pre-confederation times of land surveyors who were accredited by a board of examiners appointed by the governor. With the incorporation in 1860 of the Association of Provincial Land Surveyors and of the Institute of Civil Engineers and Architects, the state withdrew, leaving these associations to govern themselves. The same course was followed in 1869 for the medical profession when the Ontario College of Physicians and Surgeons was incorporated with the right to pass on the credentials of practitioners. In 1873 a School of Practical Science was set up as a provincial institution, supervised by the Education Office (later the Department of Education). Twenty years later a School of Mining was founded and soon attached to Queen's University to become the basis for its Engineering Faculty. The power of accreditation conferred in 1883 on another professional group, the Institute of Chartered Accountants, was also important to a public service afloat in financial statements whose dubious quality required professional attention – although no provision for accreditation of the provincial auditor was made when the Office was created in 1886. The profession of forester had to wait for its formal recognition until 1907 when a Faculty of Forestry was established in the University of Toronto. Finally, capping this combination of governmental initiatives and private associations in the preparation and accreditation of sundry professionals, there were the teachers. Their training, accreditation, and subsequent professional performance were subjected to the ministrations of the Department of Education.[26]

Although the demands on professionals were not extensive in the late nineteenth-century civil service, the developments just noted clearly paved the way for meeting the growing requirements of the factory inspectorate. The coming of the automobile and the accompanying revolution in road-building was to turn this trickle of professionals into a major influx as the regulatory administrative mode was overtaken by a direct hands-on involvement of relevant sectors of the public service. The mining engineers and professional foresters would join the civil and mechanical engineers recruited for road building, to transform the small and generally non-professional nineteenth-century public service.

Public health was another policy area that gave further impetus to the professionalizing trend to which the various branches of engineering were making the most substantial contribution. The emergence of the *Provincial Board of Health* in 1882 was a response to the perceived inability of municipal authorities to deal with public health problems that had no respect for local boundaries. The new board was to provide a province-wide, ongoing administrative response in place of the hitherto sporadic, ad hoc attempts to grapple with frequent outbursts of epidemics.[27]

In deference to the sensitivity of the local authorities, the administrative mode adopted by the new board was only moderately coercive. It relied more on information/education and persuasion, particularly when it came to the introduction or upgrading of municipal sewerage and water supply systems. Probably because of the importance of this work, both the chairman of the board and one of his unpaid colleagues were professors of sanitary science, while another member was professor of civil engineering at the School of Practical Science.[28]

Only in one area did the board seek to adopt a firmer regulatory mode and that was – surprising at first blush – in respect of its responsibility for collecting vital statistics. The interconnection between the board's concern for public health and sanitation and statistics on deaths and their causes, for example, had been foreseen as early as 1837. The great English advocate of public health regulation, Edwin Chadwick, had made this connection, although he had been opposed 'by the clergy and uneducated masses.' Fifty years later, as the secretary of the provincial Board of Health was to proclaim, it was the 'registration of death that made sanitation possible.'[29] No doubt it was this interrelationship that induced the government in 1889 to append to Dr Bryce's secretarial duties the title of deputy registrar general. In this capacity he reported to the provincial secretary who had been made registrar general in 1869. However, the real headquarters' work fell on an inspector of registry offices who, after Bryce's appointment as deputy registrar general, reported through him to the provincial secretary.

From the outset, the collection of these important data suffered from two defects, neither of which appeared to have been remedied by the introduction of a deputy registrar general. First, as an early report of the registrar general complained, there was initial uncertainty 'as to whether the collection of vital statistics is to be performed under Dominion or Provincial auspices.' Some fifteen years later this problem was still preventing the adoption of a logical division of labour and expenses so as to 'greatly exceed the present partial and necessarily imperfect methods.'

Greater and even more enduring concern was expressed for the inability of the provincial authority to apply leverage on the municipally appointed divisional registrars to produce more complete and more accurate returns. As with Langmuir's failure to deal satisfactorily with the staffing of the common gaols because of built-in local powers, so too the municipal clerks who were appointed as divisional registrars had no incentive to shoulder this added burden, as they were prohibited from accepting extra remuneration.[30] Moreover, the fact that physicians had been equally and notoriously remiss in complying with legislative requirements to report births and deaths merely compounded the frustrations of the inspector. Bryce lectured his fellow professionals in no uncertain terms: 'It is a fair question for consideration,' he wrote, 'whether the privileges which are by the Medical Act given to physicians should not bear some relation to the duties which they owe the State in this important matter of making prompt and complete returns of deaths.'[31]

Despite the clear relationship which timely and accurate reports bore to the development of drainage, sewerage, and water systems that would counter such endemic diseases as malaria and diphtheria, the complaints of the 1890s concerning the unreliable services of local officials were still being voiced well after the turn of the century.[32] By that time, however, a more direct provincial involvement was being signalled with the strengthening of the central inspectoral role of the Board of Health. In 1900 a medical inspector was appointed as chief assistant to the secretary of the board and in 1905 a provincial analyst was added to head the all-important Testing Laboratory.[33] In the 1920s a full-blown Department of Health would be created with corresponding enlargement of the professional staff of doctors, nurses, and chemical analysts as well as increased organizational complexity.

By the turn of the century the early reliance on enabling and regulatory administrative modes was beginning to be displaced or heavily supplemented by a direct hands-on mode that turned the hitherto modest movement towards centralization into a rising and irreversible flood that produced today's enlarged and complex public service. Before the organization of the service began to register the impact of these transformations, the Offices delineated in the BNA Act were used to cope with the limited administrative needs and associated modes of the time. This process to which we now turn involved the gradual emergence of a departmental system out of the Offices, supplemented by small satellite agencies rotating in loose orbit around them.

3
Offices as Departmental Building Blocks, 1867–1905

The act creating the Canadian federation in 1867 made a formal allocation of policy arenas to the new Dominion and to the several provinces.
For Ontario, this dispensation was to have an important impact on the
development of its departmental organization. The call for the creation
of five named Offices necessitated an immediate response; the longer-
term consequences were to consecrate the initial organization as the
legal basis for a roster of departments that was to endure for close to
four decades.

Legal Foundations

It is understandable why, as opposed to the other provinces, Quebec and
Ontario required particular attention: they were emerging as separate
entities from their previous uneasy partnership in the Province of Canada and required new constitutions. However, it is not clear why Ontario was assigned the particular five Offices. The inspiration for this
provision may have come from a letter written in 1847 by the colonial
secretary, Lord Grey, which had reference to Nova Scotia.[1] For 'small
and poor communities,' he wrote, 'which must be content to have their
work cheaply and somewhat roughly done,' the governor might need as
advisers only an attorney general, a provincial secretary, and a solicitor
general. If the revenue base could sustain the cost of extra advisers, he
thought a chief of public lands and works, and a financial secretary
might be added. In the event, the constitutional disposition for Ontario
was not far off Lord Grey's mark: an attorney general, a provincial
secretary, a provincial treasurer, a commissioner of crown lands, and a
commissioner of agriculture and public works.

The pains taken in prescribing the composition and status of the
Executive Council had relevance for the confirmation of a system of

responsible cabinet government in Ontario. The roots of that system go back to early eighteenth-century England. Beginning in 1705, a series of so-called Place Acts had permitted the development of that most singular feature of the Westminster model of parliamentary government: a fusion of executive and legislative branches which was made possible by permitting only the named heads of the executive departments of state to hold seats in Parliament. These ministers of the crown directed the affairs in Parliament with the developing understanding that their entitlement to govern depended upon their ability to retain the support of a majority of followers in the legislature.

At the outset, the Place Acts reflected the legislature's concern to minimize the influence of placeholders beholden to the monarch and therefore always a potential threat to the independent deliberations of Parliament. As the monarch's personal influence waned, the Place Acts came to be viewed as the means by which political office-holders could be separated from strictly administrative officials. When the Province of Canada came to emulate the British model for fusing the executive and legislative branches, its concern for making this separation between the politician and the administrator was expressed in an Act to Secure the Independence of Parliament, promulgated in 1844.[2] The colonial legislature followed the precedent of the mother country by naming the offices making up the Executive Council, appointment to which was deemed compatible with holding an elective seat in the legislature.

The British North America Act perpetuated in section 83 the same formula that the Province of Canada had used in its 1844 statute: 'any person accepting or holding employment, permanent or temporary, at the nomination of the Lieutenant Governor to which an annual salary, or any fee, allowance, emolument or profit of any kind or amount is attached shall not be eligible as a member of the Legislative Assembly.' However, the prohibition was not to apply to the named officers who comprised the Executive Council, provided that each was elected while holding such office.[3] An Executive Council Act passed in 1872 by Ontario's Legislative Assembly, and steadily amended thereafter, re-iterated this provision so as to accommodate the enlarging membership of the council.

In practice, the constraints imposed by this provision made little impact on the ability of the premier to juggle the membership of his Executive Council. While the re-election provision applied on first appointment, when a member of the Executive Council was shifted to another office, exchanged or doubled up his portfolios, there was no need to seek re-election. Thus, rather than being an impediment, the formula actually provided a flexible mechanism for facilitating the rearrangement and transfer of duties to and among the always loosely defined portfolios of the 'founding five' BNA Offices – a flexibility that was much in evidence during the formative years.[4] Many years later, in 1926, the Legislative Assembly Act was amended so as to abolish the requirement of re-election. Ironically, this same legislation permitted MLAs to accept additional employment 'as a member of any commission, committee or other body, entitled to remuneration' without sacrificing their legislative seat. Over the years, liberal use of this provision has done little to safeguard the line that separates the political from the administrative official.[5]

The BNA Act's formal requirement of five specified Offices necessitated the creation, from scratch, of the three Offices of the Attorney General, Provincial Secretary, and Provincial Treasurer. In the absence of any specific departmental enactments for these three Offices, the provisions of the BNA Act constituted the only legal basis for their existence. In the case of the Attorney General's Office, there appears to be no statutory reference to the Office as a departmental organization until as late as 1968 when the title was changed for a brief time to Department of Justice. Even so, that is precisely all that legislation has to say about this department, its functions, or its organization. Considering the primary position of the Office – its early frequent combination with the premier's functions and its administrative responsibilities for the province's judicial system, and the responsibility for law and order – it is remarkable that there is not a more elaborate statutory statement of its structure and functions.

The Office of Provincial Treasurer reveals much the same situation; only with the enactment of a Financial Administration Act in 1954 is there a statutory recognition of the organization and of its important adjunct, the Treasury Board. Thereafter, because of the various experiments with locating such related activities as revenue collection, planning, intergovernmental affairs, and economics, the department's statutory base has become more visible and the legal prescription of the core elements fully elaborated.[6]

For the Office of Provincial Secretary and Registrar, the same reliance on the bare-bones BNA Act authorization served until a major internal reorganization in 1925 necessitated the passage of its first genuine 'departmental' statute. The statute of 1925 essentially gave organizational recognition to a lengthy process by which the Secretary's Office had come to have jurisdiction over health and welfare as well as correctional services – in addition to its historical registration functions.[7] The organizational adaptations to these cumulative responsibilities signalled a succession of acts that were ultimately to dismember this historic BNA Office. Of the five founding Offices, the Provincial Secretary's has been the only one which has failed to weather the winds of change.

The story of the commissionerships for Crown Lands and for Agriculture and Public Works, the other two Offices designated by the BNA Act, is much more typical of the legal foundations established for the new Dominion's departmental system. Because the BNA Act did not specify the offices to comprise the Dominion's Executive Council, as it had for Ontario and Quebec, immediate legislative provision had to be made for each new department. Only the Office of the Privy Council existed – and persists to this day – without its own departmental act and is entitled to be termed a 'prerogative department' (i.e., founded on the original royal discretionary power, rather than on parliamentary enactment).[8]

In Ontario, the Office of Commissioner of Crown Lands was based on legislation passed by the Parliament of the old Province of Canada in 1860. This reliance on a legal foundation created by a previous political regime appears to be the only case where Ontario's legislators took advantage of the authority of section 129 of the BNA Act to carry over pre-confederation laws, as it applied to major public departments. The 1860 enactment provided a detailed description of the tasks assigned to the commissioner and spelled out the role of a permanent assistant commissioner who was to preside over the department and discharge the duties of the commissioner in his absence. The transference of this pre-confederation statute to apply to Ontario's public service was of particular importance because of the role prescribed for the assistant commissioner. This position was to become accepted as that of deputy minister – the permanent head of the department – and was to become a standard feature of every department.[9]

The last of the five designated Offices, the Commissioner of Agriculture and Public Works, also had an elaborate statutory base that carried back to pre-confederation enactments. In this instance, the progenitors had been separate departments, each with its own statute which after confederation was virtually re-enacted by Ontario's Assembly. For Agriculture, as might be expected of a policy arena characterized by the arm's-length enabling administrative mode, the statutory prescription focused on the organization of societies, associations, and their overall coordinating body, the Board of Agriculture, in lieu of any governmental machinery. Thus, the enactment of 1868 was very much a replay of the pre-confederation act of 1853 that laid out the supervisory responsibilities of separate boards of agriculture for Upper and Lower Canada. An amendment to the Executive Council Act in 1874 permitted a separation of Agriculture from Public Works; but it was not until 1888 that a clear-cut statutory foundation for a Department of Agriculture was finally provided.[10]

The statute providing for the organization of the public works side of the double-barrelled mandate of the commissioner was assented to on 23 January 1869, its provisions marking a departure from agriculture. Again, as with crown lands, there is a detailed description of the commissioner's functions, with an elaboration of the duties of no less than five senior officials of the department: an architect, engineer, secretary, law clerk, and accountant, no one official being singled out as permanent head.

The Continuity of the BNA Act Offices

This initial disposition persisted with surprisingly little change for close to forty years. Despite repeated use of the phrase 'until the Legislature of the Province otherwise provides,' that permissive note sounded in the BNA Act was quite definitely not interpreted as an open-ended invitation to tamper with the five designated Offices. Indeed, this constitutionally imposed limit was reinforced in 1872 when the first Executive Council act explicitly stated that the council 'shall be composed of such persons as the Lieutenant Governor thinks fit' but not more than six could be appointed. This constraint was not formally lifted until 1888; indeed, for all practical purposes, it remained in effect until 1905 when Premier Whitney's reorganization touched off the modern era of department-building.[11]

In 1874 a section was added to the original Executive Council Act that was intended to give effect to a decision to permit the Commissionership of Agriculture and Public Works to be divided between two members of the council while leaving intact the magic limit of six councillors. The section read: 'any of the powers and duties [of an executive councillor] ... may, from time to time, by Order in Council, be assigned or transferred either for a limited period or otherwise, to any other of the said officers by name or otherwise.'

This provision not only addressed the immediate problem of separating agriculture from public works but also provided the flexibility that accounts for the surprising longevity of the maximum size of six that was imposed on the Executive Council. It is best to think of at least three of the BNA Offices (of Attorney General, Provincial Secretary, and Provincial Treasurer) as generous containers ready to be filled with assorted functions, variously administered by 'departments,' 'branches,' 'bureaus,' 'boards,' or 'inspectorates.' Each of these compartments from time to time would be made the recipient of duties authorized by legislation, but often such duties bore little relationship to the title attached to the Office to whose care they had been consigned. In these circumstances, the terms of the Executive Council Act were naturally calculated to accommodate this kind of free-wheeling allocation.

Many instances of the use of this flexible provision are to be found. The fact that legislation conferred on the provincial secretary the additional title of registrar did not prevent, for example, the function of registering vital statistics being transferred to the new Department of Agriculture in 1888, where it remained for a decade before returning to the provincial secretary who throughout continued to carry his joint title. Again, when the one genuinely new department, that for Education, was created in 1876, it was done on the understanding that the limit of six executive councillors would not be breached. The move received general public approval when it was known that the highly respected provincial treasurer would also become the first minister of education. The Office of Commissioner of Agriculture, once detached from Public Works, also proved a generous absorber of assorted functions, thereby actually mirroring its pre-confederation counterpart's tendency to be a 'departmental potting shed.' Thus, for many years Immigration (variously characterized as a branch or a department) was housed in Agriculture; a Bureau of Industries was really the core of the department; the Factory Inspectorate found a home with Agriculture for a number of years; and for briefer periods a clerk of forestry and an instructor in road building were also accommodated. Public Works was equally compliant, becoming home for such unrelated activities as Fish and Game, and a Bureau of Labour.

Reliance for so long on the capacity of only five designated Offices to embrace willy-nilly additional administrative tasks and to transfer them about as circumstances and ministers' abilities dictated, was probably only possible because the total enterprise was so small. In retrospect, however, there surely has never been a closer approximation to the conditions favouring the principle of ministerial responsibility than that provided in the first few decades of Ontario's public service. Today's bureaucracy of large staffs and complex structures provides reason to question the practicability of adhering to this basic precept of parliamentary democracy. In these early years, however, the intimacy created by simple structures and the close collaboration of political heads with a handful of permanent officers raised no such fears.[12]

Education: From Office to Department

When a decision was made in 1876 to transform the Education Office into a ministry, early conceptions of the doctrine of ministerial responsibility, coupled with the effort to preserve the limitation on the size of the cabinet, evoked prolonged debate. Clearly, the addition of this department to the basic building blocks specified in the BNA Act marked a new departure. That its arrival was not permitted to affect the number of members on the Executive Council may be attributed to its pre-confederation structure and the controversy surrounding its trans-formation into a 'ministerial department.'

The essential issue was whether such a transformation could achieve greater accountability to the elected representatives of the people while at the same time not exposing the administrators of educational policy to undue political/partisan pressures. In contemporary parlance, the concern was with the possible politicization of education. Thus, in examining the process by which the old Education Office became the Department of Education, its addition to the roster of departments is perhaps more important for the light it throws on the basic problem of finding the most appropriate means to separate the political from the administrative, where the linchpin is the responsible ministerial head.

Although the BNA Act assigned the field of education to the prov-inces, it was not amongst those matters provided for in the five named Offices. The omission can only be explained by the understanding at the time that education was one of those responsibilities which would be carried on under the already existing Education Office for Canada West, presided over by its permanent superintendent, Egerton Ryerson, and an appointive Council of Public Instruction.

Ryerson was certainly amongst those who felt the new federation would bring no change. In mid-December of 1866 he reported from London, where he had watched the delegates to the London Conference debating the Canadian act of union, that 'Nothing will be introduced in the Articles of Confederation which will, in the least, affect our School system.'[13] The subsequent addition by the imperial Parliament of a 'remedial' section 93, protecting the rights of denominational schools, somewhat discounted Ryerson's prognosis. However, the addition did not affect his main concern for preserving the discretionary powers built into the system. This system he described as favouring a few general rules in the legislation, 'leaving all the details to be carried out by Regulations made by the Council of Public Instruction with the approval of the Government.'[14]

Such an arrangement that permits the executive to put the flesh and blood onto the skeleton of legislation provided by Parliament is the ideal recipe for bureaucratic domination. If, in addition to such discre-tionary powers, one adds the vesting of the Education Office's finances in the person of Ryerson and the fact that the presiding council was appointed and not clearly accountable to any elective official or body, that is not only a recipe for bureaucratic domination but also for irresponsible administration.

These defects in the arrangements for administering education were not long in surfacing in the post-confederation debate over the Education Office. The most immediate issue was with respect to the practice of depositing the total appropriation for education in the personal account of Egerton Ryerson, to be spent at his discretion under a system of 'accountable warrants.' In the pre-confederation Province of Canada, the auditor, John Langton, had waged perpetual war on this practice, with Ryerson one of his chief and, from Langton's perspective, most recalcitrant culprits. The issue was still unresolved when the new federation came into being and Langton became a Dominion civil servant, no longer able to pursue his vendetta with Ryerson.

In November 1868, however, the Public Accounts Committee of Ontario's legislature took up the matter of Ryerson's personal accountable warrants. Although the committee cleared Ryerson of any misuse of the substantial funds put at his disposal – the sum of over $200,000 actually amounted to more than the total allocations for the 'Civil Government' (i.e., the headquarters staffs of all other departments) – the committee was not prepared to recommend continuation of the practice of using personal accountable warrants. Ryerson registered his disapproval of the proceedings by tendering the first of three resignations he was to proffer before his final retirement in 1876 (all of which were rejected). Nevertheless, after 1870 he was obliged to bow to the inevitable loss of his discretionary control over the education budget, when a regularized system of cheque disbursement through the Office of Provincial Treasurer was instituted.[15]

Lurking beneath the surface of the struggle to induce Ryerson to abandon his personal control over the public funds allocated for educational purposes was the broader issue of a general lack of accountability of the Council of Public Instruction. Interestingly, Ryerson's reluctance to forego the system of personal accountable warrants did not stand in the way of his advocacy of a system of ministerial responsibility for education. It may be surmised that he came to this apparently contradictory view because of what he considered to be the unwarranted aspersions cast upon him during his battle with John Langton and others over the accounting for public funds deposited to his own account. Thus vulnerable to speculations about his moral rectitude and lacking a responsible ministerial head to speak publicly for him, Ryerson was obliged to defend himself. During the thick of the battle to create just such a ministerial department for education, Ryerson wrote bitterly of 'the responsibility and labour, and often odium and collision' of explaining and defending publicly the educational policies and programs of the Office.[16]

Ryerson's own conversion to the notion of a department headed by a politically accountable minister appears to have come in stages and to have been simply a particular application of a more general principle he had been promoting. On the eve of confederation, for example, Ryerson had published an admonitory address to the people under the banner, 'The New Canadian Dominion: Dangers and Duties of the People in Regard to Their Government.' In it, he had reverted to a long-held conviction that government by party was evil, other than as an ad hoc combining of forces to achieve a specific objective, such as free trade or the attainment of responsible government. For the general conduct of affairs, however, party government resulted in partisan appointments to public office and to the organization and maintenance of the entire machinery of government 'as an engine of party.'

By 1869 Ryerson had somehow converted his antipathy to party government into an argument for a 'system of Government, under which every head of a Department shall be made as directly and fully responsible to the Legislative Assembly, as I proposed ... the Head of the Education Department should be – a System which will make the individual Heads of Departments the Servants of the Legislature, rather than its Dictators, – a System which will abolish the oligarchy of party tyranny and corruption, and give Parliament its true dignity, and to the people their real majesty.'[17]

Even after the downfall of the coalition government which must have inspired Ryerson's initial faith in a non-party form of government, Ryerson nevertheless urged on Premier Blake (despite his ongoing verbal battles with both Blake and George Brown) a non-partisan approach to education which, he claimed, was 'as much the property and work of one party as another.' This plea was followed by a second letter of resignation in which Ryerson once again argued for a ministerial head, and with J.G. Hodgins, his assistant, as a deputy minister. The Public Accounts Committee, approaching the issue from a much more mundane perspective, also supported Ryerson's recommendation. As early as 1868 it had suggested that education be placed under a 'Minister of Public Instruction' and in 1871 was 'of opinion that, in order to secure a more efficient control over the expenditure of money, through the Education Office, that Office should be made directly responsible to some member of the Government.'[18]

The appointment of Oliver Mowat as premier in late 1872 created a fresh opportunity to press the cause of reform with a more sympathetic listener. At this point, however, the debate moved beyond the specific concerns of the accounts committee over financial accountability and even bypassed Ryerson's somewhat idealistic notions of a non-party system in which ministers of the crown, including one for education, would somehow be answerable to a non-partisan assembly representing the true voice of the people.

The focus of debate now became the nature and status of the Council of Public Instruction which, with such egos as Goldwin Smith and Daniel Wilson as members, became increasingly difficult for Ryerson to 'manage.' Ryerson's growing disillusion with his council as adviser and public defender of his educational initiatives undoubtedly nourished his interest in substituting a single politically responsible ministerial head in place of the council. An added factor contributing to the general lack of faith in both Ryerson and his council was the considerable discretion they exercised to make educational policy through changes in regulations. These, of course, required approval of cabinet by order-in-council, and now a less sympathetic government was proving to be more reluctant to accept the council's recommendations and was even prone to issue orders-in-council on its own initiative, without reference to the superintendent or his council.

It was in this context that committee hearings on governmental proposals for reform were held in February 1873. Ryerson was so appalled by the excessive partisanship of these proceedings that he urged Mowat to embrace the concept of a minister of public instruction (even proposing that the provincial treasurer, Adam Crooks, be named). As for the Council of Public Instruction, its work could easily be performed 'by the Executive Council on the report of one of its members.' Although this arrangement was in fact to be incorporated into the legislative provisions for a Department of Education in 1876, Mowat was not prepared to abandon the council forthwith. He converted it into a hybrid of eight appointed members, six representatives of the universities and colleges, and three elected members. This outcome precipitated Ryerson's third letter of resignation and a repetition of his standard complaint – the need to bring education 'more immediately under the review and guardianship of the representatives of the people.'[19]

In the end, Ryerson was to prevail, as the new council proved unworkable in its mix of elective and politically appointed elements which 'vitiated and ultimately destroyed a sound and successful institution.'[20] His final solution, 'a Minister of the Crown with the Cabinet as advisers on general policy and officials to assist with technical information' was adopted in the enactment of 1876.

The defenders of the old system feared that its abandonment and replacement by a politically responsible ministerial head would inject undesirable political considerations into the educational system.[21] Despite the fact that this point of view failed to prevail in the debate over the bill to create the Department of Education, the Conservative opposition leader, William Meredith, renewed the argument in 1883. But even the *Globe*, which had been lukewarm about the original act of 1876, considered the case against the new department unconvincing. Premier Mowat, leaning heavily on Ryerson's original recommendations, remained adamant in support of the ministerial department. As he had remarked at the time of the passage of the act of 1876, 'since the Chief Superintendent has been virtually a Minister without a Minister's responsibilities, it was better to introduce into education the same principles of responsibility as prevailed in other departments.'[22]

The opposition were to make one more attempt to revert to the old system of a 'non-political head' in 1891 when a major consolidation of the Education Act was before the legislature. This proposal, like its predecessor, was also rejected and appears to have been the last direct attempt to turn the clock back.

The curious formula used for defining the Department of Education in the legislation of 1876 reflects the concerns which the opposition persistently put forward for nearly two decades. The department was declared in the act to be 'the Executive Council' or 'a committee of Council.' This unique and aberrant legal formulation must surely be attributed to the worry about politicization and reluctance to stray too far from the collegial arrangements provided for so long by the Council of Public Instruction. This anomalous legacy of casting the Executive Council or its committee as 'the department of education' remained on the statute books until the Education Act was amended in 1909.[23]

A more enduring legacy of the Education Act of 1876 was the introduction of the titles of 'minister' and 'deputy minister.' Despite the idiosyncratic definition of 'department,' a 'minister' was to be selected from the membership of council (undoubtedly a formula for keeping within the statutory limit of six members) and powers were assigned to the minister, not to the department. In short, here in concrete legal terms was the formula for individual ministerial responsibility set out, paradoxically, against a definition of department that emphasized – as no other departmental act then or since has ever done – the collective nature of the responsibilities embraced by the department. It is likely that this particular legal formulation of the doctrine of ministerial responsibility, as applied to education, was a product of the uncertainties surrounding creation of the department. Since the exercise of the most important responsibilities conferred on the minister of education entailed, in any event, confirmation by cabinet through order-in-council, the potential contradictions between a department defined in collegial terms and a minister assigned powers for which he was to be individually responsible, created no problems.

The application to the other BNA Offices of the terminology of minister and deputy minister first used in 1876 took some time to register. The commissioner of agriculture was the first of the original Offices to be re-designated as a minister of a department, with the permanent head's title shifting from that of secretary to deputy minister in 1888. With the major reorganization of 1905, both the commissioners of crown lands and of public works were retitled ministers, respectively, of the Department of Lands and Forests and the Department of Public Works; the permanent heads now assumed the title of deputy minister. The other named Offices of Provincial Treasurer, Attorney General, and Provincial Secretary and Registrar retained these titles, although their permanent heads would increasingly be referred to as deputy ministers rather than assistants.

4

Early Departmental Satellites, 1867–1905

By 1876, with the addition of a Department of Education, the primary departmental building blocks were in place and were to remain for the first four post-confederation decades the basic structural mainframe of the bureaucracy. However, within and around this static group of core building blocks more than a dozen separate administrative entities came into being, the progenitors of the modern congeries of agencies, boards, and commissions – literally, the 'ABCs' of today's governments. These discrete administrative units were nurtured by the original BNA Act Offices, their varying modes of attachment to the emergent system of politically responsible ministerial departments reflecting the initial efforts to grapple with the contemporary problem of designing organizations with a so-called arm's-length relationship to the political executive.

It is probable that this early growth of agencies occurred as a means of circumventing the restrictions placed on the number of Offices by the terms of the BNA Act. It is equally probable that the early resort to such satellites demonstrated a reluctance on the part of the province to trespass on the preserves long thought to be municipal responsibilities if they were not deemed purely private or non-governmental concerns. In a sense, the tenuous attachments of these satellites to the departments made it possible for the province to intervene as inconspicuously as possible.

In hindsight, it is obvious that not a single one of the dozen or so satellites proved redundant; on the contrary, most of them were concerned with matters that sooner or later became so significant that they qualified for admission to the central constellation of departments. During their progress to such status, however, they needed to be held within the constitutional orbit of ministerial responsibility. Somehow, if that principle were to obtain, the relationship of the political executive to each of these varied administrative agencies had to be addressed.

Although nearly all the early organizational accretions were added by legislation, their statutes were either silent or inconsistent in the attention paid to prescribing their respective relationships to the central core of the executive. However, for those agencies that lacked formal statutory requirements, one finds reassuring evidence that some form of ministerial connecting link was either assumed or simply taken for granted. Nonetheless, the inescapable impression remains that both individual and, most particularly, collective ministerial control over these assorted administrative bodies was loose enough to suggest a picture of small, relatively autonomous administrative fiefdoms. The loss of a genuine sense of accountability that might otherwise have been expected to occur under such conditions may have been effectively offset by the tiny size of these organizations, their reliance on one or a very few tremendously energetic senior officials, and the prospect of establishing close working relationships between such officials and their political chiefs. In short, the scope and scale of governmental activities was such that the linkage of administration and politics provided by a politically responsible head could be preserved by the close personal contacts that only a bureaucracy of such limited size could allow.

As one inspects these assorted administrative entities, they appear to fall into three categories, based on the nature of their arm's-length relationship to the central core of departmental Offices. In the first category were the agencies, usually designated as 'Bureaus' and having the clearest connections with one or the other of the existing departments. A second category comprised the 'Inspectorates,' which in due course were also drawn into the departmental system. The third category, made up of regulatory and operative agencies, had few representatives in the early period. After the turn of the century this category became the most comprehensive repository for all the so-called agencies, boards, and commissions, or ABCs. These, unlike most of the agencies in the other two categories, managed to retain their distinctiveness through their possession of some version of an arm's-length relationship with a parent department.

The Bureaus

Three bureaus were created by statute during this period. In each case, the statutes were much clearer about the respective departmental connections than was true of other organizations added during the same period. For the *Bureau of Industries*, created in 1882, the formula had already been established by the Bureau of Agriculture and Arts which the new bureau replaced. The bureau, the statute of 1882 read, was 'to be attached to the Department of the Commissioner of Agriculture,' the lieutenant-governor-in-council appointing the secretary (permanent head) and such other officers as might be required. The legislation that created the *Bureau of Mines* in 1891 not only stated that the bureau was to be 'in connection with the Department of Crown Lands,' but its director, appointed by the lieutenant-governor-in-council was to 'act under direction of the Commissioner of Crown Lands.' A similar formula was applied at the turn of the century to a *Bureau of Labour*, where the legislation provided that it 'shall be attached to the Department of the Commissioner of Public Works.'

It is interesting that all three bureaus were engaged in the fact-collecting and dissemination functions characteristic of the earliest enabling administrative mode. It is also noteworthy that from the outset the three bureaus were integrated into the existing departmental portfolios. In particular, the Bureau of Industries served as the central operating core of the Department of Agriculture until in the early 1900s its mandate evolved far beyond its original role as fact-gatherer and educator.[1] The same outcome awaited the other two bureaus in the second decade of the twentieth century; each outgrew its branch status within its 'mother department' to emerge as a full-blown department with its own ministerial head. This final move from satellite to full member of the departmental constellation was made possible by the legislative acknowledgment of 1888 that an Executive Council limited to six members was no longer tenable.

Another organization dealing with *immigration* deserves to be placed in the first category along with the three bureaus, although it did not share their specific statutory foundation. In the assignment of functional areas provided by section 95 of the BNA Act, immigration along with agriculture was made a shared or concurrent jurisdiction between the Dominion and the provinces. In the Province of Canada immigration had been placed under the Department of Agriculture and this arrangement was continued in Ontario under the wing of the now combined Commissionership of Agriculture and Public Works. Apart from an 1873 statute providing for the commissioner to designate districts and appoint an inspector for Immigration Aid Societies in the province, the only formal recognition of an administrative arrangement to deal with immigration was an order-in-council of 13 November 1874, making provision for a commissioner of immigration 'to be attached to one of the executive offices.' The apparent casualness of this arrangement for a program area to which as much public funding was being devoted as to the total headquarters' civil establishment was offset by the unusual care that was taken two weeks later on 26 November to secure the Assembly's approval of the order.

The public attention thereby focused on immigration matters was a testimony to the aggravations arising out of the constitutional provision for concurrent jurisdiction. Already the attempt to resolve the problems that were to continue to plague this shared jurisdictional arena had produced what was to become one of the federation's favourite instruments for conflict resolution, a Dominion-provincial conference. Convened apparently at the insistence of the hard-working provincial treasurer, Adam Crooks, the conference produced a sort of five-year plan, encapsulated in a memorandum of agreement which formed part of the order-in-council which the Assembly approved in November 1874.

The memorandum sought to establish a cooperative scheme that 'should profit from the experience of the past few years.' Then it elaborated: 'That experience emphatically pronounces for a system based upon and practically worked out according to the principles requisite for the success of any business undertaking. The proper Agency should exist ... and there should be no waste of strength or expenditure and each person employed should be personally efficient for work to which he should be called to devote his whole time and energies. The immigration service demands the same zeal, fidelity and intelligence as any other and it has ceased to be the subject of experiment.'[2] In the event, as so often happens with the enthusiastic instigator, Adam Crooks added the Commissionership of Immigration to his treasurer's portfolio. From him it passed for a time to the provincial secretary but finally returned to Agriculture in 1888 when it became a ministerial department. Despite frequent references to a 'department of immigration' during this period, immigration remained the administrative responsibility of David Spence, who was listed as secretary. He supervised a small group of agents at home and shared the services (as the memorandum provided) of Dominion agents abroad.[3]

The emergence at the turn of the century of New Ontario as a prospective domain awaiting settlement brought about the creation of a *Bureau of Colonization* in 1900 with its own director. Immigration was subsumed in the bureau but thereafter tended to be associated with efforts to 'colonize' the north. For most of the time, until its abolition in the mid-thirties, the bureau came under the aegis of the minister of agriculture. Unlike the three bureaus already noted, Immigration was never to become a department in its own right but always remained a subordinate – sometimes almost neglected – adjunct to a parent department.

One of the program areas with which immigration was briefly associated was forestry. The administrative arrangements for forestry evolved from the appointment of a single officer to serve as *Clerk of Forestry* in 1883. Even less formal than the legal arrangements attending the creation of an Immigration Branch, there was nothing more than the provision in the estimates for R.W. Phipps, the first appointee, whose annual reports were addressed to the minister of agriculture. Again, the familiar pattern of the gathering and dissemination of information is reasserted, Phipps's labours being characterized by the official historians of the Department of Lands and Forests as 'really one of protection and propaganda.' Phipps himself described the purpose of his sixth annual report as intended, as were his previous ones, to 'check the deforestation of Ontario and encourage replanting.'[4]

Accumulating knowledge and a growing professionalization amongst foresters brought about a change, beginning in 1896 with the appointment of Thomas Southworth as clerk of forestry. Described as the 'founder of Ontario forest policy,' Southworth came to embrace a concern for forest reserves and forest protection, as well as the previous concern for restocking the depleted southern reaches of the province. The administrative recognition of this shift in policy emphasis was the transfer of the clerk from Agriculture to Crown Lands, which as Southworth remarked in his first report would bring his office 'under closer supervision of the Government than was previously the case.' He went on to say that 'This change indicates an alteration in the policy of the Government in recognition of the growing importance of the question of forestry. The position, the duties of which in its earliest stages had been altogether educational, is now entrusted to some extent, with the wider and more important functions of forestry proper in relation to the crown domain.' The change, he concluded, 'contemplates the establishment of a bureau under the direct control of the Department [of Crown Lands], with a well-defined sphere in the work of administration.'[5]

Southworth's expectations were met in 1898 with the transformation of his office of clerk of forestry to a bureau. But his hope that there would now be a well-defined sphere for forestry administration was cast in doubt by the bureau's merger with the Bureau of Colonization in 1900 and its subsequent return, as noted above, to Agriculture. It was not until 1906, when the old Department of the Commissioner of Crown Lands was converted into a Department of Lands, Forests and Mines, followed in 1908 by the creation of a Forestry Branch, that Southworth's expectations were fulfilled. Even so, Forestry, unlike Mines, never achieved separate ministerial representation.

Judging from the casual way in which the province first slipped into its responsibilities for road construction (apart from colonization roads), one might have anticipated subordination of this function within the existing BNA Act Offices similar to that which we have observed for immigration and forestry. The initial step could not have been more modest, with the appointment in 1896 of A.W. Campbell to the lone position of *Instructor in Road Making*. This move was prompted by the vigorous proselytizing over the previous four years by the Good Roads Association, of which Campbell had become such a leading light that he had won the informal title of 'Good Roads Campbell.' His official title of instructor speaks yet again to the pervasiveness of the enabling and facilitative mode of administration so characteristic of the period. Nor was his original attachment to the Department of Agriculture any more illogical than using that same department as the initial locus for forestry. After all, the motive propelling the Good Roads Association was the urgent need to facilitate the farmers' task of getting fresh food to the growing urban centres.

Even before the introduction of the internal combustion engine, the growing importance of road construction and the necessity for direct provincial involvement began to be reflected within the bureaucracy. The first timid intrusion of the province into an arena hitherto occupied by municipalities and private toll companies was achieved by order-in-council appointing Campbell as instructor.[6] By 1900 Campbell had become commissioner of highways, no longer in Agriculture but in Public Works. Shortly after, indicating the importance of highways in the Public Works portfolio, Campbell was elevated to the permanent headship (assistant commissioner). Not until 1915, however, was Highways accorded full departmental status with its own deputy minister but sharing its political head with Public Works until 1930 when formal statutory provision was made for a separate minister of highways.

The Inspectorate

The second category of administrative entity, with more ambiguous relationships to the core departments, comprised the inspectorate. The various inspectorates played an important role in implementing the regulatory administrative mode of the period. Indeed, through their activist approach to the discretionary powers conferred, several of the inspectors foreshadowed the emergence of the more direct, operational role most characteristic of the present-day bureaucracy.

Only one of the inspectorates, that created by statute for an *Inspector of Insurance* in 1879, appears to have had a clear statement of the officer's relationship with the parent department. In addition to the usual provision for lieutenant-governor-in-council appointment, the legislation went on to specify that the inspector was to operate 'under instructions of the provincial treasurer.' The costs of the inspectorate were to be partially defrayed (to the limit of $3,000) by the recipients of the inspector's attentions – a somewhat backhanded way of making the clients pay for the upholding of the public interest. Nonetheless, it ensured that the minister took the responsibility for confirming any decisions made by the inspector.

In 1868 the first and most influential inspectorate, for *Prisons and Public Institutions*, was placed by statute firmly under the collective authority of the Executive Council for the exercise of an extraordinary range of powers. Holding office 'at pleasure' but with a statutory salary of $2,000, the inspectorate appears to have been uniquely invested with an independent life outside the walls of any existing ministerial office. Subsequent legislation reinforced this sense of independence, the inspector being made a 'corporation sole' in 1871, capable of suing or being sued in his own right. Three years later, he also acquired the power to institute inquiries and enforce attendance 'like any court in civil cases.' His magnificent reports, whose detailed contents were prescribed in the statute of 1868, were addressed to the lieutenant-governor for submission to the Assembly, but without the conventional intermediary covering letter from a responsible member of the Executive Council. On the other hand, from the reports themselves and from Inspector Langmuir's publicly expressed views, it is clear that he worked hand-in-hand with the provincial secretary and considered himself accountable to that minister.

As time went on, and especially after Langmuir's office became a two-man enterprise in 1881, the inspectorate was more and more incorporated within the orbit of the Office of the Provincial Secretary. Nevertheless, given the grab-bag nature of the secretary's portfolio, the inspectorate tended to be merely contained rather than controlled or coordinated by the secretary's office. Even within the inspectorate, a division of labour between what had become three inspectors before the turn of the century began to mark the preliminary stages of an amoeba-like parturition. In the two decades following the First World War no less than three major departments were to mature from these separate elements: health, public welfare, and correctional services.

When statutory provision was made in 1884 for a *Factory Inspectorate*, the legislation was somewhat more precise in defining the inspectors' relationship to the responsible minister. Initially the commissioner of public works (replaced in 1900 by the minister of agriculture) signed the certificate of appointment which authorized each of the inspectors to exercise substantial discretionary powers to enter premises and ascertain whether employers were living up to the specified requirements for safety and for the employment of women and children. The inspectors' power to exempt owners of factories (and subsequently shops) from certain regulations was subject to the minister's approval.

A comparable evolution awaited two other inspectorates, both of which began as rather 'loose fish' but with ties assumed to be with that most accommodating Office, the provincial secretary and registrar. The first of these, the *Board of Health*, entered the scene in 1882 with much the same investigative and educative functions as those exercised by the several bureaus, but with none of their formal attachments to existing ministerial Offices. No statutory provision for reporting was made for the board, although in practice reports went directly to the lieutenant-governor without a covering signature of a minister. This practice continued for over twenty years before reports came to be submitted through the provincial secretary. Despite the lack of formal provisions, however, he was apparently considered from the outset to be the responsible minister. This connection was made quite explicit when the secretary of the Board of Health was made deputy registrar general, serving the provincial secretary in his secondary ministerial role of registrar general. With the accumulation of more direct operating responsibilities, the Board of Health moved by stages from satellite to full departmental status in 1924.

The act for the prevention of cruelty and better protection of children, approved in 1893, created yet another administrative body bearing somewhat elusive relations with the responsible ministry. Following the unvarying practice of other statutes, the lieutenant-governor-in-council was empowered to appoint the chief officer, the *Superintendent of Neglected and Dependent Children*, and to approve any exercise of the educational and inspectoral powers conferred on the superintendent. The statute also prescribed an annual report which was to be made to the Assembly but without specifying which member of council should be responsible for its transmission. From the outset, J.J. Kelso, the one-man organization, reported through the provincial secretary and by 1900 was listed under the civil government expenditures attributed to the secretary's Office. However, its passage to full ministerial departmental status did not occur until the Department of Welfare was created in 1931.

Regulatory and Operative Agencies

Rounding up the last of the stragglers that initially were loosely affiliated with the BNA Offices, we come to the third group of regulatory agencies. Since these were to experience their full flowering later, beginning with the Railway and Municipal Board of 1906, they will receive fuller treatment in a subsequent chapter. However, during the first thirty years under consideration here the regulatory board or commission was just beginning to be adopted. Both the Dominion and the province were aware of the deployment of such agencies in the states to the south and, in particular, the emergence in 1887 of the United States Interstate Commerce Commission to regulate rail transport.

Ontario's reluctance to resort at an early stage to extensive use of the regulatory commission can be attributed to the persistence of the belief in the efficacy of local self-government. In the two policy areas where regulatory agencies came to be used – regulation of the liquor trade, and regulation of the exploitation of such natural resources as mining, forestry, fish and game – the strength of this belief in local government frustrated the half-hearted attempts by the province to grapple with these problem areas.

In truth, leaving regulation to the local authorities was tantamount to having no effective regulation. For example, in the field of public health where the situation was found to have deteriorated to a state that could no longer be tolerated, the province moved in with an agency of its own, but with a muted, measured response that acknowledged the sensitivities of local interests. In its first report, the Board of Health, commenting on what it believed appropriate relations with its clients should be, expressed it thus:

It is the recognition of the principle that the State may and ought to exercise a paternal care over the health and lives of the people, not in any fitful or accidental manner, as during epidemics of disease, but in a daily supervision of the habits and manner of living of individuals and communities, in everything that tends to affect favourably or unfavourably the national well-being of the people, to speak of nothing more.

This was the function the government had delegated to the board, they concluded, and it was in their view to be exercised with the same discretion as that which characterized the doctor-patient relationship.[7] In other spheres, such as the regulation of the liquor trade, the focus on the revenue-raising potential of regulation left little room for using the regulatory administrative mode in the way it has come to be employed – that is, as an instrument for influencing behaviour.

Uncertainties concerning the jurisdictional preserves of the Dominion and the provinces also contributed to the slow development of potent regulatory instruments. Two of the main problem areas were the liquor trade and certain elements of resource administration, notably the fisheries. For the liquor trade, the administrative means to achieve regulatory goals was that of licensing. The means chosen fell afoul of the interpretation of the respective taxing powers conferred by the BNA Act on the provincial and national governments.[8] While court decisions ultimately resolved the particular issue of the licensing power in favour of the province, of greater interest was the way in which respect for local government traditions was preserved by the organizational arrangements made for implementing regulation of the liquor trade.

Beginning with a *liquor licensing* act of 1874, amended in 1876 and 1877, three-member boards of licence commissioners were appointed by the lieutenant-governor-in-council, to serve a year at a time on an unpaid basis. These commissioners were vested with enormously important discretionary powers to determine the qualifications for securing a tavern licence, licences for retailing liquor, determining the number so licensed, and so on. Under each local board were inspectors of licences appointed and paid by the lieutenant-governor-in council – an extraordinarily generous patronage pool, considering that inspectors were appointed for every city, county, union of counties, and electoral district. It is little wonder that, from the mid-1880s on, the Conservative opposition railed against the centralizing tendencies of the Mowat government through its access to such patronage plums.

When the Conservatives came to power in 1905, Premier Whitney would complain of the endless stream of importunates seeking government jobs, amongst the available offerings being some 275 licence commissioners and inspectors.[9] While patronage was formally centralized, the structure of local boards dispensing local favours and paid inspectors indebted to the governing political party for their appointments marked the epitome of parish pump politics. The troubled administrative history of this means of regulating the liquor trade was to play an important part in the administrative reform movement that came to a head just at the close of the First World War – a movement which curiously combined the interest in 'abolishing the bar' with the elimination of political patronage.

In the regulation of the exploitation of *natural resources*, much the same deference to local sensibilities was displayed. In the case of mining, pre-confederation legislation was re-enacted for Ontario in 1868, its implementation being confided to provincially appointed inspectors vested with the justice of the peace powers of summary conviction.[10] A measure of the singular lack of impact of this legislation is to be found in the 1889 report of a royal commission on the mineral resources of Ontario. Throughout its otherwise comprehensive findings, no reference is to be found to regulatory issues, other than the observation that there were no provisions covering the health or safety of miners.

In the commission's view, 'To instruct, to inform, to ascertain and publish facts, to lighten the industry, to enlighten the men employed in it and deal with them in a generous spirit – such ... is the true national policy for governments to pursue in promoting the development of our mineral resources.'[11] It was from this perspective that the commission went on to recommend: 'the establishing of a bureau of mines for the purpose of making a complete geological survey of the Province, and a museum of geology and mineralogy to represent its rock formations, minerals and metallurgical products, together with an efficient plan for the collection of yearly statistics of the mining and metallurgical industries of the Province.'[12]

The commission's recommendations and the mandate assigned the *Bureau of Mines* in 1891 reflected what we have seen to be a constant in every new initiative: first, know thyself before extending the reach of government. For this emphasis, the royal commission had to thank the influence of one of its members, Archibald Blue, who as secretary of the Bureau of Industries had in effect become the province's official statistician. Unusual for a royal commissioner, he was to be given the opportunity to implement his own commission's recommendations when, with the creation of the Bureau of Mines, he was made its first director.[13]

With Blue at the helm, the regulatory administrative mode was not emphasized until about the time of his departure for the federal civil service just at the turn of the century. It was at this time that the minerals of northern Ontario began to yield their treasure to the active exploitation of entrepreneurs and speculators. The explosive nature of this development, reflected in such empire-building as that of Francis H. Clergue around the Soo, drove even J.P. Whitney, the Conservative leader, to consider going beyond mere regulation: 'it will be a case of Government ownership,' he proclaimed.[14]

In the case of mining, Whitney was never to go that far, but his own 'Minister for Northern Ontario,' Frank Cochrane, was to be responsible for bringing in a revised mining act with real regulatory powers assigned to a departmental inspectorate and a quasi-independent *Mining Commissioner* who was empowered to make decisions on disputed claims that could then be routed to the courts rather than to the minister for final arbitration.

For the regulation of *game and fisheries*, there was the same early preference for leaving implementation in the hands of local authorities or, in the case of the fisheries, leaving the federal government to cope.

The 1867 dispensation had ordained that the fisheries branch was the only unit of the old Crown Lands Department of the Province of Canada to remain with the new Dominion.[15] As with mining, a royal commission reporting in 1891 on game and fisheries revealed an even more urgent need for provincial government action to compensate for years of neglect. 'It would have been well,' the commissioners concluded, 'if the Commission ... had been issued years ago,' for 'on all sides from every quarter has been heard the same sickening tale of merciless, ruthless, and remorseless slaughter.' Like the buffalo, the commissioners lamented, they 'had reason to fear extinction for the others.'[16]

The organizational response which the commissioners believed the situation called for was, in effect, the institutionalization of their own ad hoc body in the form of a permanent *Fish and Game Commission.* Noting particularly their difficulty in addressing the problems with fisheries regulation, they considered it was work of a permanent commission, for 'it cannot be done quickly, and will require the most careful thought and research that it is possible to give it.'[17] Matching the success rate of other royal commissions, the legislative response in 1892 followed closely that recommendation in its provision for a five-member Board of Fish and Game Commissioners.

Whether the royal commission or the government which acted on its recommendation were conscious of breaking new ground is difficult to say. In hindsight, it is possible to see that the statutory provisions made for the new board were unique and foreshadowed the regulatory commissions that were to emerge in full array in the twentieth century. Ironically, disillusion with the experiment of regulating natural resources by means of the Board of Fish and Game Commissioners would lead to its abandonment and reconstitution as a regular branch within a department. In view of the subsequent popularity in the later period of the semi-independent regulatory agency, an account of the relatively brief fifteen-year experience with its presumed progenitor is in order.

In general terms, the prescription contained in the act of 1892 for the composition and powers of the Board of Fish and Game Commissioners was very much in line with what was to become a fairly standard formula for the quasi-independent regulatory board. The five-member board was to be appointed by the lieutenant-governor-in-council for three-year, staggered terms, subject to renewal. It was vested with law-making powers, to be promulgated as rules and regulations, to govern the actions taken by game wardens and fisheries overseers – subject, of course, to confirmation by the Executive Council. It was to recommend the chief officer of the board, referred to as the 'secretary and business agent,' and authorize the appointment of wardens and such deputy wardens as were deemed appropriate for any part of the province.[18] With respect to both the terms of appointment and the independent powers conferred on the board over staffing, one finds the makings of the criteria one looks for in ascribing an independence to an agency that differs from that of a branch within the normal departmental hierarchy. The board is thus 'distanced' from a departmental ministerial head and, while far from enjoying the independence accorded a judicial body, has been granted a special status that is presumed to be consonant with the quasi-legislative and quasi-judicial powers conferred on it.

The Board of Fish and Game Commissioners commenced operations with somewhat unpromising prospects. To begin with, its founding legislation also declared that the board's exercise of powers was not to conflict with any authority previously vested in the commissioner of crown lands. Although in the end it was the commissioner of public works who was made the minister to whom the board reported, it became increasingly clear that the minister's department was undertaking the responsibilities initially imposed on the board, thereby rendering it redundant. Reviewing the experience with the board, a one-man commission reporting in 1910 attributed its failure to what he considered to be its purely 'advisory' nature, the scattered membership and unwieldy size of the board that made meetings difficult, and the fact that the chairman 'was immersed in other occupations.'[19] It is significant that, despite these strictures, the commissioner found such damaging evidence of the consequences of leaving matters to departmental management under a political head that he recommended a restoration of the board, but a leaner and more powerful version of the 1892 model.

Apart from the lack of success in developing the appropriate working relationship between the board and the parent department, the prolonged jurisdictional dispute over the fisheries further unsettled the already weak regulatory capacities of the board. When, the province determined that it could no longer leave regulation to Dominion officials, in 1885 a Fisheries Act was approved by the Assembly to provide for fisheries overseers vested, like the mining inspectors before them, with powers of justices of the peace, and fishery guardians to issue licences.[20] By 1892, as the royal commission on game and fisheries discovered, the sad consequences of relying on local administration and disengaged Dominion officials had been compounded by the difficulty of getting cooperation from the regulatory officers of the several American states bordering the Great Lakes. The problem could worsen should the United States administration decide to assume control of the Great Lakes fisheries – a prospect raised by one Michigan official who testified before the commission.[21]

Under such circumstances, Ontario pressed forward with the preparation of a case to be placed before the courts with a view to clarifying the jurisdictional issue. The case was finally determined in 1898 by the then court of last resort, the Judicial Committee of the Privy Council. Like the wisdom of Solomon, their verdict sought to divide the indivisible by conferring on the province the right to license, exact fees, and impose conditions on licensees, while the Dominion's power to legislate rights enabled it to regulate the time, manner, methods of fishing, and the kinds and classes of fish to be caught.[22] Ten years after this decision, a federal royal commission on the Georgian Bay Fisheries was to ventilate the litany of complaints arising from overlapping and conflicting regulatory regimes which the Judicial Committee's decision clearly had done little to resolve.[23]

At the time the decision was made, however, Ontario was so assured that the jurisdictional issue had been settled to its satisfaction that it promptly passed a measure in 1898, calling upon the Dominion government to transfer to the province all documents, books of account and the like 'relating to the fisheries.' This measure was followed a year later by a statute providing for a deputy commissioner of fisheries and the appointment of such other officers as were deemed necessary for what was to become a Fisheries Branch, attached to the commissioner of public works. The first report issued by the new branch optimistically declared that 'the prerogatives of the respective Governments had been so clearly defined by their Lordships [of the Judicial Committee] that there need be no serious apprehension of any conflict of authority in the exercise of their several functions.' That these words were probably written by F.R. Latchford, the commissioner of fisheries, is somewhat ironic in view of Latchford's later elevation to the highest court in the province and of the subsequent findings of the royal commission on the Georgian Bay Fisheries that, if anything, the jurisdictional problems had become more exacerbated with the passing years.

With the fisheries thus given an administrative arm of its own, no longer under the regulatory Board of Fish and Game Commissioners but a branch within Public Works, the board's role was reduced to maintaining supervision over the chief game warden and his deputies. It was only a matter of time before even that role was incorporated within the Fisheries Branch and the experiment with a regulatory board, bearing a somewhat arm's-length relationship to the parent department, was abandoned. The board's demise was officially registered in the statute of 1907 which also provided for the creation of the Game and Fisheries Branch in Public Works; the circle was completed in 1914 when it was enacted that the branch 'be deemed a Department' with its own deputy minister.

In retrospect, it would appear that the experiment between 1892 and 1907 with a semi-independent regulatory board was probably conducted without any articulated conception of the need for conferring a special status on the board because of its peculiar licensing and regulatory functions. Such a conception was to evolve later through efforts to establish an appropriate arm's-length relationship, but at this stage it was probably conferred for purely pragmatic reasons. For example, the uncertainties over jurisdiction, particularly in the fisheries, may have fostered a reluctance to set up administrative machinery within a regular department. But once it was believed that the decision of the Judicial Committee had resolved the jurisdictional questions, the province was quick to establish its regulatory apparatus *within* a department, thus depriving the board of its reason for existence. It is also probable that the desire to 'take it out of politics' would have encouraged the move to create a board set up at arm's length from the central political establishment. Certainly in this arena of the hunter and fisherman, government was loathe to interfere with the seasoned individualism of a pioneer community accustomed to thinking of the resources from land and water as inexhaustible, infinitely expendable and, above all, its own to exploit as it pleased. In the event, this first experiment with the use of a semi-independent regulatory board underwent the same transformation into the normal ministerial department which we have observed to be the ultimate outcome for all the other satellite agencies.

Operative Boards. Even as this experiment in organizational design was being abandoned, steps were being taken to create new forms of satellites that would reflect a much more deliberate effort to grapple with the designing of an arm's-length relationship appropriate to the special nature of the functions conferred on each agency. After the turn of the century, expansion of state activities was reflected not only in an enlargement of the regulatory administrative mode but also in a direct involvement in the provision of goods and services by means of organizations akin to those established in the private sector to perform much the same functions. Although sometimes confused with the regulatory agencies, their primary administrative mode is operative. Unlike regular departments, their mandates are viewed as akin to those of private business enterprises and are deemed to warrant an arm's-length relationship to a parent ministerial department in order to secure 'businesslike' procedures and results.

While the setting up of the great hydroelectric enterprise in 1906 must be taken as the major exemplar of the business-type governmental agency existing apart from the regular departmental constellation, there were at least two forerunners that emerged in the early period here under consideration: the *Queen Victoria Niagara Parks Commission*, created in 1887, and the *Temiskaming and Northern Ontario Railway*, set up in 1902. The Parks Commission, with its unpaid board that included such notables as John Langmuir, its chairman (by now general manager of the Toronto General Trust Company), and Sir Casimir Gzowski, was rather like a board of trustees vested with responsibility for acquiring the land and the subsequent construction and upkeep of associated park facilities. It was later to acquire significance in conjunction with the hydroelectric power developments at the Niagara Falls but, of course, was never to achieve the prominence of the agency created in 1906, the Hydro-Electric Power Commission, to develop the great electricity grid which continues to serve municipal utility companies.[24]

Much more in the commercial role of that giant enterprise, for which the private sector was increasingly serving as the model, was the Temiskaming and Northern Ontario Railway. It may be considered the first organizational reflection of the contemporary interest in 'state ownership.' At the turn of the century this issue began to be much discussed, particularly in England, where 'municipal trading corporations' were the locally based harbingers of the national government's corporate entities that later were to comprise the organizational framework for giant nationalized undertakings.

In Ontario, this early 'gas and water socialism' made its impact not only on the organization of municipal water and gas utilities but was bruited as the basis for operating the new technology created by the telephone, the operation of electrified railways, and for the production of hydroelectric power. The intensity of interest in these questions in Ontario just after the turn of the century was indicated by the Legislative Assembly's appointment of a select committee on Municipal Trading and Municipal Ownership of Public Utilities that in its report of 1902 commented extensively on developments not only within the province but in the United States and Britain.[25]

The T. & N.O. Railway was the first province-wide agency to emerge out of this growing interest in state involvement in the entrepreneurial field. However, the board of three to five commissioners set up to construct and operate the railway in 1902 was not endowed with an extended arm's-length relationship to the government of the day. On the contrary, the tenure of the commissioners was 'at pleasure' of the crown; for all its actions the board was subject to 'any direction from the Lieutenant-Governor in Council,' today, a much-debated restriction on the autonomy deemed appropriate for the managers of business ventures. Decisions with respect to the laying of tracks and setting of rates were also subject to cabinet approval. Even the power to employ engineers, accountants, and other staff was subject to the same over-riding approval of the executive. Finally, as with any ordinary department, the provincial auditor was empowered to audit the accounts.

Clearly 'state ownership' meant 'state control,' for the special legal status which set the agency apart from the regular departments brought with it no great operating freedom, unlike its private-sector counterparts. Indeed, it is fair to conclude that by taking away with one hand all the presumed attributes of the private business model with which the agency had been endowed by the government's other hand, the new railway company had been placed in the worst of both worlds.

The structural problems of the government-owned and operated railway company were to become issues for general debate when similarly organized administrative agencies were subsequently created. At the time, however, the railway's ability to fit into the administrative system of the day, despite organizational features that might be said to run against the grain of contemporary sentiment, is best expressed by the official historian of the T. & N.O. Railway. 'Ownership by a government Commission,' writes Albert Tucker, 'implied no socialist methods or goals. Rather the public character of the Commission was incidental to the basic ideology of capitalist enterprise.' Tucker goes on to say that the new venture was seen to be in 'safe' hands because of the party nexus that related board members not only to the premier who maintained a close oversight from the beginning but to his successors, regardless of party, who perpetuated this tradition.[26]

After the first decade of this century, these early precursors were followed by many and varied structural heretics that created a disorderly organizational galaxy that grew like Topsy. The reordering of this universe was not to be properly addressed until after the Second World War.

This assessment of the early period may be fittingly rounded off by examining the nature of the tasks facing nineteenth-century public servants, the technical means available for the performance of these tasks, and the number and quality of personnel recruited for the administrative branch of government.

5

Early Tasks and Administrative Means: Mostly Men and No Machines

The administrative modes which dominated the nineteenth-century public service in Ontario were highly dependent on the tasks associated with the creation and processing of paper. If this conjures up the image of the quill-pushing clerk, one would be perfectly on target. It was very important for a developing community to collect and disseminate the information upon which future policies could be based as well as provide the means by which administrative agents of these policies could be supervised and controlled. The early public service was awash in a sea of paper, fed by the activities of legislative committees (although an official *Hansard* was still a century away), of royal commissions, the reports of public departments and grant-supported associations, detailed returns from the municipalities, from land agents, from the superintendents of colonization roads, or the sociological treatises emanating from the elements of the small empire over which the inspector of prisons and charities presided – and on and on.

Voluminous as was this published evidence of what preoccupied a majority of public servants, also to be included was the internal paperwork which, though largely invisible so far as the public record was concerned, nevertheless required the lion's share of attention in all public departments. It is not surprising, therefore, that on the two occasions, in 1878 and 1893, when replies were made to legislators' requests for information on the amount of business undertaken by each department, the guideline employed invariably related to the quantity of paper processed.[1]

Such a quantitative measure was particularly appropriate for the Office of the Provincial Secretary and Registrar and for the Attorney General's Office, where the emphasis was on routine fact-gathering, tabulating and collating from forms, and the maintenance and checking of accounts. The clerks in the Provincial Secretary's Office had the particularly burdensome duty of requesting, collecting, and tabulating detailed statistical returns from the municipalities, a task which had been temporarily undertaken until 1872 by the Dominion Audit Office.[2] Its function as the central repository and recorder of legal documents, such as patents and commissions, was a natural outcome of its double-barrelled responsibilities expressed in the dual title of Secretary and Registrar.

The registration function assumed a much higher profile after the enactment of legislation in 1869 which made the provincial secretary the registrar general for the province, responsible for the collection and maintenance of the vital statistics on births, marriages, and deaths. This function was of such importance to the development of a public health program that, after the creation of the Board of Health in 1882, its secretary was made deputy registrar general reporting to and using the staff of the Provincial Secretary's Office for administering this responsibility. The paperwork generated by the performance of the registration function may be demonstrated by just one aspect – the issuance of marriage licences that had to be taken over from the Dominion government in July 1874. Forty district registrars had to receive the hundreds of licence forms prepared by headquarters for distribution to 596 local registrars. Two years later, the district registrars were dropped as intermediaries and headquarters now had to correspond directly with some six hundred local agents. In the late 1870s, in order to compile the full range of vital statistics, the small Toronto headquarters was having to maintain communication with 2,100 postmasters, nearly 2,900 clergymen, and over 1,500 medical practitioners, seldom with their enthusiastic cooperation.

The maintenance of complex accounts to keep track of the expenditures and to allocate the revenues between municipalities and province arising from liquor licensing tasks assumed by the province in the mid-1870s was yet another source of paperwork. All these records had to be compiled for the edification of a legislature where parish pump politics gave special relevance to such detailed accounts. The impact of these and other recording and accounting activities associated with the incorporation of joint stock companies after 1874 or the maintenance of the divisional court jury fund was revealed by the accumulation of an estimated 75,000 files.[3]

In the Office of the Attorney General the pervasiveness of paperwork was attributable only in part to its responsibility for the administration of justice, which involved much correspondence on the appointing and advising of justices of the peace, crown attorneys, the registrars of various courts, and the like. Where provincial judicial districts existed, as in Algoma, Thunder Bay, Muskoka, and Parry Sound, the Attorney

General's Office maintained a direct supervisory responsibility that extended beyond mere routine paperwork; the administrative officers at Osgoode Hall, the centre of the court system, also came under the more direct control of headquarters.[4]

However, the correspondence files of the Attorney General's Office were expanded less by these responsibilities for judicial administration than by the de facto combination of the Office with that of the Executive Council, since both served the needs of the premier. The two offices were not separated until 1905, when a central agency was developed to serve the needs of the premier as well as the collective needs of the cabinet. Even so, thanks to the fact-compiling proclivities of the time, we know that a separation was made from the outset between the business of the premier (the Executive Council component) and the regular business of the Attorney General's Office. In 1871, for example, 1,000 letters as against only 152 'official' letters were considered to be related to the premier's business; by 1892 the premier's portion was 5,500 as compared with 2,372 'official' letters associated with the Attorney's Office. Within that same twenty-year period the number of files had tripled from 806 to 2,142 and the number of orders-in-council recorded by the Executive Council staff had grown from 250 to 741.

This description of the work typically associated with two of the five original BNA Offices could be elaborated to extend to the others, especially Crown Lands and Public Works, where the detailed reports and accounts from scattered agents in the field became the stuff of workaday life for the clerical and book-keeping staff at headquarters. The more extended the account the more the initial perception is reinforced: the production and processing of paper comprised the daily tasks of a public service that was largely geared to the enabling and regulatory administrative modes.

This conclusion confronts today's observer with a fascinating paradox: faced as they were with voluminous work of a routine, repetitive nature, civil servants of the day were having to cope with such tasks equipped quite literally with an office technology still dominated by the quill pen. Trying to place ourselves in their shoes, we have to visualize a period where the typewriter was a curiosity and where, even by the 1890s, the fountain pen was a long way from displacing the steel-nibbed pen, which had still to replace the quill.[5] Even as late as 1897, among the items supplied to each member of the legislature were included stationery, pens, corkscrews (which we are assured were for opening ink bottles), and knives which, if not used as of yore for sharpening the quill nib, would have served to sharpen the pencils with which the members' kits were also amply supplied. Whatever the arcane uses to which the penknife had been put, it still seemed to have a powerful symbolic value, not only for the members of the legislature but also for each clerical worker, for whom it was standard issue. Even the judiciary were not above acceptance of a penknife, though theirs, at $2.50, were apparently of superior quality. The miscellaneous expenditures of most departments also generally carried a separate item, often for as little as 15 cents, to cover the cost of 'sharpening erasers.'[6]

Other means of communication in the public service were equally constrained. The telephone was just emerging with the incorporation of the Bell Company in 1880, the automobile would not appear until after the turn of the century, and of course aircraft and radio were very much in the future. For the regulatory and inspectoral administrative mode, where these means of transportation and communication are today so taken for granted, there were available only the expensive and somewhat inflexible means of transportation by train and communication by telegraph.

These facts of life for civil servants working in the last thirty years of the nineteenth century tend to be overlooked by today's investigator because the most visible records available are products of the printing press. One tends to forget that the material with which the compositor had to work was laboriously collected, compiled, or copied by hand. Our admiration for these early employees of the state must surely be heightened by the amazement that so few could produce so much with such primitive means. To take but one example: how could John Langmuir, the indefatigable inspector of prisons and charities, conduct his extensive inspectoral duties and yet find time, with the help of no more than a couple of clerks, to compile reports running often to several hundred pages, replete with detailed statistics that are formidable sociological documents of the time?

Such feats were achieved in spite of the indifferent quality of some of the employees responsible for compiling the returns required by the legislature. One fascinating vignette of such work and its performers was presented in 1894 to the Public Accounts Committee of the Assembly.[7] The item under consideration was the expenditure on a group of 'Sessional Writers' many of whom, like their supervising officer, David Spence, held down permanent offices in the public service but were permitted to moonlight for the two months during which the Assembly was in session. As their title indicated, they were employed at a fixed rate of two dollars a day as writers, one of their assignments being to copy a sample letter prepared by Spence requesting certain information which the municipalities were required to provide for the provincial legislature. For those whose writing was poor, there were forms to be ruled in a way which presumably did not lend itself to being printed. For others in the pool of some forty to fifty writers, frequent leaves of absence could be approved – the foreman apparently receiving a gift from the group in gratitude for liberal interpretation of the workday rules that called for attendance from ten in the morning to four in the afternoon, with an hour for lunch. (One is reminded here of Charles Lamb's likening of the British civil servant to the fountains in Trafalgar Square: they both play from ten until four, save that the civil servant stops an hour or more for lunch.)

The picture of four dozen or more sessional writers, still ensconced in the reception room of the old Legislative Buildings rather than in the recently completed Parliament Buildings at Queen's Park, laboriously copying or ruling forms, the more competent collating the responses sent in by sundry correspondents, nicely epitomizes the nature of the workplace for civil servants in the late years of the nineteenth century.[8]

That things were about to change might have been gathered from the queries of one member of the Public Accounts Committee as he endeavoured to discover whether there might not be more efficacious means of performing such routine tasks.

QUESTION: Have you a typewriter?
A: No, we don't use a typewriter.
Q. Why not?
A: I don't know anything as to that.
Q. You are simply finding work by writing these letters for the sessional writers to copy; is not this just a means of finding them work?
A: Of course, everything put before them provides them with work.

Further probing elicited the grudging admission that 'if a typewriter had a copy set for him he could block a number of letters' but that much of the work of tabulating statements did not lend itself to the 'typewriting machine.' To the query, why not send typewritten requests to the municipalities in lieu of the hand-written copies of a form letter, the answer was that a hand-written letter was not as likely to be thrown out by the recipient and besides, 'most men can write as fast as typewriters.' But the clinching argument for sticking with the old technology was 'the clerks I have are not fitted to run typewriting machines, and I have none for them to use.'

The witness before the Public Accounts Committee in 1894 was not alone in excusing his reluctance to move with the times on the lack of machines. W.T.R. Preston, the librarian in charge of purchasing books for the library of the Education Department, revealed to the Accounts Committee in 1896 that the typewriting machine was still very much a curiosity. Declaring that he had found very little use for a typewriter presented to him five or six years ago by friends, he offered to sell it to the government.[9] Preston's offer came some dozen years after both the Offices of Attorney General and of Provincial Secretary had each purchased a typewriter. By 1886 both these offices had added a second machine; the Education Department, the Audit Branch, Public Works, and Crown Lands had also made requisitions, often through the back-door route of supplementary estimates, the principal supplier being the firm of Thomas Bengough.[10]

In 1887 Archibald Blue, secretary of the recently created Bureau of Industries and a leader in the field of statistics collection, recommended the purchase, at a cost of $200, of a 'counting machine' which had attracted his attention while on a visit to Boston. Other than an item in the public accounts of 1883 for the purchase by the Attorney General's Office of a 'caligraph' (at $95.75 coming close to the cost of a typewriter), there was little indication to the close of the century that office work in the public service differed much from pre-confederation times.[11] Nor do figures as late as 1922 reveal a particularly extravagant dedication to the new mechanical helpmates: for a headquarters staff now numbering about fifteen hundred, the purchase of 184 new and replacement typewriters does not strike one as excessive.[12]

However gradual the acceptance of the new office technology represented by the typewriter, it had impressive repercussions on the hitherto overwhelmingly male composition of the public service of Ontario. As in England, where the so-called 'boy copyists' (some of whom were over ninety because of the absence of a pension plan for the class) were giving way at this same period to 'female typewriters,' the new machine opened employment opportunities in the public service hitherto unavailable to women. Significantly, in England the use of the term 'female typewriter' not only conveyed the notion of an exclusive identification of woman with the machine she operated, but also perpetuated a segregation of female employees from their male counterparts in public service which was to endure despite the breakdown of barriers in the First World War.

In this respect the 'colonies' proved more liberated. Although women tended to outnumber men in the typing and clerical-typist categories in Ontario, they were never designated as a class apart and certainly no evidence has been found to match the paranoia shown by at least one old-line British ministry which incarcerated its female workers in a separate room lest their mingling with the vulnerable (and no doubt venerable) boy and men copyists might lead to unwholesome behaviour. This policy was not formally abandoned until passage of the Sex Disqualification (Removal) Act of 1919.[13]

In Ontario a category of typist, clerk/typist, or stenographer/typist began to appear on the pay lists of the public service by the turn of the century. Their growing acceptance and value were reflected in weekly salaries that had at least doubled from ten to twenty dollars during the first decade. Although no formal segregation between male and female typists appears to have been made, from the outset women clearly predominated. A royal commission report on unemployment published in 1916 noted the emergence of the new category of stenographer. Some 26,000 stenographers were claimed to be at work in the province, close to half being employed in Toronto; of these, only a small fraction of the total were men.[14] The preparation of this new category of worker had become a thriving business; no less than twenty-eight schools and business colleges had been created in Toronto alone. Interestingly, in a period before government employment agencies displaced privately run agencies, graduates of these schools had to resort to agencies run by the major typewriter manufacturers, whose products the successful applicants were expected to push with their employers.

Of course, the typewriter alone was not responsible for the transformation in the composition of the public service workforce at headquarters, where women made up some 30 per cent of the workforce by the early 1920s.[15] Nevertheless, women were employed almost exclusively on the clerical and paperwork with which the typewriter was closely associated, not only in the public service but in private sector business offices. The female employee had to settle for whatever satisfaction she could derive from lower-order appointments in ministers' or senior male officials' offices. However, it requires no great leap of the imagination to conjure up the dependency of a senior executive or a ministerial head upon the support of a dedicated female secretary/clerk/typist.

There were, no doubt, exceptions to this built-in state of subserviency, as the career of Miss Vera Glenney could demonstrate. First hired in 1918 as a clerk/typist to serve as the lone permanent support staff to Dr J.M. McCutcheon, the first civil service commissioner, Miss Glenney edged up the hierarchy to become secretary and ultimately, in 1957, one of the commissioners. Miss Glenney's accession to the senior ranks, one should observe, took place long after the Second World War. Even then her career was an exception, for the broader societal forces had done little to alter the bias that relegated women to the positions which the advent of the typewriter did nothing to rectify. On the contrary, the presumed affinity of the female employee for the typewriter, and the routine, repetitive work associated with it, sustained a bias that proved resistant to change. Only in the last decades of this century, with the advent of equal opportunity and pay equity programs, have the disparities come to be addressed.

Only in one administrative arena was the male order explicitly breached when, in 1895, an amendment to the factory legislation provided for the appointment of one female inspector. Clearly, extension of the legislation beyond the factory to include shops and mercantile establishments where so many young women were employed prompted the need for a female official. Subsequent expansion of the inspectorate tended to preserve this ratio of approximately one female to three male inspectors: in 1923, for example, there were five women and thirteen men on the inspectorate.

In one respect, the bias remained: Margaret Carlyle, on first appointment, received a salary roughly half that of her male colleagues and even after twenty-five years of service her salary of $1,100 was still out of line with the $1,600 paid the most recent male recruit. The women who later joined her in the inspectorate received precisely the same treatment, despite the fact that, judging from their reports, there was no difference in their workloads that would justify the salary differential. Nor was there strong evidence for a prevalent view that a differential was warranted because women were bound to have short careers. Miss Carlyle's long tenure compared well with any of her male colleagues. Mrs J.R. Brown, the next woman to be appointed in 1904, enjoyed almost as lengthy a career, her married status apparently not being considered a cause for concern.

While the introduction of the typewriter had important repercussions on public offices dedicated to paperwork, the other indispensable instrument, the telephone, probably had more relevance for those engaged on inspectoral work. However, its acceptance as more than a luxury item for public officers was so tardy that even the inspectorates of the early 1900s had no ready access to a telephone. A modest item in the budget for the Attorney General's Office in 1879 – $100 to cover the cost of renting 'a battery, bell and box' – seems to be the first reference to Bell's apparatus. This was quite daring, considering that the first experimental transmission had occurred as recently as 1876. More than a decade was to pass before the public accounts for 1892 made reference to a sum for 'Bell rentals' for the entire headquarters civil service, amounting to $1,337.32. Ten years later, the total telephone bill for the government amounted to only $4,500.[16]

The explanation for the slow acceptance of an instrument that would have been so obviously useful for the performance of the kind of tasks then confronting public officials such as the inspectors is to be found in the unresolved issues surrounding the introduction of the telephone. There was a question of jurisdiction to be settled between the provinces and the Dominion. There was also heated debate over the desirability of making the telephone a public utility, and if so whether ownership should be vested in municipalities, the province, or the Dominion. With Ontario Hydro already in place as a monument to provincial/municipal ownership for the production and distribution of electrical power, one might have assumed a similar outcome for the telephone. However, just before the First World War, the provincial treasurer reported against direct provincial ownership as a result of a fact-finding mission he had undertaken in Europe.[17] Thus, unlike the western provinces where government ownership was established, Ontario permitted a proliferation of private companies whose 79, 000 telephones represented one-third of the total owned in 1915. It is probable that these disputes over jurisdiction and ownership contributed to the slow expansion in government's use of the instrument. Undoubtedly the confused situation dictated the necessity of regulation over and beyond that applied by Dominion regulatory authorities on the Bell Company. The availability after 1906 of the Ontario Railway and Municipal Board provided the necessary provincial instrument.[18] Thus, the coming of the telephone was a mixed blessing: even as its proliferation advanced the work of public servants, that same uncoordinated sprawl posed new regulatory burdens on the public service.

The advent of the automobile, the other great technological breakthrough in the means of communication and transportation, came too late to benefit the itinerant public servant of the late nineteenth century. J.W. Langmuir's account in 1874 of his manifold duties as the lone inspector of prisons and public charities, contains an illuminating sentence: 'I travelled upwards of 10,000 miles last year, and made more than 150 statutory inspections.' All this was done without benefit of telephone or automobile, and with the assistance of a clerk or two working at best with steel-nibbed pens. Even when Langmuir's work came to be divided between three inspectors, their bailiwicks continued to be equally sprawling because they were determined by the type of institution to be inspected, rather than the location.

Although the factory inspectors were assigned specific regions rather than being required to cover the entire province, they were still so few in number in relation to their large districts and expanding duties that they could have benefited enormously from the telephone and automobile. Dr Peter Bryce, secretary of the Board of Health, who with his board colleagues frequently travelled to sites of epidemics or to inspect municipal water supply facilities, would also have welcomed assistance from the new technologies. Even at the turn of the century these were not available to Dr Charles Hodgetts, appointed first medical inspector under Dr Bryce. In his report covering the first fifteen months after his appointment on 1 October 1900, Dr Hodgetts revealed that his duties had taken him out of his Toronto office for 277 days, during which time he had travelled 25,000 miles in the course of visiting 176 municipalities.[19]

There is a striking absence of complaints about what must have been horrendous hardships encountered during the course of all these inspectors' labours. The matter-of-fact acceptance of the difficulties associated with the performance of the varied duties with which each inspector was vested tells us something of the character of these pioneer public servants. From their reports it is clear that without exception they were independently-minded, vigorous, self-reliant individuals. The environmentalist might argue that such qualities were engendered by the conditions under which they were required to work. Without testing the validity of this hypothesis, it nevertheless remains clear that the paucity of administrative means did not prevent Ontario's early public servants from coping by a display of personal effort far beyond the call of duty.

From this conclusion springs a fresh paradox. When, in course of time, new office instruments and new communication and transportation technology were introduced into the public service – all labour-saving devices or conducive to efficiency one would have thought – instead of exerting a moderating influence on the growth of the bureaucracy, they conspired to expand it. Parkinson's law in this case might be reformulated to posit that paperwork expands to meet the capacity of the machines available for processing it. Thus, while the typewriter opened up opportunities hitherto unavailable to women, the presence of the machines also triggered a more general growth in clerical work associated with the production, manipulation, and storage of the paper so created and thereby further expanded employment opportunities for women.

The interrelation of administrative means and administrative tasks that produces automatic (and, presumably, unnecessary) growth in the public service is open to another, less cynical, interpretation. Placing new facilities such as the telephone and the automobile at the disposition of the public service may have opened up opportunities to regulate more effectively or provide services that, in the absence of such administrative means, would have been beyond the capacity of public servants to provide. From this perspective, for example, the thrust of centralization, which we have seen evidenced in the progressive intrusion of the provincial government into the affairs of its municipal authorities, would have been aided and abetted by the arrival of the new office technology and the new means of communication and transportation.

With a province the size and sprawl of Ontario, improvements in the means of communication and transportation must certainly have encouraged the province to assume a more direct, hands-on administrative mode that fostered growth of the public service. A most obvious instance of this interconnection was the use of aircraft by the Foresty Service to cope with devastating forest fires as well as conduct surveys of foresty resources in the relatively inaccessible northern regions of the province. This program was introduced, not without initial misgivings, largely because of the availability after the First World War of a pool of aircraft and pilots looking for civilian worlds to conquer.[20]

Somewhat earlier, the impact the automobile was to make on improving the capacity of the bureaucracy to face new obligations was registered in 1910 with Ontario Hydro's purchase of four cars, presumably to facilitate the constant travelling of its engineers – although a new Pearce Great Arrow at a cost of $5,000 appeared to sceptical members of the Public Accounts Committee an unnecessary luxury. Ten years later Ontario Hydro was still the leading user, its 150 cars and trucks outnumbering the 95 cars and 41 trucks owned by all other departments combined.[21] Among the heaviest departmental users listed in a 1920 return were the 'district representatives' of the Department of Agriculture, newly created officers representing a more positive move on the part of the province to trespass on municipal ground. The allocation of forty-nine automobiles to this group (as well as nine more to the district health nurses) may be taken as evidence in support of the view that the availability of a new technology provides the necessary incentive for adoption of a direct hands-on administrative mode.[22]

These illustrations suggest that access to new means of communication and transportation made it possible for the province to proceed with consolidating its control at the centre and simultaneously to disperse the implementation of programs. Thus, during the years immediately preceding and following the First World War the reciprocal relationship between administrative means and administrative modes found expression in the increased emphasis placed on the hands-on administrative mode. The importance of the connection between initiation of governmental policies and the availability of means for their successful implementation is confirmed by the dependency of today's welfare state upon the electronic gadgetry of the contemporary office.[23]

It is important, also, to recognize that the form of the new technology, such as the automobile, created problems in its own right which called for further governmental intervention. The practical spin-offs from the advent of the automobile, for example, forced a revolution in the province's approach to road construction and, more indirectly, necessitated a growth in other bureaucratic quarters in order to cope with the consequent problems of environmental damage and (sub)urbanization. These external consequences of the arrival of new technology belong rather to the story of the growth of the public service departments in response to the full array of societal pressures, of which those promoted by new technologies as applied to the office workplace constitute but a part.

6

Personnel and Personalities in the Early Public Service

Numbering the Public Service

The staffing of the departments and satellites that made up the structural framework of the early public service was, with the exception of the Crown Lands and Education Offices, almost entirely a matter of recruiting from the ground up. Until the early 1890s, members of the Legislative Assembly displayed unremitting interest in the public service – probably fuelled by their suspicion that the executive was abusing its appointment prerogatives and failing to meet their expectations of a share in the loaves and fishes. Testifying to this interest, the government produced elaborate responses to members' questions concerning new appointments, growth in numbers, and even descriptions of workloads.

The returns for the staff located at the seat of government were extraordinarily detailed, identifying by name everyone from the lowliest fireman to the most senior official. Unfortunately, the attempt to enumerate the outside service of the central Offices and their agencies is fraught with much uncertainty. Not only are the records of employment scattered throughout the public accounts, but the varying terms of employment – seasonal, part-time, *per diem*, or fee basis – give rise to definitional problems that produce significant variations in the head count of public servants. Such uncertainties are reduced after the creation in 1918 of the Office of Civil Service Commissioner and the subsequent adoption of a superannuation scheme that required a clearer definition of a public servant. Even so, wide variations in the official figures published from time to time throughout the 1920s and onward reveal the persistence of the definitional problem.

The firmer figures for headquarters staff are provided in Table 1. Since the satellite agencies tended to be shifted about amongst the Offices, each has been arbitrarily listed under the parent Office with

TABLE 1
Headquarters Staff of the Public Service

Department	1871	1881	1892	1905
1. Att'y Gen'l & Exec. Council	4	5	10	8
a. Judicial Admin'n	24	27	42	52
2. Prime Min. & Exec. Council				4
3. Education	19	16	17	26
4. Crown Lands	24	23	33	44*
5. Public Works	15	9	15	22†
6. Treasury, inc. Audit Office	10	8	12	22
a. Insp. of Insurance	0	2	3	5
b. Queen's Printer	0	2	3	4
7. Prov. Sec'y & Registrar	7	6	11	15
a. Regis. General	2	7	11	19‡
b. Insp. of Prisons etc.	2	6	7	12
c. Licence & Justice Acc'ts	1	4	7	8
d. Insp. Div'n Courts	1	2	3	4
e. Insp. Registry Office	1	1	1	1
f. Sup't. Neglected Children				5
g. Munic. Auditor				1
8. Agriculture	2	1	9	22
a. Immigration	1	3	3	7
b. Factory Inspection	0	0	3	7
c. Forestry Branch	0	0	1	7
Total inside Service	113	122	191	295

* Includes 4 in Mines Branch.
† Includes 7 in Fisheries Branch, 2 in Game Protection Branch, and 2 in Labour Bureau.
‡ Includes 6 in Provincial Board of Health.
SOURCES: *Sessional Papers*: 1869, No. 31; 1871–2, No. 45; 1873, No. 40; 1874, Nos. 11 and 56; 1881, No. 22; 1894, Nos. 43 and 99. *Public Accounts* for various years.

which it was most regularly associated. Until the late 1880s, Agriculture also tended to be treated as a subordinate adjunct to one of the Offices, but in the table it is given its separate status, including Immigration as a subsidiary.

It is appropriate to start the examination of headquarters establishments with the estimates that were submitted by the government in 1881 in compliance with provisions of a civil service act of 1878.[1] That act called for the classification of the headquarters' staff into officers and various clerical grades and then imposed on the government the duty of formulating establishments for each department in each category and presenting the results to the Assembly for its formal approval. No attempt was made to classify the lower order of employees such as messengers, caretakers, or other minor menial or custodial groups. In short, the classification and tabulation presented in 1881 showed only the permanent, salaried headquarters establishment. It came to a grand total of 122.

Reflecting the as yet still incomplete organization of the departmental system, only five deputy heads were authorized – for the Offices of Attorney General, Provincial Treasurer, Provincial Secretary, Commissioner of Crown Lands, and the Department of Education. Public Works was to continue to operate without a single permanent head until after the turn of the century, its three most senior people being classified as 'officers.'

The classification revealed a disproportionate number of senior officials. More than one-quarter of the total held senior positions: five deputy heads, twenty-five officers, and six chief clerks. If the seventeen first-class clerks are added, the proportion is closer to half. It is worth noting that, within the ambit of the Attorney General's Office, classification required the inclusion of the staff needed for the administration of the courts of justice at Osgoode Hall. This accounted in no small measure for the imbalance. No less than twenty-seven classified staff were in this judicial administration group, accounting for one-third the entire 'officer' category and eight out of seventeen in the first-class clerk category.

Comparing the total of 122 with the number shown shortly after confederation in 1871,[2] one observes the extremely modest growth in the first decade. In 1871 the equivalent total (including the Education Office and administration of justice) is 113, bolstered by some twenty permanent messengers, housekeepers, firemen, and the like (personnel that were not among those classified in 1881, although by that time there were not many more of them than in 1869).

Advancing another decade beyond the 1881 base, a remarkably detailed return in 1894 presents the situation for the year 1892.[3] Once again deleting the messengers, caretakers, etc., who were not part of the 1881 figure for the classified service, total headquarters' staff has grown to 191, most of the increase being attributable to administration of justice and Crown Lands.

Figures for the 'outside' or field service (see Table 2) are much more difficult to pin down. Three of the original BNA Offices conducted their affairs entirely from headquarters: the Attorney General, the Treasurer, and the Provincial Secretary and Registrar. However, the Provincial Secretary's Office had loose supervisory responsibilities for the inspector of prisons and other public institutions, and his administrative domain did embrace a sizeable group of prisons, asylums, schools for the

TABLE 2
Outside Staff of the Public Service

Department	1871	1892	1905
1. Att'y Gen'l & Exec. Council	0	0	0
2. Prime Minister & Exec. Council			0
3. Education, incl. staff of SPS, Normal, Model Schools, Inspectors	100	150	250
4. Crown Lands incl. Mines	100	150	200*
5. Public Works, incl. Fish & Game, Labour Bureau, Highways	10	20	90
6. Treasurer, incl. Audit Office	0	0	0
7. Prov. Sec'y & Registrar	0	0	0
a. Staff Prisons, Asylums, other Schools & Institutions	230	245	250
8. Agriculture: Agric. Coll., dairy instructors, etc. & Immig/Colonization	0	60	160
Total outside Service	440	625	950

* Estimate only because of the fee for service, seasonal, part-time, or as with wood rangers, shared-cost mode of payment.
SOURCE: Relevant *Public Accounts,* and *Sessional Papers*: 1871–2, No. 45 and 1894, No. 43.

the deaf and for the blind, whose combined salaried staffs in 1871 numbered approximately 230. The Education Office had a salaried, travelling inspectorate of some eighty persons and a full-time staff of around twenty at the Toronto Normal School. The field staff of Public Works – lockmasters, engineers, and superintendents of works – were nearly all temporary or seasonal and totalled only ten in 1871.

The figures for Crown Lands are best stated as the number of persons drawing on the public purse, for most were on per diem and expense accounts, like the ten inspectors for colonization roads, the two examiners for the Board of Surveys, the eighteen wood rangers, and the twenty land evaluators. Added to these were some two dozen land sales agents, the timber agents' offices at Quebec and Ottawa (where the province paid one-third of the salaries of the staff of eight), and the fifteen surveyors paid on the basis of five to seven dollars an acre, who would appear to have done very well out of this arrangement. Thus in 1871 the number claiming some form of stipend for public services rendered outside the seat of government would have totalled somewhat above four hundred.

By 1892, in contrast to the slight growth of personnel at headquarters, very substantial expansion had taken place in the field service. In the

Education Department, the inspectorate was little changed in numbers. But a second Normal School and a Model School, together with the staff of the School of Practical Science (listed with the department, although to be affiliated with the University of Toronto in 1906) brought the number of permanent salaried staff to 150, with another several dozen temporary employees. Public Works, with some two-dozen employees, had about double the number of lockkeepers, dam caretakers, and clerks of works it had in 1871, divided evenly between permanent and seasonal employees. The sprawling domain of Crown Lands had added fire rangers and fisheries overseers to the expanding group of land agents, surveyors, colonization road inspectors, and the like, adding at least another fifty to the estimated total of one hundred in 1871.

The staff for the institutions under the care of the inspector of prisons and charities – the asylums, the central prison, the reformatories, and the schools for the deaf and the blind – increased only marginally to some 245, although there were many daily hired help, such as the laundresses, that were not included in these figures. A new entry came from the Department of Agriculture which, beginning in 1873, had assumed charge of the Agricultural College at Guelph with its experimental farm. By the 1890s the college was beginning to launch travelling lecturers to the farmers' institutes and instructors in dairying. Some 125 of these employees were temporary, but there were eighteen professional staff at the college, supported by thirty-two permanent 'domestics,' and there were some twenty permanent employees on the farm.

In sum, a total of about 625 'outside' employees in 1892 would appear to be a fairly substantial advance on the figure of around 440 in 1871. If the officials engaged in judicial administration are included, the province's control over patronage is seen to be much enlarged. Such figures are presented in a request in 1894 for a detailed return of all employees, showing the proportion of Catholics to Protestants.[4] This comprehensive picture of total governmental enrolment includes staff of the Assembly and the enormously extended group of officials responsible for the administration of justice and the maintenance of the peace – sheriffs, registrars of courts, police magistrates, bailiffs, licence inspectors, and so on. If it was the intention of the Protestant Protective Association to prove discrimination in governmental hiring practices by promoting such a query, the result must have been disappointing: statistics showed that Catholics made up one-sixth of the population but accounted for a lesser proportion of positions and consequently fared badly in the apportioning of the total salary bill.

Of greater interest here is the check provided by this comprehensive return on the calculations produced above. Clearly, the second return covered far more ground than what has here been taken to represent the public service proper. Thus, the grand total presented is 1,738, of whom 409 were considered to be 'inside' employees. This figure is more than double the total previously calculated for headquarters personnel in 1892. It may be explained by the inclusion of the staff of the Assembly and the treatment of sizeable staffs of institutions based in Toronto as part of the 'inside service.' The same virtual doubling of the figure calculated for the outside service (625 as against 1,329) is caused by the inclusion of the array of officials concerned with judicial administration, many of whom were not salaried. The figures are also swollen by the inclusion of seasonal and temporary workers employed largely in Public Works and Crown Lands. However, as the most comprehensive assemblage of statistics of public service employment in all its aspects, the grand total of over 1,700 presents the truest measure of the extent of patronage available to the government of the day. Only the core component at headquarters – perhaps not more than two hundred or so in the 1890s – appears to have been immune from the baneful influence of partisan appointment.

Finally, looking at the public service in 1905 when the Conservative administration of J.P. Whitney brought the long Liberal regime to an end, the total headquarters establishment numbered about three hundred, an increase of about one hundred over the previous decade. In this period the five original BNA Offices had been expanded to eight through the conversion of the Education Office into a department in 1876, the formal separation of Agriculture from Public Works, and Whitney's own decision to split off the Presidency of Council from the Office of Attorney General. This became the Office of the Prime Minister and President of the Executive Council.

Contributing further to this growth was the integration of satellite agencies into the BNA Act Offices and the move towards a more hands-on administrative mode. The Agriculture Department began to develop its headquarters establishment; a Municipal Auditor's Office was added, as was the Office for the Superintendent of Neglected and Dependent Children; a Succession Duty Branch was added to the Treasurer's Office; Public Works accumulated a Fisheries Branch, a Game Protection Branch, and a Labour Bureau as well as harbouring a Roads Branch that in due course would become a department in its own right. Since all of these were initially small enterprises with limited staffing needs, the growth of headquarters staff was far from spectacular.

The estimation of the staffing requirements for a progressively widespread field service is, again, elusive; they were dispersed through virtually every heading of the public accounts, beyond the 'civil government' category. For three of the eight departments, all personnel were located at headquarters: the new Department of the Prime Minister and President of the Executive Council (a staff of four); the now separate Department of the Attorney General (six); the Treasury Department, including the Audit Office (seven) and a new Succession Duties Branch (four), had a total staff of twenty-two. The Provincial Secretary's Department had a central office of fifteen, while its appendages of a Licence Branch (six), Audit of Criminal Justice Accounts (two), Registrar General's Branch (thirteen), Provincial Board of Health (six), and Inspectorate of Public Institutions (twelve), were all centralized, save for the last-named agency. Here the permanent staff required to manage the nine asylums for the insane, the central prison, and the Mercer reformatory numbered about 250.

The remaining four departments had field services of varying sizes. The two dozen or so central staff of the Department of Education presided over an Inspectorate of some seventy-five persons. In addition to the staffs of the Normal Schools and the School of Practical Science, the department had inherited the schools for the deaf and for the blind from the Inspectorate of Public Institutions – all told, some 250 full-time teachers, support staff, and inspectors, together with at least another fifty part-time employees.

The total headquarters staff of the Department of Agriculture came to twenty-two and represented but the tip of the iceberg when contrasted with more than one hundred full-time and some fifty part-time employees at the Agricultural College, the Experimental Farm, dairying instructors, and the staff of an experimental fruit farm.

In the Department of Public Works, a headquarters staff of thirteen (three of whom dealt with colonization roads) were outnumbered by the full-time staff of eighteen required for the maintenance of the Parliament Buildings alone. Seasonal lockmasters, caretakers, and bridge tenders numbered twenty-seven, while there were 225 overseers of colonization roads and twenty-three road inspectors. The Fisheries Branch, illogically placed within Public Works, had a headquarters staff of five permanent and two temporary employees who presumably looked after the salaries of well over two hundred overseers and the captain and twelve-man crew of the steamer *Gilphie*. A Game Protection Branch, also mysteriously associated with Public Works and with a staff of three, supervised seven seasonal game wardens in the field. The final appendage, a Labour Bureau with a staff of two, as yet had no field staff.

The Department of Crown Lands, renamed Lands and Mines in 1905, had the most far-flung and elusive staff of field agents. The old core of the Crown Lands Department, which historically had dealt with lands

and timber, had a headquarters staff of forty to cope with some fifty
salaried land agents. (The fact that the official lists showed a dozen of
these as having been 'removed' on the advent of the Conservatives in
1905 is indicative of their vulnerability to patronage.) In addition, there
were seventeen timber agents, seven homestead inspectors, some
seventy-five wood rangers, and well over 350 fire rangers, most with
tiny amounts attached to their names by way of stipends and for
'expenses.' Then there were the timber agents offices in Quebec City
and Ottawa, adding another four to the staff. Reflecting a relatively new
initiative, there are the full- and part-time staff of Algonquin and Ron-
deau parks – another dozen or so. Bringing up the rear were several
hundred cullers who had been licensed by the department but were not
regarded as its employees, even though each was dutifully listed.

The Colonization and Forestry Branch, which had been set up within
the old Crown Lands Department in 1900 and was to be transferred in
1905 to Agriculture, had a headquarters staff of seven to deal with the
Liverpool Emigration Office (staff of two) and, on the immigration side
at home, to deal with a host of 'settlers' guides' hired at two dollars a
day. The forestry connection with colonization was to be found in the
policy of removing land deemed unsatisfactory for settlement and setting up forestry reserves. More than forty-two temporary or part-time
staff were by this time associated with the creation and preservation of
these reserves.

The Bureau of Mines, incorporated in 1905 as the second component
of the department, had at the outset a tiny headquarters' staff of four
and had as yet to build up a field force to go with it. Instead, it relied
on contractual relations for 'services' from a variety of firms and individuals.

One final element of the public service in 1905 has yet to be dealt
with – the administration of justice and the policing function. The Civil
Service Act of 1878 had included among its classified service the staff
required for the administration of the central courts. In 1905 the various
courts – the Supreme Court of Judicature, the Court of Appeals, the
High Court, Central Office, Registrar's Office, and Surrogate and
Weekly Court – employed a staff of over fifty. The appendage of employees in the field must be an approximate figure. Many were locally
supported, paid by fees, and employed part-time. However, counting
only those who were salaried, there were close to two hundred involved
in the administration of justice and policing. In addition to ten local
masters of title, there were some forty deputy clerks of pleas, often
jointly appointed as local registrars. There was also the staff in all the
ten districts awaiting conversion to counties for which the province was

responsible: police magistrates, sheriffs, clerks of the peace, district attorneys, constables, gaolers, matrons, and so on. Conservatively, 125 full-time personnel would appear to have been necessary to cover these varied categories. The provincial police, with but a dozen chief constables for the Niagara and Detroit River district and three inspectors of criminal investigation (i.e., detectives), was just emerging as a significant force.

In summary, the headquarters staff in 1905, including those involved in the administration of justice, totalled 295, as against 113 in 1871 and 191 in 1892. A calculation of the totals employed in the 'outside service' is more problematic. For example, the Civil Service Commission, in a retrospective 1954 report, claimed that the civil service numbered 704 in 1904. Clearly, this figure would have included the headquarters personnel, here calculated to be a little under three hundred. It would also have included only the permanent, salaried employees in the outside service. These would have represented probably less than one-third of the 1,600 employees who were engaged on every conceivable employment arrangement. This larger and scattered component of the public service provided the main source for patronage.

The Personalities in the Early Public Service

The Crown Lands Department

The staff of the Crown Lands Department of the new province of Ontario was in the main carried forward from the pre-confederation public service. It was headed by Andrew Russell, who had risen from the ranks to become assistant commissioner in 1857. Unlike many of his associates who were to continue well on into the post-confederation era, he was replaced in 1869 by Thomas H. Johnson.[5] As if to compensate for the strong sense of continuity imparted by the extensive carry-over of pre-confederation personnel, Johnson was an 'outsider' who had been a member of the legislature from Prescott from 1847 to 1854 and then a stipendiary magistrate for Nipissing.

Johnson was to be followed as assistant commissioner in 1887 by Aubrey White who is described by the official historians of the department as representing a shift towards a developing professionalization within the department and new policy concerns for conservation and protection of the valuable forestry resources of the province. Though White had been born in Ireland, he had come to Canada at the age of seventeen, and had been active in the lumber business. From about 1876, he had been casually employed by the department as a wood ranger and land agent before becoming a full-time clerk in the Woods and Forests Branch in 1882. Within five years he had become the deputy head, a position he was to hold until 1915.[6] Thus, despite his somewhat late start at the age of forty-seven and unlike his predecessor, White could be considered a genuine 'insider' whose twenty-eight years' service as assistant commissioner/deputy minister was surpassed only by longevity of service of the men holding down the headships of the major subdivisions of the department. No less than ten of these officials, each with at least fifty years of service in the department, availed themselves of the newly-instituted superannuation plan to retire in 1921. The most senior of these was D.G. Ross, the chief accountant who had first been appointed on 15 April 1861. Lagging just a few years behind was Major J.A.G. Crozier, who had been a new addition to the department in December 1867.[7]

Of all the original BNA Offices, unquestionably Crown Lands carried the heaviest baggage of its pre-confederation past into the service of the new province. That sense of departmental tradition imparted by the long unbroken careers of both senior and junior staff ultimately came to be symbolized in the adoption of a uniformed field service – all contributing to create an esprit de corps to which no other element of the public service, save for the provincial police force, could aspire.

The Department of Education

Although the Education Office was not formally included among the original BNA Offices, it became a full member of the departmental team in 1876. As with Crown Lands, there was a carry-over from the pre-confederation regime and even more continuity with the past because there was not even the need (as in the case of Crown Lands) to undergo the trauma of physical removal back to Toronto from Ottawa. Thus it was that Egerton Ryerson and his long-time assistant, J.G. Hodgins, each after twenty-three years of service to the old provincial Board of Education for Canada West, were able to preside over the conversion of the board to a Department of Education.

Ryerson was born in Upper Canada of United Empire Loyalist parents in 1803. He embraced the Wesleyan Methodist faith and became a saddle-bag preacher. An early advocate of a common school system, in 1844 he was drawn from his position as the head of the newly created Victoria College to become superintendent of the Education Office.[8] The man who was to be so closely associated with him, John George Hodgins, was born in Ireland in 1821. He arrived in Ontario at an early age and was educated at Cobourg's Upper Canada Academy, which in 1841 was to become Victoria College. Hodgins was appointed chief clerk in the Education Office in 1844 and became Ryerson's deputy in 1855. With the transformation of the Office into a department, Ryerson retired, leaving Hodgins to preside until 1890 as the first deputy minister of education. Hodgins would pursue his literary aspirations as librarian and historiographer of the department until 1904 – in all, an astonishing sixty years of service.[9]

The staff of the Education Department was also largely a carry-over from pre-confederation years. Alexander Marling, for example, who became chief clerk in 1854 when Hodgins moved up to become Ryerson's deputy superintendent, succeeded to the deputy ministership in 1890. He died less than three months after taking office, though not before he, too, had completed a fifty-six-year career in the department. His successor, John Millar, who was to serve for fifteen years as deputy minister, had also progressed through the ranks of teaching, had held an inspector's certificate, and had had administrative experience as a school principal.[10] This tradition of staffing and promotion from within the educational system was and would continue to be a feature of the department's recruitment policy.

Public Works

Ontario's combined Office of Public Works and Agriculture had pre-confederation counterparts in separate departments of Public Works and of Agriculture for the Province of Canada. However, their personnel remained in Ottawa to staff new Dominion departments rather than being dispersed to Quebec and Ontario. The major exception was Kivas Tully, who was appointed in mid-1868 to the most prestigious position in the department, that of architect and chief engineer. Tully had been born in Ireland in 1820 but had come to Canada in 1844, where he had become a leading architect. He was responsible for such buildings as Trinity College in Toronto, Victoria Hall in Cobourg, and other governmental buildings with which he had been so involved at the time of confederation that there was some question as to whether he would be on staff in Ontario or with the new Dominion. The decision to appoint him chief architect was to have an enduring impact, for Tully held the post for nearly thirty years, continuing as consultant until close to his death in 1905.[11]

There was also statutory provision for a separate chief engineer in the department. Thomas N. Molesworth was appointed in 1870, first as assistant engineer and then in 1874, when Tully surrendered his joint title, as chief engineer. Molesworth died in 1879 and was replaced by Robert

McCallum who had entered the department as a draughtsman in 1873 and was to remain chief engineer until 1903.

The same tendency to appoint from within the department, once the first appointees had been retired, applied also to the third senior post in Public Works, that of chief accountant. In 1872 F.T. Jones was appointed both law clerk and accountant, a position he retained until 1885, though surrendering the accountant's role to J.P. Edwards in 1880. Edwards was definitely an insider, having joined the department as a clerk in 1868 and remaining as accountant until 1914 – in all, forty-six years of service.

The fourth senior position was that of secretary. For three decades that position was held by William Edwards, whose background qualified him much more for the agricultural concerns of the originally combined office of commissioner of agriculture and public works.[12] Born in England in 1818, Edwards had become a resident of Toronto by 1836 and thereafter had combined twenty-two years in business with a stint on city council and active involvement in the Mechanics' Institutes and the pre-confederation Board of Arts and Manufactures, with its numerous attachments of agricultural societies. It was this experience which Edwards drew upon when, at the age of fifty, he was appointed secretary in 1868. His initial contributions were related to the agricultural side of the department's joint responsibilities. It was he who not only prepared the separate pieces of legislation designed to re-establish the pre-confederation regime of agricultural associations and the various societies for fruit growers, dairymen, and the like, but also served as secretary in charge of immigration until 1873. Despite this background and initial focus on agriculture, Edwards remained as secretary to the Public Works side of the Office rather than going with Agriculture in 1874, when the Office became two separate entities. Judging from the lower salary paid the secretary in comparison with the professional engineer and architect, Edwards's position was in no sense equivalent to that of deputy head but rather constituted little more than that of office manager. Not until A.W. Campbell was appointed assistant commissioner of public works in 1900 did the department acquire a permanent head.[13]

With Campbell's appointment, the Department of Public Works finally caught up with the practice long since adopted by the other BNA Offices. Campbell came to the position with an engineering background, having graduated in civil engineering in 1885. He had been apprenticed to municipal engineering firms in southwestern Ontario and had become city engineer for St Thomas. After 1891 his leadership of the 'Good Roads' movement brought him into government service in 1896 as instructor in road making. The growing importance of roads led to his elevation to the director of a roads branch and almost simultaneously his confirmation as the first permanent head of the department in 1900. Described as 'a man of a high order of administrative ability' whose 'reports on roads and streets have become textbooks in the hands of engineers and road makers,' he was 'looked upon as one of the most reliable authorities in such matters on the continent.' With credentials such as these, Campbell became a prize catch for the Dominion public service; in February 1910 he became deputy minister of the federal Department of Railways and Canals.

For the Ontario department which Campbell left, his initial appointment reaffirmed a tradition, dating back to pre-confederation times, wherein the professional engineer was the dominant senior member of the department. This practice, for example, had contributed to the scandals associated with construction of the Parliament Buildings in Ottawa: the engineer in charge of the Department of Public Works simply pursued his own professional agenda, regardless of costs, leaving the amateur political head of the department to face the unpleasant fallout from his cavalier approach.[14] Despite this practical confirmation of the old British adage that it is always better to have the expert 'on tap rather than on top,' this opposing departmental tradition of giving pride of place to the expert was carried forward in Ontario with the appointment of officials such as Tully, Molesworth, and Campbell as the dominant figures in the department. The tradition survived through the early 1900s when Public Works was lumbered with irrelevant responsibilities for Labour and Game and Fisheries. Consequently, when Highways broke free as a separate department on its own in 1915, W.A. McLean, who had been chief engineer of the previous Highways Branch (having entered the department in 1903 as a clerk), was confirmed as deputy minister – a position he held until 1924–5.

Meanwhile, the traditional responsibilities of Public Works for construction, maintenance, and upkeep of public buildings, roads, canals, and bridges were directed by another engineer. R.P. Fairbairn, who had started his career with the department in 1880 as an engineering draughtsman, became chief engineer in 1903 and replaced Campbell as deputy minister in 1910. This tradition of promoting from within was continued when George P. Hogarth, yet another engineer who had also come up through the Highways Branch, succeeded Fairbairn.

Agriculture

Quite a different tradition developed with the Department of Agriculture, after it was separated from Public Works in 1874. Initially, the staffing

requirements were of the leanest order. In 1874 Professor George Buckland took over the task of servicing and monitoring the grants to agricultural associations which William Edwards had initiated while he was
secretary of the combined department. Immigration, which remained
loosely attached to Agriculture, was initially part of Edwards's secretarial responsibilities. In 1874 David Spence assumed Immigration responsibilities which he carried until his death in 1902.

Although Buckland was assigned the title of assistant commissioner
of agriculture after 1882, it was not until 1889, four years after his death,
that a position equivalent to that of deputy minister was established with
the appointment of Archibald Blue. He had first entered the service as
secretary of the Bureau of Industries when it was made the chief component of the Commissioner of Agriculture's Office in 1882.[15] Blue had
been born in Scotland in 1840 and educated there before coming to
Canada as a public school teacher. By the time of confederation he had
moved into journalism and was working for the *Toronto World* when he
was appointed to the Bureau of Industries. Blue's fact-collecting proclivities ('he possesses great executive ability and just revels in figures'
was one contemporary characterization of him) led him on to be founding secretary of the Bureau of Mines in 1891. After nine years, his
success attracted the interest of the Ottawa bureaucracy. In 1900 he was
appointed chief of the Office of Census and Statistics, a post which he
held until his death in 1914.

Blue's successor as deputy minister of agriculture was Charles Canniff
James who held office from 1891 for more than twenty years.[16] Described
by Sir George Ross as 'one of the best men we have in the Ontario public
service,' James had been a gold medallist in natural science on graduation
from Victoria College in 1883. He had been professor of chemistry at the
Ontario Agricultural College for several years when summoned in 1891
to replace Archibald Blue. A cultivated man (he was a fellow of the Royal
Society of Canada) who wrote widely on agricultural matters, James had
extensive outside interests as a golfer and a member of the Canadian
Olympic Committee. His broad scientific and literary background made
him a most appropriate head for a department that only at the end of his
tenure had begun to extend its reach beyond the strictly facilitative and
educational/fact-disseminating roles that had characterized its operations
from the beginning. Thus, unlike Public Works, which relied on the
expert to serve as permanent head of the organization, Agriculture tended
in its early years to favour a more broadly trained generalist.

Attorney General's Office

The staffing for the Office of the Attorney General had to begin from scratch since there was no carry-over of personnel from the departments of the old Province of Canada. Because the Office, save during Blake's short regime and George Ross's tenure as provincial treasurer, was held by the premier, there were two mandates to be supported by the staff – that of chief legal officer for the province and that of providing secretarial services for the Executive Council. The first of these tasks fell to the most senior official in the Office whose title was soon elevated from chief clerk to deputy attorney general, while the second duty was in the hands of the clerk of the Executive Council.

Until Premier Whitney's reorganization of 1905, which provided for separate offices for the attorney general and the president of the Executive Council, one senior official carried both titles, with a subordinate bearing the title of assistant clerk of the Executive Council. J.G. Scott was the first appointee to assume the mantle of deputy attorney general in 1870, following a succession of three short-lived chief clerks.[17] Although Scottish born, he was educated at the Toronto Academy, called to the bar in 1862, and at age thirty-four was appointed to the post he was to hold for fifteen years until 1885. His successor, E.F.B. Johnston, was also born in Scotland but educated at Osgoode Hall. He was called to the bar in 1880 and, at the age of thirty-six, assumed the joint office previously held by Scott.[18] His tenure lasted only three years as he moved first to the Inspector of Registry Offices and then back into private practice, where he became a noted prosecutor.

His replacement as deputy attorney general and clerk of the Executive Council was John Robison Cartwright, born in Kingston in 1842 and a cousin of the more politically visible Sir Richard Cartwright. Educated in England at Rugby and Oxford before being called to the provincial bar in 1871, he entered directly into the administration of the judiciary as clerk of process, Osgoode Hall.[19] He appears to have become Premier Mowat's secretary in 1881, at first on an eight-month basis, and by 1886 on a full-time basis. In March of 1889 he became deputy attorney general and continued in that position until 1919 – a lifetime career of forty-eight years of service.

Cartwright also held the position of clerk of the Executive Council until 1904 when, with the anticipated separation of the Attorney General's Office from the Presidency of the Council, the assistant clerk, James Lonsdale Capreol, was promoted to clerk, a position he retained until his retirement at age seventy-one in 1919.[20] Born in Toronto in 1848, Capreol had been educated abroad at the Lycée France and then at the Royal Military School in Kingston. After being called to the bar in 1869 he practised law in Cobourg with Colonel J.H. Dumble, his father-in-law, until he was appointed assistant clerk of the Executive Council in 1879 at the age of thirty-one. Clearly, the attorneys general and premiers in their roles as both chief law officer and head of government were well served by the legal specialists of considerable repute who directed the five or six-member staff that made up the Office of the Attorney General until well after the turn of the century.

Provincial Treasurer's Office

For the first decade after confederation, the Provincial Treasurer's Office had as its most senior officer a chief accountant, W.R. Harris, who headed a tiny staff of two clerks and a messenger. In 1879 Harris was made assistant provincial treasurer (the equivalent of deputy minister) and continued to preside until 1888 when his successor was brought in to restore confidence in a department that for the previous two years had been pilloried by the Public Accounts Committee of the legislature for failure to detect major defalcations dating back to the early 1870s. For all his twenty years of service, Harris appears to have been somewhat of a nonentity and, though himself not touched by the scandal, nevertheless demonstrated administrative ineptitude in doing so little to prevent, let alone detect, the defalcations. D.E. Cameron, the man who was brought in from outside the service to rectify the situation in May of 1888 as assistant treasurer, remained only until October 1894.[21] During his six-year incumbency he made much progress in patching up the procedures for monitoring both the receipts and expenditures relating on the one hand to revenue collecting and licensing agencies, and on the other, to the disbursements on government account by all agencies in the public service. At the age of thirty-seven, Cameron came well equipped to undertake this salvage operation by virtue of his private banking experience. He was known as an active campaigner and effective speaker in the Liberal cause, having been one of the founders and a first vice-president of the Young Liberal Movement of Montreal. The maintenance of this open political connection seems not to have raised concerns about his public service status as deputy head and troubleshooter for the Treasurer's Office. His subsequent departure in 1894 to become general auditor of the Mutual Reserve Fund Life Association of New York indicated that both S.C. Wood, the able provincial treasurer, and Cameron himself looked upon his appointment as a way of responding quickly to the crisis in the department and not as a permanent career prospect.

One of the factors contributing to that crisis was the inadequacy of the audit system, which from the outset was viewed simply as an adjunct of the Treasurer's Office. When provision was made by order-in-council in 1869 for the Office of Provincial Auditor, the Honourable

William Cayley was appointed.[22] Born in Russia in 1807 and educated in England and coming to Canada in 1836, Cayley was called to the bar of Upper Canada in 1838. From 1846 to 1861 he served as a member of the Assembly of the Province of Canada and for a period held the portfolio of inspector general of accounts. It was during his tenure as provincial auditor, which lasted until his retirement in 1877, that the defalcations took place and went undetected for close to another ten years by his successor, Charles Hood Sproule.[23]

Cayley's errors of omission were attributed to poor health during the last years of his tenure. On the other hand, Sproule could only fall back on the defects in the system itself which accorded to the auditor none of the independent status we have come to take for granted today. Some steps were taken to rectify this situation with a formal audit act of 1886. So strong were the historic ties binding the audit to the Treasurer's Office that in 1905, apparently without any adverse reaction, Sproule was transferred from the post of provincial auditor, which he had held since 1878, to the position of assistant provincial treasurer. This position he was to hold until 1920, thereby completing some fifty-two years of an association with the Treasurer's Office that had began on 1 December 1867 when he was first appointed as a junior clerk.

Provincial Secretary's Office

When the Office of Provincial Secretary was established, Thomas Charles Patteson was the first to be appointed assistant provincial secretary.[24] Oxford educated, he had come to Canada in the late 1850s and set up a law practice in Cobourg. His was a brief tenure, for he left his position in 1872 to become editor of the Conservative *Mail* and subsequently joined the federal public service as postmaster for Toronto. His successor, I. Robert Eckhart, had been appointed Patteson's chief clerk in 1867 and was to serve from 1872 to 1880 as assistant secretary. George Edmund Lumsden, born in Canada of Irish parents, was a journalist and editor of the Hamilton *Times* when he was called upon to replace Eckhart in November 1880 as assistant secretary, a position he held until 1903.[25] His successor, Thomas Mulvey, also had journalistic interests, being one of the founders of the *Canadian Magazine*. Mulvey was a man of extensive talents, having graduated as a gold medallist in physics from St Michael's College and become a barrister in 1889. The Dominion was ultimately to claim his services; in 1909 he left to become undersecretary of state for Canada.[26]

The Satellites

The responsibilities of the successive assistant provincial secretaries cannot have been particularly arduous. Usually they called more for the talents of a publicist or liberally educated generalist rather than an aptitude for business or administration. The tendency to use the Provincial Secretary's Office as an umbrella or all-purpose repository for a variety of satellite entities imposed few burdens other than the core responsibilities of a clerical, bookkeeping nature. It was in the satellites, particularly the several inspectorates, that real administrative challenges had to be faced by a small group of dedicated officials.

The most remarkable of these was surely John Woodburn Langmuir, who single-handedly ran the *Office of Inspector of Prisons and Charitable Institutions* from 1868 to 1882.[27] Langmuir had been born in 1835 and educated in Scotland before coming to Canada, where he joined a business firm in Picton. Demonstrating more precocity than was common even for his time, he became mayor of Picton at the age of twenty-four and was only thirty-three when appointed inspector. Although he was to leave his position after fourteen years to become managing director of the Toronto General Trust Corporation, he continued to make his contribution to the public service of the province, as a member and then chairman of the Niagara Parks Commission, as chairman of a royal commission on the prison and reformatory system of Ontario as well as a member of a Dominion royal commission on life insurance. Reflecting his earlier interests as inspector, he was founder and president of the Homewood Retreat Association of Guelph.

The triumvirate who gradually succeeded Langmuir all retired just as the Whitney government replaced the Liberal regime in 1905. They were also able men. Dr W.T. O'Reilly was appointed to assist Langmuir in 1881 and, on the latter's retirement, Robert Christie joined O'Reilly. Christie had been a member of the Assembly prior to his appointment, and another former member joined him ten years later with the appointment of T.F. Chamberlain. With the virtually total replacement of the inspectors in 1905, S.A. Armstrong, a barrister, who had been educated at Trinity College and was connected through his mother with Joseph L. Cory, then the federal deputy minister of finance, was appointed senior inspector at the age of thirty-one. Five years later Armstrong replaced Mulvey as assistant provincial secretary, a position he held until war's end in 1918.[28]

Amongst this all-male enclave the name of Dr Helen MacMurchy warrants special attention. She was appointed inspector of the feeble minded in 1906 and was to hold this position until 1920, when the Child

Welfare Division of the new federal Department of Health commandeered her services as director, a position she was to hold until 1934. Born in Toronto in 1862, Helen MacMurchy taught school before studying medicine. Graduating from the University of Toronto with honours, she then worked under Sir William Osler at Johns Hopkins. Her impressive curriculum vitae was summed up in these words: 'One of Canada's best known and best informed advocates of social and racial betterment.'[29]

Another inspectorate that floated between the Offices of the Treasurer and of the Attorney General but in the later years of the nineteenth century was attached to the Office of Provincial Secretary was that of the *Inspector of Insurance and Registrar of Friendly Societies*. J. Howard Hunter was the first appointee, replacing Dr O'Reilly who, before he had time to act, was transferred to assist Langmuir.[30] Hunter was born in Ireland but came to Canada and completed his education at the University of Toronto. He became renowned as a teacher, school principal, and champion of the Grammar School Association, fighting against the alleged proclivities of Upper Canada College to steal the best students and starve the grammar schools outside the city centre. With the help of Robert Christie, Hunter was instrumental in getting increased appropriations for the grammar schools. More generally, he was involved in the discussions leading up to the creation of the School of Practical Science in 1873 and of a department of education in 1876; he participated in the setting up and then was put in charge of the Brantford Institute for the Blind in 1874. It was from this position that he was appointed inspector of insurance, where his knowledge of mathematics and science enabled him, among other duties, to set up Canadian life mortality tables with corresponding premium rates which became the basis for his regulatory duties and gained recognition well beyond the province. Hunter's meticulously detailed reports were submitted annually to the legislature until his retirement thirty years later in 1910.

The Inspector of Registry Offices was, like the Prison Inspectorate, an early post-confederation creation that had particular relevance for the Office of Provincial Secretary in view of the inclusion of Registrar in that Office's title. For the first twenty years the inspector was the Honourable Sydney Smith.[31] He had been postmaster general for the Province of Canada and had been appointed inspector of registry offices for Upper Canada in November 1866, an appointment which was simply reaffirmed when the new Province of Ontario was formed. E.F.B. Johnston succeeded Smith in 1889, leaving the more prestigious position of deputy attorney general to take on the inspectorate, presumably as a means of effecting a transition back to private practice five years later.

Another satellite agency loosely affiliated with the Office of Provincial Secretary was the *Provincial Board of Health*, created in 1882. The leading figure here was its secretary, Dr Peter Henderson Bryce, who was the prime animator in the field of public health and, in his dual role as deputy registrar general, a dedicated advocate for the collection of vital statistics.[32] Graduating as a gold medallist in natural science from the University of Toronto in 1876, Bryce went on to secure his medical degree while teaching science and applied chemistry at the Ontario Agricultural College and then, laden with awards, did advanced medical studies in Edinburgh and Paris. It was while he was practising medicine in Guelph that he was appointed, at the age of twenty-nine, first secretary of the Board of Health in 1882, continuing in practice for the next seven or eight years before his joint activities as deputy registrar general and secretary to the board required his full-time attentions. He retained these positions until 1904 when he became chief medical officer for the federal Department of the Interior and the Department of Indian Affairs.

Equally distinguished was Bryce's successor, Charles Alfred Hodgetts, who, after performing specific assignments beginning in 1894, was appointed in 1901 the sole medical inspector for the Board of Health. He assumed Bryce's position in 1904 which he held until 1910.[33] Dr Hodgetts had secured his M.D. from Victoria University in 1886. He had been house surgeon at the Toronto General Hospital in 1886–7, at the Stafford Infirmary, England, in 1888, and had then done the obligatory tour of Birmingham and London hospitals. Extolled by the *Ottawa Free Press* as 'the foremost public health authority in Canada,' Dr Hodgetts was to go on, after his departure from the Board of Health in 1910 at the age of fifty-one, to become head of the health division of the federal Conservation Commission, with a special interest in public housing as it related to the nation's well-being. He was also heavily involved with the International Red Cross and the St John's Ambulance Association.

The tradition of having medical men with broad attainments in charge of the Board of Health (even though the board itself had non-medical members) was sustained in 1924 when a Department of Health was created; its two senior officials, J.W.S. McCullough and R.W. Bell were both doctors with long connections with the Board of Health. This tradition of placing expert professionals at the head of this department has proven as durable as the dominance of engineers in Public Works.

A late-blooming agency, also with an attachment to the Office of Provincial Secretary, was that of the *Superintendent of Neglected and Dependent Children*. John Joseph Kelso was the founding father of this position, having proselytized as a philanthropic worker from the days in the mid-1870s and 1880s when he reported for the Toronto *World* and then the Toronto *Globe*.[34] Born in Ireland, Kelso had come to Toronto at the age of ten and received his education there before undertaking the journalistic work which launched such philanthropic endeavours as the creation of the Toronto Humane Society in 1886, the Toronto Fresh Air Fund in 1888, and the Children's Aid Society in 1891 – all preparations for his assumption of the post of superintendent in 1893. This position he was to hold for over thirty years, long enough to have the satisfaction of seeing his inspectorate become the nucleus of a Department of Public Welfare in 1931. Midway in this long career, the *Toronto Star*, with pardonable hyperbole, claimed that he 'had performed a more valuable service in preventing crime than half the police force of Ontario.'

Kelso's career typified the contribution of the amateur impelled by a vigorous social conscience and reliant on the support of similarly dedicated philanthropic and religious groups. Although a School of Social Work was instituted at the University of Toronto as early as 1914, it was not until the ravages of the great depression propelled governments into the forefront that the demand for trained professionals as well as a department dedicated specifically to the provision of social services made their appearance. Unlike the field of public health, where professionally trained persons were involved from the beginning and where a tradition of their administrative dominance was early established and perpetuated, in the field of social work and social services there was no such tradition. The result was that at least into the 1920s much reliance was placed on concerned individuals volunteering their services on the local boards of children's aid societies, or on mothers' allowances boards, or the provincial minimum wage board.

One other satellite agency was the *Factory Inspectorate*, created in 1887. Initially, three appointments were made to cover the three districts into which the province had been divided: Robert Barber, James R. Brown, and O.A. Rocque. Curiously, though they remained in office until 1901–3, biographical details are sketchy. On the other hand, the first woman inspector appointed under specific provisions of a statute of 1895 was given recognition in Morgan's second edition (1912) of *Canadian Men and Women of the Time*. Margaret Carlyle, whose career carried forward until 1920, was born and educated in Glasgow and then employed in manufacturing establishments in Scotland and business in Canada before her appointment as the first female factory inspector (and indeed one of the first women to hold a senior position in the provincial bureaucracy). Among the cross-border fraternity that comprised the International Association of Factory Inspectors, Miss

Carlyle's status and unusual competence were recognized in her appointment as one of the association's vice-presidents in 1903. Her feisty reports amply justify the Toronto *Globe*'s description of her as 'a woman of strength of character, good judgment, sound discretion, and a sympathetic disposition.' Judging from the reports of her colleagues, this description aptly epitomized the qualities required of the factory inspector who, apart from having to act with tact and discretion, often had to cooperate with medical personnel in the Board of Health, the statistics-gatherers in the Bureau of Industries, and the legal profession in respect of workers' compensation. In addition, as indicated by the professional engineering qualifications of James T. Burke, an appointee of 1901 who was to become chief inspector in 1909 and retire in 1933, familiarity with the new technologies being imported into the factories along with their accompanying hazards became an indispensable asset.

The foregoing review of the senior personnel comprising the early public service reveals that, on the whole, the province was remarkably successful in attracting and retaining highly competent people. Where professional requirements were demanded, the senior appointees brought impressive credentials to their offices. In the field of public health the province was equally well served by the highly trained young doctors who contributed their talents to the Board of Health.

Where there were not the same accredited professionals available, reliance was placed on experienced practitioners, pending the time when new professions would be recognized. Such, for example, was the situation in Crown Lands until schools of forestry and of mines were created. On a somewhat different basis, some administrative situations were met by drawing on gifted amateurs who, interestingly, nearly all came to office with prior experience in journalism.

A Look Forward

This parade of nineteenth-century senior public servants reveals at least two general features that were to carry forward from Whitney's time until the Second World War. First, most senior officials enjoyed remarkably lengthy careers in the public service, usually with one agency. This longevity might well be attributed to the Liberal regime that lasted from 1872 to 1905, except that when party fortunes changed there was no wholesale changing of the guard at headquarters, as was customary in the United States. Indeed, as we shall see later, governments of all political stripes took considerable pains to divorce themselves from the

'Yankee Spoils System' and complimented themselves for retaining their predecessors' senior appointments.

A detailed examination of the personnel, comparable to that presented in this chapter, would bear out the conclusion that, up to the Second World War, the tradition of lengthy tenures for senior personnel was continued.

In the Office of the Attorney General, for example, the forty-eight-year career of J.R. Cartwright in the most sensitive positions of deputy attorney general and clerk of the Executive Council continued beyond Mowat and his Liberal successors to an equally lengthy service with the Conservatives under Whitney and Hearst. Edward Bayley, his successor, had joined the Office as solicitor in the early 1900s and retired when Hepburn assumed office in 1934. The tradition of appointing from within the experienced ranks of the Attorney General's Office has continued.

In the equally sensitive position of deputy to the premier, Whitney's first appointment, Horace Wallis, served all Conservative leaders until Hepburn's time, and was equally acceptable to Premier Drury. In the Department of Education, the pattern of choosing long-term insiders persisted; A.H.U. Colquhoun, Whitney's selection as deputy minister in 1906, was only replaced in 1934 when he reached retirement age. Similar long terms were accorded the chief policy officer, the superintendent of education, held successively by John Seath and F.W. Merchant, both with long experience in the department.

In the successor departments to the old Crown Lands Office, Aubrey White, the deputy minister of lands and forests, carried over from Mowat's period until 1915. Although his immediate successor, Albert Grigg, was an outsider, in 1921 Walter C. Cain, who had been with the department since 1903, was appointed deputy minister and remained through Hepburn's regime until 1942. The adjunct Department of Mines was headed by T.W. Gibson from the time it started as a bureau in 1899; his retirement as deputy minister came in the natural course of events when Hepburn assumed office, but his services as a consultant continued for several years after.

In Public Works and Highways, the dominance of the engineers persisted, as W.A. McLean and George Hogarth were promoted from the engineer's branch to the position of deputy minister, Hogarth being one of the few senior officials proving unacceptable to Hepburn in the latter's sweep of the lower rank of the bureaucracy in 1934. In Agriculture, the twenty-one-year career of C.C. James as deputy minister was followed by the eighteen years of service in the same position by W. Bert Roadhouse, ending in 1930.

The same longevity and continuity of service through changing governments is also found in the Provincial Secretary's Office. At the end of the First World War F.V. Johns replaced S.A. Armstrong, Whitney's appointment as assistant secretary in 1905. Johns was to remain until after the Second World War. The dual senior position of deputy provincial secretary provided the base from which its first holder, H.M. Robbins, moved over to become deputy minister of hospitals in the Health Department in 1930. His successor, C.F. Neelands, continued through the war years and then became deputy minister of the new Department of Reform Institutions in 1946.

The pattern of long service rising to permanent headship persisted until after the Second World War. By this time there was emerging a pattern of more mobile, even transient appointments to the senior ranks. No doubt this change has been brought about by the postwar multiplication of departments and agencies, along with the demand for more and better educated personnel. The break in tradition cannot be attributed to frequent changes in the governing party, for it coincided with the long uninterrupted period of Conservative governments. The change would appear to have been brought about in a more deliberate fashion, based on a management philosophy that sees value in frequent rotation of personnel and a broader source for their selection than long service in one agency.

A second generalization stemming from the biographical sketches presented above is that the qualifications and capacities of a significant number of the senior personnel were such as to induce the Dominion government to lure them to its own public service. This transfer of talent was particularly noticeable where professional qualifications, as in engineering (especially road construction) and medicine were in demand, although the federal government was equally interested in drafting such gifted all-rounders as Archibald Blue and Thomas Mulvey.

In retrospect, perhaps in only one area, the Office of Provincial Treasurer, does one have a sense of weakness at the top. But this weakness can be ascribed to the slow development of professional competence beyond that of routine bookkeeping. The emphasis on keeping complicated, often redundant, sets of books and the entanglement of the auditing function with the pedestrian verification of accounts of revenues and expenditures characterized the work of the Office. Even so, the limited capacities of the staff were over-taxed. Only gradually does the Treasurer's Office begin to assume the trappings of a proper financial ministry, beginning modestly after the turn of the century with a Succession Duties Branch that required a trained treasury solicitor. For subsequent tasks related to budgeting, economic forecasting, and planning, the economist as well as the tax expert were required, and these were not to enjoy their salad days until after the Second World War.

Before that time arrived, however, as the inexperienced Drury government was to find in the early 1920s, the continuing deficiencies in the Treasurer's Office, coupled with the inept if not dishonest leadership of its permanent head and the naïveté of its minister, touched off a scandal that shocked the financial community, particularly since it involved Aemelius Jarvis, one of its most respected members.

In his wonderfully detailed and balanced assessment of the famous 'Jarvis-Smith Affair,' Peter Oliver concludes that the scandal was but a specific demonstration of service-wide inadequacies in the face of increasing expenditures and mounting postwar demands on government. 'In old Ontario,' he writes, 'in the days of Mowat and even of Whitney, the demands on the expertise of the civil service had been relatively slight.' In relation to the new demands, Oliver is left with 'the impression that the level of professional expertise and education [in the public service of the twenties] was not high. Its standards and practices remained those of an earlier day.'[35]

This judgment, however tentatively couched, would appear to do less than justice to the qualities and capacities of most of the senior personnel whose lengthy service to the departments and agencies up to and beyond Whitney's time have been reviewed in this chapter. Given that the selection procedures, even for the most senior personnel, were conducted on a patronage basis, the results appear to have been surprisingly good.

Drury had to endure the consequences of entering office in 1919 just as a superannuation plan was introduced. Many in the senior category, admittedly grown long in the tooth, took advantage of the plan, thereby compounding the difficulties of Drury's inexperienced cabinet ministers. The loss of civil servants to the military call-up may also have added to the sense of shifting sands in an institution renowned for resistance to change, but the availability of a pension rather than war service appears to have had the greater impact on changes in the top command.

Confronted by the evidence of ineptitude and downright criminal actions that extended well beyond the Office of Provincial Treasurer, it is difficult to contest Peter Oliver's claim that in the aftermath of the First World War the province's public service would face demands on its organization and its staff that would require major changes.

7

Organizational Response to the Hands-On Administrative Mode, 1905–1940

With the arrival of Premier James Pliny Whitney in 1905, the earlier era of indirect administration begins to shift into the more hands-on administration so characteristic of today's public service. The early reliance on private associations to perform public tasks – the enabling administrative mode – now becomes subordinated to, if not displaced by, the more direct involvement of the province. Not only is the provincial public service beginning to place greater emphasis on both the direct operative and regulatory administrative modes, but its workload is being expanded by a more vigorous effort to supplement, supplant, or direct services provided by the municipalities.

During the opening decades of the twentieth century the impact on the public service of these new thrusts of centralization and altered administrative modes was registered both by the increase in numbers of civil servants and by the growth of government departments and their satellites. The organizational response was reflected in a measurable expansion of personnel and organizations and in the development of a more coherent departmental structure. A gradual integration of the various components previously only loosely affiliated with the BNA Offices was undertaken, applying a more logical basis for assembling work units within each ministerial portfolio.

Despite the claims of the scientific management movement (which would come to command respect in the 1920s) that there was 'one best way' of grouping work units, the history of departmental formation and re-formation in Ontario, as in other governmental jurisdictions, suggests quite otherwise.[1] If one thing is certain in reviewing the structuring of work units in departments, it is that there is no final resolution of a situation that is so vulnerable to and reflective of the changing priorities of the public agenda. The departmental system, then, becomes a kind of barometer for gauging, at any point in time and over time, both the extent and the nature of a government's involvement with the socio-economic conditions affecting the lives of its citizens.

There is also a side effect to growth and expansion of public servants and public service organizations. The more numerous the personnel and the more complex the organizations, the more attention must be diverted from the primary goals in order to attend to what, in the vernacular, we could call 'the care and feeding' of the administrative machine and those who work within it. Rather like the fast-breeder reactor, there would seem to come a point in the life of most bureaucracies when their growth becomes self-generating. This process, in turn, creates the need for increasingly sophisticated instruments with which to direct the entire enterprise and to coordinate the structural ensemble. In short, the maturation of the public service organism gives rise to differentiation, which necessitates the creation of functionally specialized organs.

While such developments are more visible in the fully matured public service of today, in the organizational changes initiated in Premier Whitney's regime one can readily discern the beginnings of that structural integration and functional differentiation which was to characterize the slow maturation of Ontario's public service. An amendment to the Executive Council Act in 1905 directly addressed the need for a strengthened central office to support the premier and the collective needs of the cabinet. It also indicated the manner in which the original BNA Act Offices would evolve into the contemporary system of departments – a process with which it seems logical to begin.

Consolidation and Evolution of the BNA Act Offices after 1905

Along with a search for more coherent combinations of work units within expanding departmental walls, developments after 1905 were clearly designed to respond to the rapid growth of government responsibilities. In essence, the problem was how to incorporate the early satellites into the departmental framework and yet preserve the small number of portfolios bequeathed by the BNA Act. Superficially, the immediate changes created by the legislation of 1905 appeared to be little more than terminological: the titles of the political heads of the Crown Lands and of the Public Works departments were altered from commissioner to minister, with corresponding changes in the titles of the permanent heads from assistant commissioner to deputy minister. The historic title of Crown Lands was changed to the Department of Lands and Mines. An amending act of the following year added Forests to Lands and Mines, while introducing a unique provision for both a deputy minister of lands and forests and a deputy minister of mines.

The use of a dual permanent headship under a single ministerial head clearly provided a restraint on the growth in size of the cabinet. An alternative and subsequently more favoured method of achieving this objective was to double up the portfolios held by cabinet ministers. During the Second World War, for example, George Drew's first cabinet contained only ten individuals, even though the number of ministerial portfolios had grown to fifteen. Only because six executive councillors, including the premier, assumed responsibility for two portfolios was this containment possible.[2] Of course, even this solution, when coupled with the contemporary expansion in the number of departments, has only ameliorated the growth of the cabinet to a size normally double that which Drew was able to maintain.

In Whitney's time and beyond, however, the cabinet was kept at a modest size not by having ministerial heads perform double duty but by continuing the tradition of loose holding-company types of 'Offices.' This approach to organizational design was characterized by an ad hoc assignment of particular administrative units to parent offices. It was workable only as long as governmental activities involved administrative modes that placed light demands on government. These responsibilities could be met by a handful of civil servants, presided over by a select group of senior officials who enjoyed notable longevity in their offices. For many years the tradition of a small cabinet proved resistant to the pressures of successive accretions of new functions and expansion of old responsibilities. There was a price to be paid for the tradition – a loss of administrative efficiency and accountability that was the consequence of casual, rather personal, assignment of tasks to omnibus portfolios, a process encouraged by the original provisions in the BNA Act.

Crown Lands: Omnibus Resource Department

The reorganization of the agency for administering all lands (aside from agricultural lands) that was undertaken in the legislation of 1906 was consistent with this tradition. In a curious departure from all the tenets of ministerial responsibility, the act also conferred on the deputy(ies) 'in the absence of the Minister or in case of a vacancy in the Office of Minister' the capacity to 'discharge therein the duties of the Minister' in so far as they pertained to mines and mining, lands and forests. While other enactments traditionally conferred on the deputy minister 'the care and management' of the department, *under direction* of the minister, this particular statute appears to be unique in conferring much broader ministerial powers on the deputy minister.

Curiously, when the government's supply motion to give effect to this new arrangement was before the legislature, the opposition's criticism as reported by the *Globe,* 7 March 1906, was muted. Indeed, former premier George Ross spoke approvingly of the government's decision to abandon its original intention of creating two separate departments as 'not practicable.' As the new minister, Frank Cochrane, argued, lands and forests and mines were 'too closely connected to admit of it.' George Ross concurred, making the arguable claim that the creation of two deputy ministers 'left things precisely as they were.' Even on the important issue of conferring on the deputy minister the capacity to exercise the statutory powers of his minister, Ross merely commented that 'this seemed to be going a little too far.'

The practice of employing two deputy ministers in the omnibus department concerned with administering land was to persist until 1920. In that year, bowing to the inevitable splintering-off process but still under its original deputy minister, T.W. Gibson, Mines gained the status of a separate ministerial portfolio. Accordingly, unless the cabinet was to increase in size, a doubling up at the ministerial level would now have to occur. As it happened, the enactment of 1920 simply formalized an arrangement that had already been made, whereby a minister without portfolio, Harry Mills, had been taking responsibility for the Bureau of Mines while it was still technically a part of the Department of Lands, Forests and Mines. Interestingly, the legislation of 1920 not only created a separate department of Mines but retained that unusual feature of the 1906 enactment whereby the deputy minister was empowered to act in the absence of the minister or in the event the office was vacant. This arrangement was not abandoned until 1972.

The organizational manoeuvres initiated in 1905 and 1906 for Crown Lands can be interpreted as efforts to find administrative solutions for a multifunctional portfolio obliged to assume an ever-growing number of responsibilities. In this instance the overload was not attributable to the build-up of a random collection of ill-assorted functions; rather, it occurred because of the effort to combine all the operative and regulatory activities associated with the crown lands and their forest and mineral resources.

Even without Game and Fisheries, which had been assigned to Public Works and were to create problems of their own in that portfolio, the ability of the Crown Lands Department to preserve its omnibus character was undermined by the wave of responsibilities that swept over it in consequence of the seismic changes in the remoter reaches of the Laurentian Shield, now featured as New Ontario. Not only did mining and forestry issues burgeon to the point of forcing the organizational innova-

tion of the double-barrelled deputy ministership and ultimately a separate ministerial portfolio for Mines, but the optimistic vision of the
opening of a new frontier of settlement introduced another administrative conundrum that further unsettled the evolving departmental system.

The conundrum was a classic demonstration of the precepts preached
by the scientific management movement, precepts that related to the
most efficient way to 'aggregate work units.' The emergence of New
Ontario, where most of the natural resources were located, raised the
prospect that work units might be aggregated on the basis of location or
place (i.e., a department of northern affairs) rather than on the basis of
purpose (i.e., a department of resources).

The initial response to the challenge posed by the emergence of New
Ontario was typically to add the new program to the omnibus 'purpose'
portfolio of Lands, Forests and Mines. That program was inaugurated
in 1912 under terms of the Northern and Northwestern Ontario Development Act, which provided a loan fund to encourage settlement and a
commissioner to administer the fund. Subsequent amendments in 1915
and 1916 sweetened the fund without altering the administrative arrangement whereby the commissioner and small staff operated under the
minister of lands and forests.[3] However, in 1924 the lieutenant-governor-in-council was authorized to appoint a legislative secretary for
Northern Ontario 'from among members of the Assembly representing
the electoral districts in the provincial judicial districts.' The duties of
this political officer were 'to furnish information to the Legislature as
to the requirements and resources of the said districts and to assist the
members of the Executive Council in the Assembly, and more particularly the Minister of Lands and Forests and the Minister of Mines.' The
statutory salary of $6,000 was the same as for full-fledged ministers.

The perception that this move was indeed intended to symbolize the
arrival of New Ontario in the seats of executive power at Queen's Park
was further buttressed by an act in 1926 that provided for a department
of the 'Civil Government of Ontario' for the Development of Northern
Ontario, complete with its own deputy minister and 'such commissioners, officers and clerks' and the like as were deemed necessary.
Simultaneously, the merging of soldiers and sailors' land settlement acts
with the northern development fund marked the effort to integrate as
much as possible all administrative activities associated with the place
where they were conducted. This included the construction of public
works, roads, development of water power, along with the original
emphasis on encouraging settlement and colonization by means of a
variety of agricultural and reforestation projects. In short, this 'place'
portfolio was so constructed that it would inevitably overlap with the

existing mandates of nearly all the other 'purpose' departments, particularly the resource departments concerned with lands and forests, mines, agriculture, and public works.

The unusual experiment with a legislative secretary was not abandoned until 1937, when Northern Development was merged with the Department of Mines. However, the issue of whether to give special status to a region by organizing its administrative services on a place basis has continued to be a never-quite-resolved problem in organizational design yielding various permutations and combinations of 'place' versus 'purpose' aggregations of work that persist to the present day.

Public Works and Its Satellite Offshoots

Public Works, like Crown Lands, had inherited a clear-cut set of operating responsibilities at confederation. It was responsible for the construction and maintenance of public buildings and the erection and upkeep of locks, dams, bridges, and drainage works. In 1874 legislative permission was granted to sever the combined Commissionership of Agriculture and Public Works, thereby freeing the larger partner to concentrate on its engineering functions. By the 1890s these were performed by a staff that had remained virtually unchanged since its inception.

At the turn of the century, however, the coherence of Public Works was disrupted by the intrusion of a number of satellite agencies that were spin-offs from other portfolios or responses to new governmental initiatives. In nearly all instances – with the notable exception of road construction – there seemed to be little administrative logic in loading these units on Public Works. It is difficult, for example, to see why a newly created Bureau of Labour should have been summarily added to the department in 1900, or why, three years later, a Fisheries Branch and a Game Protection Branch should have found Public Works to be an appropriate administrative home. In the event, Public Works was able to free itself of these seemingly unrelated satellites after the First World War, but not before a familiar pattern of structural adaptation was deployed in an effort to preserve the 'holding company' portfolio that Public Works had now come to comprise.

Game and Fisheries. In the case of the fisheries and game protection, the first effort to bring order into this domain had led to the creation of the ineffectual Game and Fisheries Commission in 1891. The first signs of consolidation at the centre came with the appointment of E. Tinsley as chief game warden in 1896 and of S.T. Bastedo, former private secretary to the premier, as commissioner of fisheries in 1898. These appointments signalled the province's first real effort to provide a coordinated control over the scattered game wardens and fisheries overseers. These were the officials who, with their headquarters staff of two or three clerks, were added to Public Works in 1903, thereby rendering the Game and Fisheries Commission redundant. In the legislation of 1907 that abolished the commission, the two branches were united. In 1914, following a pattern already established in Lands, Forests and Mines, departmental status was granted and a deputy ministerial head provided – though with no provision for a separate ministerial head.[4] Not until 1947, as part of an effort to return to the days when Crown Lands had been *the* resource department, was Game and Fisheries reabsorbed into the comprehensive fold of the Department of Lands and Forests.

Labour. The progress of the Bureau of Labour – the other oddly matched accretion in 1900 to the Department of Public Works – was similar to that for Game and Fisheries, save that when expansion led to separate departmental status, it acquired a minister of its own. The rapid evolution of Labour into a full-grown ministry could not have been anticipated from its humble beginnings as yet another fact-gathering venture, headed by a secretary and even at the onset of the First World War equipped with only one clerk/stenographer.

The early bias towards an agrarian community had initially imposed on the Bureau of Industries, attached to Agriculture, responsibility for instituting inquiries and collecting 'useful facts related to the agricultural, mechanical, and manufacturing interests of the Province.' The case for separate compilation of labour statistics was made in the 1889 report of a federal royal commission on the relation of capital and labour in Canada. That commission resulted in the creation of a Bureau of Labour at the Dominion level in 1890, followed by Ontario in 1900.[5] The Dominion's bureau was elevated to departmental status in 1900 and became the proving ground for a young Mackenzie King as its deputy minister.

The proprietarial, clientele orientation implicit in the creation of the Ontario Bureau of Labour was underlined by the appointment of its secretary, Robert Glockling, a seasoned trade union official. His successor in 1906 was John Anderson, a prominent member of the Toronto Typographers Union, a member of the 1886 Dominion Royal Commission on Labour and Capital, and in 1894 an unsuccessful Independent-Labour candidate.[6]

Further evidence of the clientele orientation of the bureau was provided in Glockling's second report for 1901 where, in calling attention to two legal decisions compiled from the *Labour Gazette*, he remarked that the results 'will be much appreciated ... by the workers of the Province.'[7] Again, in a later critical commentary on the operation of free labour employment exchanges, there appears even stronger evidence of the clientele orientation: 'For while it is not the purpose of the Bureau of Labour to advise or suggest legislation concerning any subject, yet it would appear to be the duty of the Bureau to point to any seeming injustice to the working-men and women that may come under its notice, and which may serve as a guide to legislation.' One is reminded here of comparable reports from the factory inspectors who took the same proprietary interest in their 'charges.'

This modest paternalistic role soon began to appear inadequate, even in the face of the major regulatory thrust initiated in 1911 with the appointment of Sir William Meredith as a royal commissioner to work out an innovative workmen's compensation enactment which culminated in the creation in 1914 of the Workmen's Compensation Board. Even as this agency was preparing to go into operation, yet another major inquiry into unemployment was launched in December of 1914. Chaired by the publisher Sir John Willison, the commission included amongst its large membership the Most Reverend Neil McNeil, the Venerable Archdeacon Henry J. Cody, and the Reverend Daniel Strachan, as well as the University of Toronto's economist Gilbert Jackson, and mathematics professor A.T. DeLury. An interim report in mid-1915 urged the creation of employment bureaus. Its final report was a fascinating melange of social considerations and labour economics which carried the now familiar plea for better statistics. But it also contained an advanced commentary on how such data contributed to better planning and (anticipating Maynard Keynes?) how a reserve of public works could cope with periods of recession. Administratively, the commission called for a Department of Labour 'either as a separate or in connection with an existing Department of Government.'[8]

The momentum gathering in favour of a labour department also found expression in a motion presented to the legislature in April 1915 by Messrs Tolmie and Carter, two members of the legislature with strong labour connections. Acknowledging 'the growing importance of social and industrial problems,' the motion called for 'the creation of a Department of the Government, presided over by a responsible Minister, whose chief concern should be to study and promote legislation and administrative action for the betterment of the conditions of the workers.'

Although the motion was roundly defeated, its suggestions for assembling under one roof the scattered agencies dealing with the 'welfare of the industrial classes,' including the Factory Inspectorate housed in Agriculture, were in fact put into effect in 1916 with the creation of a Trades and Labour Branch, placed under Public Works.[9] The superintendent of the branch was given the status of a deputy minister but it was not until 1919 that 'an act to provide for a Ministry of Labour' was approved. Curiously, this act was silent about the pairing of Labour with Health that appears to have taken place in practice and in the budget until further legislation of 1924 elevated Health to full departmental rank with its own minister.

There can be no doubt that the rise of labour to prominence on the government's agenda was attributable to the exigencies of war and the need for coordinated control over the supply and placement of workers, particularly farm workers and women workers drafted in great numbers into munitions production. In this respect, the branch's responsibility for employment agencies was undoubtedly its most important leverage, of which the new superintendent, the young, energetic Dr W.A. Riddell, took full advantage. He had obtained his Bachelor of Divinity from Union Theological Seminary in 1912 and a doctorate in sociology and economics from Columbia University just as he assumed control of the branch in 1916. Riddell exemplified the mix of the 'social gospel' and professional welfare economist that was to leave its mark on labour policies and practices of the 1920s and 1930s. Indeed, in Riddell's case, his extraordinary performance as first deputy minister of labour in Ontario proved to be but a rehearsal for his broader, distinguished service with the International Labour Office in Geneva and as advisory officer for the Dominion of Canada to the League of Nations.[10]

Highways. While the drawn-out process of extracting programs unrelated to the basic architectural, construction, and engineering responsibilities of Public Works was going on, concern for a program of road construction began to loom on the department's horizon. Until nearly the turn of the century, the only responsibility for road construction assumed by the province was undertaken by the Colonization Roads Branch located in Crown Lands; otherwise, the municipalities or privately incorporated toll road companies assumed the burden. When the province made its first reluctant venture into this arena in 1896, with the appointment of a lone instructor in road making, the Department of Agriculture was placed in charge. This connection soon began to change as the horse-drawn conveyance and steam-driven farm equipment gave way to the internal combustion engine and the automobile. By 1900 the operation of A.W. Campbell, the instructor in road making, was transferred to Public Works, first as a commissioner in charge of a Highways

Branch, and in short order as the assistant commissioner (i.e., deputy minister) of Public Works.[11] The story of how this modest operation headed by a civil engineer and staffed by a clerk and two stenographers grew to such dimensions that it had to be awarded a department of its own is essentially to recount the history of the automobile's coming of age.

When Whitney took office in 1905 the automobile was just on the point of making its explosive entry on the scene. As 'Good Roads' Campbell had persistently pointed out in his annual reports, the campaign for road construction was not a fad promoted by the bicyclist, nor a movement to impose a burdensome tax in order to build unnecessary 'stone roads.' Historically, he claimed, the cost of road construction had always been underestimated and yet had represented perhaps the greatest outlay faced by the municipal authorities; overall, it was probably larger than the combined expenditures on waterways and the notoriously costly railway-building ventures that had beggared several local governments. The true costs of road building had been less visible because the expenditures had been meted out in dribs and drabs and the work, especially with the almost universal reliance on statutory labour, was generally performed by unskilled labour working under equally unqualified supervisors.

Although persisting in the laissez-faire belief that the province's role should be educative and, at most, facilitative by way of low interest loans to the municipalities, by 1900 Campbell was intent on overthrowing the traditional dependence on statutory labour and the customary dependence on toll roads. In Campbell's view, roads should be regarded as 'an indispensable public service, a benefit to every citizen, whether a direct user of the road or not and consequently should be maintained by a universal tax.'[12]

This line of argument provided the basis for the adoption of a provincial grant for road improvement that would be designed to equalize the burden for counties and townships. In 1912 Whitney brought the province more actively into that arena by doubling the grants to the municipalities and making the grants conditional on cabinet approval of county road construction plans and of the engineers appointed as road supervisors.[13] The centralizing implications of the conditional road construction grants were also strengthened when, in 1912, the federal government began its own grant-in-aid program for major highway construction in the province. Clearly, the automobile was beginning to make its presence felt.

As early as 1905 the growing use of the automobile was a matter of note: 'It is a machine the usefulness of which is certain to increase. At the present time the cost is excessive, but that is a matter which time will regulate ... When the highest type has been reached, the parts will be standardized, the increased use of these vehicles will cause many more to be manufactured and the price will be reduced. Each automobile comprises not a carriage alone, but horse and harness as well. When the entire outfit, represented in this way, can be produced for the price of a horse, carriage and harness, they will be used not only by people of wealth, but by the citizens generally.'[14]

Still, there were dangers, and a 1903 enactment regulating the speed and operation of motor vehicles on highways established a maximum speed of fifteen miles an hour (ten miles in town). The act also provided for a two-dollar registration fee and a list of do's and don'ts that clearly acknowledged the priority of four-legged beasts over four-wheeled vehicles – a situation that was still unchanged by legislation in 1912. Interestingly, regulation of the use of the highways, as opposed to their financing and construction, was vested in the Provincial Secretary's Office where a pool of fewer than a dozen 'automobile constables' appeared on staff. They were probably quite sufficient at the outset to cope with the 1,593 licence holders listed in 1907, of whom one thousand were residents of the United States.[15]

The situation with respect to regulation and construction of highways was to change dramatically, judging from the great increase in motor vehicles after the First World War. The revenues from automobile licences rose from $24,394 in 1910 to nearly $150,000 in 1914 and, at war's end, to over one million dollars.[16] Promoted by the ever-expanding grants provided by the province and the federal government, highway construction responsibilities also expanded greatly.

The organizational response was the creation in 1915 of a Department of Public Highways in which the licensing responsibility carried by the Provincial Secretary's Office since 1903 under the Highway Act could now be placed with a Motor Vehicle Branch, created in 1916. Equipped with its own deputy minister, the new department continued to share a minister with its late parent, the Department of Public Works. Its licensing responsibilities, under J.P. Bickell, the long-time director of the Motor Vehicles Branch, led to a mushrooming of clerical staff. Highway construction burgeoned under E.C. Drury's enthusiastic minister of public works and highways, Frank Biggs, and later the no less enthusiastic Premier Ferguson. As a result, the lone engineer on staff at the start of the century had been joined in the early 1920s by eight assistants, a highway forester, an accountant, and a large clerical staff. However, the department that would be recognized today did not emerge until the mid-1930s when a highly developed division of labour was adopted to reflect the more sophisticated technological age of road transport. It was this emerging trend that brought about the final attainment of its own ministerial head in 1930, bringing to an even dozen the number of executive councillors.

Public Works: The Final Dispensation. In summary, the omnibus portfolio of the Department of Public Works laboured for well over the first two decades of the 1900s to liberate itself from a somewhat ill-assorted collection of responsibilities in order to return to its original mandate as the government's construction and maintenance arm. At its most bloated stage, at the close of the First World War, there were no less than four officials of deputy minister rank reporting to one ministerial head: a deputy minister for the department proper, a deputy minister of game and fisheries, a deputy minister of highways, and a deputy minister (superintendent) of trades and labour. All of these were to emerge as departments in their own right, although Game and Fisheries was never to acquire a minister of its own. Thus, in returning Public Works to its original mandate by these divestitures, it became necessary to add two more ministerial members to the cabinet.

Well beyond the period under review, the traditional role of Public Works as the government's real property and construction department was vastly expanded to include the many and varied common services required by the large and complex apparatus that Ontario's public service had become. This extension of the responsibilities of Public Works was reflected by the new title conferred on it in the early 1970s, the Ministry of Government Services.

Provincial Secretary: Demise of an Omnibus Department

The third BNA Office whose accumulation of sundry satellites was to be dismembered and surface as separate departments was that of the Provincial Secretary and Registrar. This Office had tended to be viewed as the natural repository for the statistical and regulatory responsibilities relating to such matters as the registration of births, deaths and marriages, the oversight of the Inspectorate of Prisons and Charitable Institutions, of the Board of Health, and of the Office of Superintendent of Neglected and Dependent Children.

Inspector of Prisons, Charities, etc. The earliest and most enduring association of the Provincial Secretary's Office was with the inspector of prisons. Beginning in 1868 under the dominant leadership of John Langmuir, the inspectorate tended to be only nominally part of the

Office. This situation persisted even after Langmuir's departure and the increase in the number of inspectors to accommodate the specialization of work entailed in inspecting various institutions.

Not until 1925 was genuine integration of the inspectorate into the Department of the Provincial Secretary achieved. This was brought about by legislation that created the equivalent of yet another double-barrelled permanent headship. With unusual precision, a division of labour was made: that portion which dealt with the traditional responsibilities for vital statistics and other registration functions, such as the incorporation of companies, was placed under the assistant provincial secretary, the official who had held the status of deputy minister almost from the outset; the other portion, consisting of the responsibilities long exercised by the Inspectorate of Prisons, Hospitals and Charities was now assigned to a 'deputy provincial secretary.'

This new statutory officer was intended to have a status co-equal with the assistant provincial secretary and, indeed, if so authorized by the lieutenant-governor-in-council, might 'exercise any of the powers and duties conferred ... upon any other officer of the department or upon any officer of any other department or branch of the public service the administration of which is for the time being assigned by the Lieutenant Governor in Council to the Provincial Secretary.' This wording clearly reflects the traditional ad hoc reliance on the Secretary's Office to take on any number of unrelated responsibilities. However, the implication that these would fall to the new deputy secretary did not apply in practice, for it was the original permanent head who tended to attract the bits and pieces. The deputy secretary was left to cope, as originally planned, with the inspectorate's responsibilities for prisons and reformatories.

This unusual arrangement persisted until the late 1940s in the face of a constant outward seepage of other functions which, over the years, had come to be attached to the Provincial Secretary's Office. In 1946 with the creation of a Department of Reform Institutions and the transfer of C.F. Neelands, long-time deputy provincial secretary in charge of the Reformatories and Prisons Branch, to be the new deputy minister, the long incubation of the inspectorate in the Provincial Secretary's Office was brought to an end.

Although the original reason for implanting a second permanent head in the Provincial Secretary's Office would thus appear to have become less persuasive, the seemingly infinite capacity of the Office to attract to it an assortment of responsibilities necessitated the continuation of both permanent heads. In due course, however, the dual permanent headship was abandoned and the Provincial Secretary's Office itself disappeared. Thus, of all the original BNA Offices, this one not only nurtured the most numerous departmental progeny but was, in fact, the only one to expire as a result of its mothering efforts. To trace the course of this dismemberment it is necessary to return to some of the other satellite agencies which, like the Inspectorate of Prisons and Public Institutions, had an association with the Office of Provincial Secretary.

The Provincial Board of Health had a special connection with the Provincial Secretary's Office because of a joint concern for the collection of vital statistics. Shortly after the turn of the century it added to its staff a medical inspector and a provincial analyst, along with two clerks, a messenger, and two stenographers. By the outbreak of the First World War the testing laboratories had expanded and at war's end the board, now headed by a chief medical officer and with a new division concerned with maternal and child welfare and public health nursing, found itself bracketed with Labour in the new department spun out of Public Works in 1919.

In this somewhat ill-matched combination but apparently operating quite independently under its own deputy, Dr J.W.S. McCullough, the old board began to take on a distinctly departmental appearance as three new divisions were added: Preventable Diseases, Industrial Hygiene, and Public Health Education. The inevitable organizational response to this growth came in 1924 with legislation establishing a full-blown Department of Health, complete with its own deputy minister (to be chief officer of health) and its own minister. A few years later, in 1930 and 1931, a series of acts transferred to the Department of Health many of the responsibilities for licensing and inspecting hospitals and charitable institutions which had been carried by the Inspectorate of Prisons and Public Institutions, under the wing of the Provincial Secretary's Office.

Thus, in the long road leading to the creation of a comprehensive health department, the Provincial Secretary's Office was first relieved of the Board of Health and then required to hand over that portion of the inspectorate's responsibilities having to do with hospitals, sanatoria, and the like.[17] The subsequent evolution of the Department of Health to become one of the largest, most dispersed departments, ultimately succeeding highways and education as the prime spender of provincial budgets, is a story that belongs to the period following the Second World War.

Office of Superintendent of Neglected and Dependent Children. This other satellite of the Provincial Secretary's Office, in combination with the responsibilities of the Inspectorate of Public Institutions for charitable institutions and orphanages, formed the basis of a new Department of Public Welfare in 1931. The Superintendent's Office had been created in 1893 and, with few exceptions, had remained a satellite of the Provincial Secretary's Office until 1931. In the mid-twenties, under its new title of Children's Aid Branch but still headed by its founder, J. J. Kelso, the agency had grown greatly, requiring a large staff of field agents to enforce the Children's Protection Act. At the same time the Provincial Secretary's Office had been obliged to shoulder responsibility for three major social welfare programs: mothers' allowances and minimum wages, both administered by commissions set up in 1920, and old age pensions, a joint initiative with the federal government that was to be locally administered and for which provision was made by legislation in 1929 and 1930. With the Children's Aid Branch as nucleus and these programs, a new Department of Public Welfare emerged in 1931.

What precipitated the combining of these functions and bits and pieces of other social programs into a single department was the report of the Royal (Ross) Commission that had been somewhat reluctantly appointed by Premier Ferguson in 1929. The reasons for his reluctance became apparent when the commission's findings were published. They condemned the scattered, uncoordinated nature of the programs and the outmoded administrative institutions incapable of meeting needs which had been greatly altered and expanded by the growth of urbanization and by industrial and technological change. Amongst their numerous recommendations was a call for a department of welfare.

The Ferguson government responded positively to this recommendation, the new Department of Welfare being extolled as the first of its kind in Canada.[18] Nevertheless, its beginnings were modest in the extreme; it was not until 1934 that it acquired its own deputy minister, M.A. Sorsoleil. He presided over a minuscule headquarters staff of four permanent and several temporary employees, and had to wait until 1937 to gain a ministerial head of his own.

Municipal Affairs. In addition to those functions loosely assigned to the Provincial Secretary's Office which eventually came under departments of Health, of Public Welfare, and of Reform Institutions, Municipal Affairs was given departmental status in 1935. The roots of the department go back to the initial responsibility assigned the Office of the Provincial Secretary for the compilation of municipal statistics. The obligation of municipalities to provide such information was at first considered to represent the limit of the province's intervention. By the 1880s this attitude was giving way in such fields as public health and sanitation and was soon to change radically in the area of road building.

In municipal financial affairs the first sign of change came in 1897 with the statutory creation of the Office of Provincial Municipal Auditor. The annual reports of this officer were included regularly in the report of the provincial secretary as were those of a Bureau of Municipal Affairs created in 1917. The director of the bureau was made a deputy head and authorized to report through a designated minister (the provincial secretary) and amongst other matters assigned was the provincial municipal auditor.

Prophetic of jurisdictional problems to come, the legislation of 1917 went out of its way to specify the municipal terrain excluded from the purview of the new bureau – most notably, the administrative mandates of the Board of Health and of the two major agencies created in 1906, Ontario Hydro and the Railway and Municipal Board.[19] It was this luxuriance of provincial agencies dealing with various aspects of municipal affairs that delayed the emergence of a full-blown department until 1935. By that time housing had become another responsibility that had been passed on to the Provincial Secretary's Office in 1919 and had involved sufficient cooperation with the municipalities to warrant its transfer to the new Department of Municipal Affairs.[20]

Demise of the Provincial Secretary's Office. The omnibus Office that had provided a home for so many incipient departments was to expire in 1972. Before its demise it experienced one last energizing burst during George Drew's tenure as premier. At that point a number of functions that had accumulated in the Premier's Office were off-loaded to the Provincial Secretary's Office. In the initial batch of functions to be shifted was the clerk of the Executive Council, and it was from this vantage point that L.R. McDonald, the assistant provincial secretary, appears to have assumed the role of secretary to the cabinet in 1948. Once again, however, the Secretary's Office served merely as an incubator for this all-important position, for by 1949–50 McDonald was transferred to the Office of the Prime Minister, as deputy minister and secretary to cabinet.

The other agencies transferred out of the Prime Minister's Office and for which the Provincial Secretary provided a temporary accommodation address included such assorted agencies as the Office of Speaker, Clerk of the Legislative Assembly, Office of the Crown in Chancery, King's Printer, and Civil Service Commissioner. The only remnants of the historic core functions of the Secretary's Office were the Registrar General's Branch and the Companies Branch, over which R.J. Cudney presided as deputy provincial secretary. The addition of Citizenship to the department's title in 1960 apparently did little to resuscitate the flagging responsibilities of the Secretary's Office, for not until five years later do the Public Accounts show 'sundry employees' for a citizenship branch. Thereafter, with no fanfare to mark the passing of one of the five historic Offices with which Ontario's public service began, the final dispersal of the Secretary's Office was quietly consummated by the omnibus reorganization act of 1972.[21]

Agriculture: From Enablement to Hands-On

The century-long evolution of the Provincial Secretary's Office affords the best demonstration of how the original all-purpose portfolio served as the potting shed for seedling organizations that ultimately matured to departmental status. The history of the development of the portfolio of the Commissioner of Agriculture serves to demonstrate quite a different feature of departmental evolution: the move to transform the elementary structure required for the passive, facilitative administrative mode to an integrated organization required to meet the contemporary demands of a more direct hands-on administrative mode.

Before this could occur, Agriculture had to be separated from sundry responsibilities with which it had been encumbered. Undoubtedly the commissioner's early and prolonged reliance on his agricultural clientele to fulfil his limited mandate made his agency vulnerable to the pervasive practice of allocating any function remotely concerned with the land to the agricultural portfolio. Thus it was that forestry, mines, and road making found their initial base in Agriculture, although these were fairly promptly transferred to more appropriate ministries. The Factory Inspectorate, however, proved to be a much more durable partner. It remained as a branch within the department from 1889 to 1916, when it was finally transferred to Public Works as a prelude to becoming a core element of a new Department of Labour.

Immigration. Most durable was the early association of Agriculture with Immigration, which lasted as a colonization branch until 1934. In view of the importance of immigration, particularly for providing farm labourers and domestics in the early decades of this century, it is surprising that it failed to achieve much prominence in the departmental roster. This low visibility may be attributed, in part, to the sharing of responsibility with the Dominion government. The maintenance of an Ontario immigration office in Liverpool and then in London was an off-and-on arrangement that depended upon the degree of aggravation experienced with federal government efforts aimed primarily at attracting new settlers to the expanding western provinces.

In his report for 1909 D. Sutherland, the new director of the Bureau of Colonization, complained that incentives provided by the Dominion government, such as cheap railway passes for harvesters, were draining even local residents, let alone immigrants, away from Ontario. To retaliate, Ontario had to restore arrangements for dispersing immigrants from a special office set up near Toronto's Union Station. Specific directions were now given to Ontario's London agents to countermand this failed cooperative measure. But, as Sutherland's report also revealed, there were internal as well as external jurisdictional divisions contributing to the problem of administering immigration affairs. There was the difficulty of coordinating provincial and Dominion efforts to attract immigrants and disperse them once arrived in Canada. On the colonization side, the bureau was limited to an advertising and informational role; the immigrant wanting to buy a homestead had to deal with Lands and Forests and also had to cope with a Colonization Roads Branch under Public Works.[22]

This jurisdictional confusion was exacerbated when another player, the Department of Northern Development, entered the scene in 1926, with a mandate to advance settlement and colonization in New Ontario and to administer financial assistance to the settlers. In the early 1930s Northern Development tended to command the lion's share of funding for such programs as unemployment relief, workers' camps, and the Trans-Canada Highway. As a consequence, in 1934 Agriculture's involvement with immigration and colonization was abandoned with Hepburn's abrupt abolition of the bureau.[23]

Thereafter, 'colonization' disappears from the lexicon. Even 'immigration' becomes elusive as one traces its sporadic surfacing in George Drew's Ontario House (an item in the Public Accounts for 1944–5 showing expenditures 'to enhance immigration work') and its final appearance as a branch in a Department of Trade and Development in 1968. With the postwar shift away from the historic reliance on the old country for immigrants and the move to more diverse sources, the term 'citizenship' begins to emerge as the new organizational reference point and 'immigration' as such disappears altogether from the structural map of Ontario's public service.

Departmental Consolidation. Returning to the main concerns of the Office of Commissioner of Agriculture, the heart of the Office's operation was to be found in the Bureau of Industries, created in 1882 for the compiling and distribution of the statistical data provided in the main by the grant-assisted societies and associations. In the course of time there developed extensive overlap between the bureau's activities and those of the Bureau of Labour created in 1900 and the responsibility of the Provincial Secretary for municipal statistics. The conversion of the Bureau of Industries to a Statistics and Publication Branch in 1918 signalled some resolution of the problem of overlap. More importantly, it was a manifestation of the gradual integration and consolidation that had been transforming the old Office over the last decade into a modernized department.[24] This process is worth examining for the light it throws on the organizational steps involved in order to assume a more hands-on approach to tasks hitherto left to the client groups or undertaken by the municipalities.

It is possible to set a rather precise date for the point when Agriculture could be considered to have come of age as a department proper. For the year ending 30 October 1910, for the first time since its attainment of the formal status of a department in 1888, the public were given an annual report from the minister. The annual reports from the various societies and associations, which had hitherto served as surrogates for a departmental report, were nevertheless continued. The minister himself was sufficiently conscious of this ground-breaking effort that his annual report for 1910 contained an extensive and invaluable review going back, in the case of the agricultural societies, to pre-confederation times.[25]

The report reveals that by 1910 the department had been organized into branches, each a kind of mirror image of the clientele groups which over the years had been depended upon to conduct fairs, scientific research, and information-gathering in return for their modest governmental grants. Now the department, through its respective branches, assumed a more managerial or directive stance. The superintendent of the Agriculture Societies Branch, for example, now served as the secretary of the Fairs and Exhibitions Association, the Horticultural Association, and the Vegetable Growers' Association. The director of the Live Stock Branch was described as acting as executive officer for a number of livestock and poultry associations, as well as supervising grants to horse breeders, swine, sheep, and poultry societies.

For the Fruit Branch, established in 1908 under a chief inspector, in addition to the perennial preoccupation with fighting insect pests, increasing attention was directed 'to the market end of the business' – an observation most prophetic of the wave of the future. However, for this branch as well as for Dairy Products (which at the time had not quite achieved branch status), the process of taking over from the clientele groups was still far from assured. Although the department had assumed control over the instruction of dairymen in the 1890s and cheese makers in 1906 (which involved a staff of thirty-five from April to November), the association still employed its own inspectors to check on adultera- tion, paying for them out of grants from the department. In the case of the Fruit Branch, inspection for fumigation and packing houses under the Fruit Pests Act was dependent on a 'local option' arrangement whereby the municipal authorities had to be petitioned by the societies to agree to cooperate.

Indeed, the problem of getting cooperation from municipal authorities or securing approval for heavier provincial involvement was a central concern for the Farmers' Institute Branch, despite the fact that it had been set up for some twenty-five years. The organization of meetings and speakers for the Farmers' Institutes and, after 1905, the more durable Women's Institutes, was under the superintendent's supervi- sion; that this modest exercise in adult education was not enough was revealed by the observation that district agents needed to stimulate their constituents 'to do things rather than merely talk about them.'

These district agents had been set up on an experimental basis in 1907, limited to six counties and jointly supported by Education and Agriculture. When the Dominion government's grant-in-aid program for agriculture was inaugurated in 1912, the district representatives came entirely under Agriculture and in 1918 were transformed into the agricultural representatives (Ag. Reps) of today. They remained de- pendent on a county grant of $500 to legitimate their local opera- tions.[26]

Even in terms of the original interest of the department in the inform- ing and educating of its clientele, the somewhat passive assertion of the facilitative administrative mode was clearly being overtaken by more direct operative and regulatory modes. By the 1930s such modes would come to dominate, though by no means displace, the traditional depart- mental focus. The incipient interest in marketing, expressed by the Fruit Branch in 1908, was to expand and become the occasion for creating marketing boards which in turn were added to a growing crop of inde- pendent agencies.

An interesting sidelight on the impact of integration and consolidation upon the central organization of the Department of Agriculture is to be found in its pioneering deployment of an assistant deputy minister. Now a commonly used title for a member of the senior managerial team, in 1911, so far as can be ascertained, it was unique. In that year, presum- ably in conjunction with the major restructuring of the department, the long-time deputy minister, C.C. James, was replaced by W. Bert Road- house, and C.F. Bailey was made assistant deputy minister.[27]

One might speculate that the reason for initiating such an appointment was tied in with the increasing organizational complexity created by consolidation of the department. The creation of mirror-image branches to reflect the assortment of societies and associations historically comprising the department's clientele inevitably produced an overwhelming 'span of control' problem for the permanent head. Coupled with the retention of some of those satellite agencies previously noted, the supervisory capacity of a single deputy minister was presumably overextended. Nor was it appropriate to adopt the solution of using the dual deputy ministership, as occurred in other departments. It was not really a question of preparing the way for an ultimate separation of a totally unrelated activity into a separate department, but a matter of coping with managerial overload created by the expansion within one department of logically associated functions.

Nevertheless, in 1917 the dual deputy solution was made available to the department when it was enacted that the lieutenant-governor-in-council 'may appoint one or more than one Deputy Minister of Agriculture.' The same legislation also authorized the appointment of a commissioner of agriculture, 'to advise and make recommendations to the Minister' after investigating conditions affecting agriculture. In the event, the option was never exercised. The assistant deputy minister was appointed to what proved to be the short-lived post of commissioner of agriculture, since by 1921 the department had settled for a single deputy minister. Presumably a decision had been made that neither the size nor the complexity of the department warranted that increase in the number of reporting levels within the hierarchy which would become a standard feature of the post-Second World War bureaucracy with its much more enlarged and more refined division of labour.

Provincial Treasurer: Late Bloomer

The last of the nineteenth-century departmental building blocks, the Office of Provincial Treasurer and the Department of Education, were in fact the least susceptible to the incursion of alien satellites. Consequently, their consolidation and growth throughout more than half the twentieth century was much more straightforward than for the other BNA Act Offices. This is not to say that these two departments did not undergo substantial changes. However, in the case of the Office of Provincial Treasurer the responses to the need for modernization came so belatedly that they belong to the post-1945 period which effectively falls outside the range of this study. For that reason and more particularly because these developments have much to do with the modernized

Treasury as an agency of central control and coordination, such of its story as is relevant will be picked up in a later chapter dealing with financial control and accountability.

Education

Though a later addition to the five BNA Act Offices, the Department of Education has been considered here as one of the original departmental building blocks. At the outset, it will be recalled, critics were concerned that the transformation to a ministerial department would expose the educational system to partisan politics and patronage. The abolition of the appointed Advisory Council of Public Instruction at the same time as the new department came into being in 1876 was interpreted as additional confirmation of the critics' suspicions that political interference would increase. This is the context within which one can assess yet another of Premier Whitney's reform measures.

By means of a major revision of the Education Act in 1906 an advisory council to constitute an independent source of advice and expert knowledge for the minister was reintroduced. At the same time a superintendent of education was to be appointed, directly under the minister and superior in status to the deputy minister, to have 'the general supervision and direction of all classes ... professional training schools ... examinations for teachers ... inspectors of schools,' and the like.

Even the competing news of a major eruption of Mount Vesuvius could not distract the editorialist for the *Globe* from registering a strong vote of approval for the proposed reforms. 'The appointment of a Deputy Minister of Education and a Superintendent of Education,' the editorial proclaimed,

will establish executive and expert supervising [*sic*] in their respective spheres. This will leave the Minister free to make the speeches, lay the communications, and manage the political element of the work. The bill provides for an advisory Council of seventeen members, representing the four universities, the high, public and separate school teachers, and the public school inspectors. Provision is made for the appointment of a superintendent to deal with the school book question and to conduct such investigations and inquiries as may be deemed necessary. (11 April 1906)

Testifying to the importance which was attached to the new position of superintendent, the *Globe* subsequently complained that the proposed salary of $3,500 was too niggardly, being no more than that paid a chief inspector of public schools. What was required, the *Globe* contended, was 'a man of adequate scholarship, wide experience, true ideals, and that rare combination of personal qualities which make a man a leader among his followers.' In short, a person possessing 'at least the qualities of a University President' (11 May 1906).

Could this have been the same commentator who on 26 April and again on 5 May had lambasted the government's University of Toronto reform bill for giving too much independence to the new board of governors and the president, protesting that 'the right of veto is essential for Cabinet solidarity'? Why did such a veto make sense for an institution of higher learning while, in the view of the *Globe*'s editorialist,

the Minister [of Education] has no real knowledge of the educational situations, no capacity for understanding the problems, and no resources for meeting its needs. His leadership is political or it is nothing, and he has no aptitudes for grasping what is mastered for him by his subordinates ... Fortunately, the Deputy Minister has both the aptitudes and the training for managing the administrative side of the Department's work.

In the *Globe*'s opinion, the proposed superintendent would provide the lead in educational policy.

The effort to achieve for educational administrators independence from intrusion of the 'amateur' political head was by no means as clear-cut as the *Globe*'s editorialist believed. In his first report under the new dispensation, the minister of education, Dr Pyne, observed that the advisory council had 'long been discussed as a practical method for bringing the Minister of Education in close touch with the teaching profession and enabling him, whenever he desires, to seek in a regular and systematic manner the counsel and opinion of the various ranks of educationists.' Pyne went on to emphasize:

In creating this body, the Legislature has carefully guarded the responsibility of the Minister, who is not to divide or evade his duties to the Legislature or the public ... The Council will be consulted from time to time on matters concerning which I feel that the advice of professional educationists will be helpful to the public advantage. My representative upon the Council and the medium of official communications is the Superintendent of Education. [His] appointment is in harmony with the principles that underly the present reconstruction of the educational system and is intended to afford the department the constant assistance of professional experience and knowledge dissociated from the full administrative control which remains in the hands of the responsible Minister. The functions of the office of Superintendent being advisory and not executive, are exercised primarily with a view to the educational bearing of all questions submitted to him. The abstract merits of all educational problems thus receive due consideration and I am glad to have, in this important work, the aid of Dr. John Seath whose long connection with our school system and whose labours on behalf of education amply qualify him for the position of Superintendent.[28]

Despite Dr Pyne's enthusiastic endorsement of the advisory council, after the first two or three years when some use was made of it for matters of curriculum reform, it soon became such a formal façade for the real input from the senior officials in the department that it was quietly phased out of existence by an amendment to the School Acts in 1915. Effectively, the reforms of 1906 confirmed the pattern of insider domination of educational policy that dated back to Ryerson's hegemony. For close to thirty years, from 1905 to 1934, three figures were to preside over the fortunes of the department. John Seath, who at the age of sixty-one assumed supreme command at the policy level, had from his arrival from Scotland in Canada in 1861 served as principal of several high schools and then become inspector of high schools and collegiate institutes. Described as domineering and authoritarian, his clinging on to the superintendency until his death in 1919 at age seventy-five was adjudged to be a reason for the 'poor shape' of the department by that time.[29]

The office of deputy minister that was presumed to take care of the nitty-gritty of administration while Seath occupied the empyrean heights of policy was filled by A.H.U. Colquhoun. As if to emphasize the separation between the two realms of policy and administration, Colquhoun, unlike Seath and all his predecessors, did not come to office as an expert educationist. He had spent his early years after graduating from McGill University as a journalist on the staff of the *Montreal Star*, the *Ottawa Journal* and the Toronto *Empire*. He was to collaborate with Seath until 1919 and complete his twenty-nine years of service as deputy minister with Seath's successor, F.W. Merchant.

Like Seath, Merchant had come up through the educationist hierarchy by way of school principalships and the inspectorate. During Seath's regime he had become director of technical and industrial education and had made an important report on English-French schools. He assumed Seath's role as chief policy adviser to the minister, with the new title of chief director of education. When Colquhoun and Merchant retired in 1934, Duncan McArthur assumed both positions, thereby bringing to an end the interesting experiment with a dual headship of the department based on the perception that a separation could be maintained between the administrative or managerial responsibilities and the purely policy roles conventionally carried by the permanent head of a department.[30] As if to confirm the indissoluble link between policy and administration, in 1938 Duncan McArthur, in a most unusual transition, moved from the office of deputy minister to that of ministerial head!

There appear to have been no similar experiments in any of the other departments. The dual (even multiple) deputy ministerships used extensively elsewhere were adopted with quite different objectives in mind. Nor has the Department of Education reverted to the thirty-year experiment with dividing policy and administration between two senior officials. The subdivisions are now framed as multiple assistant deputy ministerships, where policy and administration continue to mingle.

Strengthening the Centre

Office of the Prime Minister and President of Council

Surprisingly, one of the most important measures taken by Whitney was a structural change destined to strengthen the directing and coordinating capacities of the leader of the government. Surprising, because the step taken in Ontario came at a remarkably early stage in the evolution of the public service. More than three decades before the Dominion government was to provide its first minister with an office and specialized staff, the position of president of the Executive Council for Ontario was formally established as a cabinet portfolio by an act of 1905 (5 Edw. VII, c.5).

Thereafter, from the combined Office of the Prime Minister and President of the Council, the premier had at his disposal the administrative infrastructure required for the exercise of authority as leader of the party and leader of the cabinet collectivity. Subsequent changes made by Whitney's successors were to bring about further refinements and a clearer separation of administrative support for the premier's personal and party leadership functions and the servicing of the collective needs of a cabinet over which the premier presided.

With the creation of the Office of President of Council in 1905 the title of premier was abruptly elevated to 'prime minister.' While the standard form of reference, for example in the press, continued to be premier, in such documents as the estimates and public accounts, the listing was consistently 'Office of the Prime Minister and President of Council' and later simply 'Department of the Prime Minister.' Not until the early 1970s did government documents revert to the term 'Office of the Premier.'[31]

Whatever psychic satisfaction may have been derived from the symbolic equation of Ontario's first minister with Canada's first minister, the title of prime minister may nevertheless have been a more accurate portrayal of an historical reality – namely, the dominance of the province's premier vis-à-vis the members of the cabinet. Of course, this dominance has always been acknowledged in the well-known maxim that the premier is 'primus inter pares.' But for most of Ontario's history, that phrase might well have been reinterpreted as 'much more primus than pares,' at least as far as concerned the premiers up to and including Leslie Frost.

Premier Frost was perhaps the last of the first ministers who was capable of exerting such personal dominance over his cabinet.[32] His successors, not necessarily because they were less able or forceful but because the universe over which they presided had become so much more demanding, were compelled to lean more and more on the collectivity making up their cabinets. These changing and more imperious demands, imposed upon both the premier and his colleagues, necessitated further elaboration of those components of the machinery of government that served both the particular needs of the premier and the collective requirements of cabinet government.

The commanding role attributed to the premier existed from the beginning, but the special demands placed on the office were thought by all but one of its early incumbents to be adequately met by the staff attached to the Office of the Attorney General, the portfolio generally held by the premiers up to Whitney's time. The exception was Edward Blake who, during his brief tenure as premier from 1871 to 1872, actually made an organizational disposition for the premier that anticipated the change legislated in 1905. Blake insisted on separating the Office of Attorney General and the Office of President of the Executive Council, assuming the latter portfolio for himself in his role of first minister.[33] So strong was the fixation on maintaining the size of the Executive Council established by the terms of the BNA Act that Blake's decision was roundly criticized and was a probable reason for the legislation of 1872 by which a limit of six was placed on the membership of the council.[34]

In the event, the experiment with a separate president of council did not survive Blake's departure. Both Oliver Mowat and his successor, Arthur Hardy, combined the premiership with the Office of Attorney General, although in the last Liberal ministry, G.W. Ross opted for the Treasurer's Office and assigned J.M. Gibson to the Attorney General's Office.

When Oliver Mowat acceded to the premiership in 1872 and with it to the Office of Attorney General, he did not altogether dismiss the point that Blake's experiment had tried to make, that the responsibilities of a first minister – particularly when associated with the workload of such an active portfolio as that of the Attorney General – might well require separate administrative facilities to serve the specific needs of the first minister. In fact, Mowat had to acknowledge this point when the opposition took issue with what they viewed as the excess baggage of two officers in the upper reaches of the Attorney General's Office. Mowat, defending the need for both, argued that the premiership and the Office of Attorney General might not necessarily be held by the same person and that, moreover, he viewed the clerk of the Executive Council as 'the deputy of the Premier.'[35]

Despite his recognition of the need of separate staff for the premier, Mowat continued to combine within his office the clerk and the deputy attorney general positions. Indeed, until formal statutory provision was made for the Office of President of the Executive Council in 1905, the two posts were merged in the person of J.R. Cartwright. When Cartwright was appointed to the position in 1889, he had already served for four years as secretary to the premier and, although Mowat and his successors continued to have a secretary, it is probable that Cartwright essentially filled the position of permanent chief adviser. Subsequently, in 1899, when the then premier, George Ross, decided to assume a portfolio other than that of the Attorney General, Cartwright continued as deputy for the new attorney general. He also retained his position as clerk of the Executive Council, presumably reporting to Ross. With Whitney's reorganization of 1905, Cartwright lost the joint title and then soldiered on as deputy attorney general, his lengthy service at this central position being about equally divided between Liberal and Conservative administrations.

Although the joint title was dropped in 1905, it took much longer to sever the association of the clerk of the Executive Council from the Office of Attorney General. The prolongation of the connection came about because of the existence of an assistant clerk of the Executive Council, a position that was held from 1879 on by J.L. Capreol. Thus, when Cartwright relinquished his title of clerk of the Executive Council in 1905, Capreol was promoted to that position, although he remained under the attorney general's supervision until 1916. Only then, with the transfer of the clerk to the 'Office of the Prime Minister and President of Council,' was a correspondence achieved between assigned administrative roles and the prescriptive title generated by Whitney's reorganization of 1905.

Those familiar with the present-day infrastructure buttressing the responsibilities of the premier will, no doubt, recognize in these organizational manoeuvres the forerunners of the current, sophisticated Office of the Premier and Cabinet Office. The dual title conveys the notion of the separation between the premier's duties as a party leader and chief spokesman for the province, as distinct from the duties associated with the management of cabinet. In less demanding times the distinction was less clear. Nevertheless, from an early date the position of secretary to the premier was established with a status (as reflected in salaries) roughly equal to that of the clerk of the Executive Council. This remained true until at least 1921: Horace Wallis, brought in as the 'Prime Minister's Secretary' by Whitney's reorganization, was awarded the same salary as Capreol – a situation that persisted even when Wallis was given the title of deputy minister. Although Capreol was replaced in 1920 by his long-time assistant C.F. Bulmer, Wallis became, and remained until his retirement in 1934, the key man in the premier's office. Wallis also appears to have enjoyed the confidence of Whitney, Hearst, E.C. Drury, Howard Ferguson, and George S. Henry.[36]

By the end of the First World War, with a deputy minister in overall command of the premier's office and the clerk of the Executive Council at the head of a minute staff concerned with the mechanics of cabinet business, the reforms initiated by Whitney in 1905 appeared to have been consummated. However, the neatness and clarity of this reorganization was countermanded by the tendency, beginning in 1919, to make the premier's office a repository for a variety of substantive matters not obviously related to the premier's double duties as party leader and chairman of the cabinet. With Wallis presiding over the main office as deputy minister, one might have supposed that a genuine department for coordinating and integrating these prime ministerial functions was in the making. However, the several components appeared to have had little to do with one another or with the deputy's office.

One of these, the Office of the Civil Service Commissioner, was placed in the premier's office from its inception in 1918 and remained until 1946 when it was transferred to the Department of Provincial Secretary. While this placement might be construed as a sign of the high priority assigned to the issue of civil service reform, it is probable that the distribution of patronage had to be kept within the benevolent but authoritarian embrace of the premier. In the late 1920s another operating responsibility, the King's Printer's Office, was added to the premier's office, as was a Publicity and Information Bureau which in Mitchell Hepburn's time became a Travel and Publicity Bureau.

The arrival of Hepburn in 1934 created a more cluttered premier's office. He took the Provincial Treasurer's portfolio himself and added his deputy treasurer, Chester Walters, to the already crowded premier's menage, conferring on Walters the additional title of controller of finance. Walters, described by Neil McKenty as 'an able man with a towering ego whose influence with the Premier over the years ... nettled not a few Liberals,' obviously dominated the premier's office; his formal status as controller of finance combined with the premier's assumption of the Treasury portfolio made the office the real power centre of government.[37] Hepburn's reliance on Walters as trouble-shooter and fiscal inquisitor of the bureaucracy is thoroughly documented in John T. Saywell's biography of Hepburn.[38]

Thus, at the end of the Liberal regime in the early 1940s, the premier's office had come to contain a curious accumulation of functions: a main office that handled the personal-cum-party elements of the premier's agenda, over which the premier's secretary presided; the Office of Executive Council headed by the clerk; the Office of Civil Service Commissioner headed by C.J. Foster, who also served as general secretary for the main office (an interesting commentary on the professed arm's-length relationship of an agency set up to guard the public service from the ravages of patronage); a Travel and Publicity Bureau whose director enjoyed a higher salary than either the clerk of Council or the civil service commissioner; and finally, the Office of King's Printer.[39]

This mix was altered somewhat but not substantially reduced when George Drew and the Conservatives displaced the Liberals in 1943. Reflecting a major interest of the new premier in encouraging ties with the mother country, the director of Ontario House in London, England, J.S.P. Armstrong, was placed under the direct supervision of Drew. Because Drew took on the Education portfolio rather than the Treasurer's Office, Chester Walters was evicted from the premier's office as controller of finance but much to Hepburn's surprise (though presumably not to Walters's) was continued as deputy treasurer under the new provincial treasurer, Leslie Frost. There Walters's influence was diminished – but only by dint of occasional reminders from a determined political head 'that he was a deputy minister, not the acting premier, and that making major decisions was not his prerogative.'[40]

This exploration of the process of department-building during the first four decades of the twentieth century reveals the organizational means by which the omnibus nineteenth-century Offices gradually jettisoned the mixed bag of administrative entities consigned to them, often with little rhyme or reason. For three of the original BNA Act Offices, absorption of these agencies was achieved by creating departments within departments and doubling up on the permanent heads until, in due course, separate ministerial departments emerged. Thus, at the outset of the Second World War, the result of these processes of parturition, growth, and maturation was a doubling of the number of executive councillors which, until 1887, had been statutorily fixed at six.

Long before this expansion of the cabinet had occurred, a prescient move by Premier Whitney in 1905 had prepared the ground for a central agency that would provide the premier with the administrative staff services which would become increasingly necessary if the incumbent was to be able to cope with the political/personal role of party leader as well as the governmental role of directing the affairs of an enlarging cabinet faced with a growing agenda. Whitney's innovations at the centre would in later years require substantial supplementation and adaptation. Moreover, the ministerial departments whose rise and consolidation have been described were in process of being overwhelmed by the growth of new forms of non-departmental agencies that by their number and significant responsibilities dwarfed their nineteenth-century satellite progenitors.

8
Twentieth-Century Satellites: Meredith's Models

The growth of departmental portfolios proceeded apace from Whitney's 1905 reorganization. Paradoxically, even as organizational consolidation and rationalization was taking place, opposing pressures were encouraging experimentation with new non-departmental forms. Before the end of the century several pioneer ventures of this kind had been launched. These included the Queen Victoria Niagara Parks Commission and the Fish and Game Commission, followed in the new century by the Temiskaming and Northern Ontario Railway Commission, the Hydro-Electric Power Commission of Ontario, and the Ontario Railway and Municipal Board. These agencies were given separate statutory identities which today are considered necessary for effective implementation of the regulatory administrative mode as well as for the hands-on administrative mode required wherever governments undertake commercial and financial activities akin to private sector enterprises.

Unlike the satellites examined in previous chapters that were nearly all absorbed into regular departments or became departments in their own right, many of the new structural nonconformists retained their separate identities. However, almost continuous debate has marked the efforts to establish the appropriate degree of independence from the parent or responsible ministerial department. As the number of such agencies has grown over the years, these concerns have intensified, not only because of the problem of classifying increasingly varied organizational forms but also because of the basic need to establish some kind of birth control.

The contemporary efflorescence of non-departmental forms endowed with a varied mix of administrative, entrepreneurial, and judicial or determining functions, with all the attendant problems of accountability and control, provides sufficient grounds to reach back to the early progenitors in order to discover what reasons were then educed for conferring special status on selected agencies.

Sir William Meredith's Bequest

The search may start appropriately in 1906 with two agencies, the Ontario Railway and Municipal Board (ORMB) and the Hydro-Electric Power Commission, both of which have persisted and give little sign of fading away. Unquestionably, the most influential sponsor of these particular non-departmental administrative structures was Whitney's political mentor and predecessor as leader of the Conservative party, William Ralph Meredith. Before his retirement from partisan politics and his elevation to the bench in 1894, Meredith had been a determined opponent of the conversion of the Education Office to the Department of Education. He had been concerned that placing education under a politically responsible minister would expose public instruction to undesirable political influence. Undoubtedly, his position as chancellor of the University of Toronto and his membership on the 1905 commission concerned with the reorganization of that institution confirmed his view of the need to establish an arm's-length relationship with the government. At the same time he was grappling with the status of the university, Meredith's political and legal talents were called upon for the creation of the ORMB and Ontario Hydro. A decade later he was to be instrumental in creating the Workmen's Compensation Board.

The first of Meredith's creations was the Ontario Railway and Municipal Board. When Whitney assumed power in 1905 he inherited from the Ross government a railway committee of cabinet as the means of dealing with regulatory problems particularly associated with the growing enthusiasm for electrified street railways. Unwilling to turn such contentious matters over to the probable log-rolling proclivities of the legislature's own railway committee, Whitney wrote to Meredith (now chief justice of Ontario) saying that he wished 'some person ... would furnish me with a memo ... showing the object and purpose of a permanent Commission to be created to deal with disputes and questions affecting Railways, Telegraph and Telephone Companies.'

The bill to create the ORMB that received first reading in the legislature on 12 March 1906 was, from all appearances, Meredith's response to Whitney's plea. Charles Humphries, Whitney's biographer, correctly marks the significance of this new venture in declaring it 'a new step in the governance of the province: dawn on the day of the board or commission had arrived.'[1]

The lion's share of this accolade undoubtedly belongs to Meredith's drafting skills and should be extended as well to the second of the great administrative innovations whose legal formulation owes as much to Meredith as does the ORMB – the Hydro-Electric Power Commission.

The measure creating HEPC moved through the same legislative session as that for the ORMB. It is important to observe that while the ORMB could claim to be the prime example of a regulatory agency, the Hydro enactment dealt with a direct operating administrative mode involving the management and development of a major public enterprise. That it was equally a device for regulating the distribution of electrical power through municipal utility companies contracted with Hydro as the wholesale producer was but an added complication for those later concerned with creating accountability and control regimes for such satellite organizations.

Ontario Hydro was the inspiration and, ultimately, the creature of its chief advocate, Adam Beck. As a neophyte member of Whitney's cabinet, Beck was faced with having to give legislative effect to the resolution approved on 17 April 1906 by a deputation of western Ontario municipalities which urged 'the necessity of safeguarding the people's interests by originating as a government measure legislation enabling the Governor in Council to appoint a permanent provincial Commission.' According to W.R. Plewman, a participant observer at the time, 'the bill he [Beck] introduced for the government largely was of Adam Beck's own phrasing. But back of Adam Beck was the Chief Justice of Ontario, Sir William Meredith, who behind the scenes worded much of the legislation desired by the aggressive leader of the Hydro municipalities.'[2]

The evidence supporting Meredith's authorship of the third important contribution to the evolution of non-departmental organizational forms is even clearer. In 1911 Meredith was commissioned to investigate the laws relating to the liability of employers and with a mandate to recommend a model Workmen's Compensation bill. Meredith pursued his inquiries between the years 1911 and 1913, drawing his inspiration primarily from British and most particularly German experience. His recommendations took the unusual but practical form of a draft bill which he then proceeded to show answered not only all requirements but, when set against all alternative proposals placed before him, could be proved eminently more suitable.[3] In 1914, faithful to Meredith's model, the bill 'to provide for Compensation to Workmen for Injuries sustained and Industrial Diseases contracted in the course of their Employment' was enacted. By this legislation another landmark, in the shape of the Workmen's Compensation Board, was added to the organizational landscape.

The functional adaptability of the agency, board, or commission form of organization is admirably demonstrated by the three very different entities that sprang from Meredith's draughtsmanship. Such flexibility was to be a feature of succeeding 'ABCs' and a major reason for extending their use to meet new responsibilities falling on government in the years after the First World War. Their popularity is attested to by their current number, while they flourish in such variety that categorization has become a real challenge. However, in general terms, the three most important species – whose administrative modes can be broadly characterized as regulatory, entrepreneurial, and allocative – are represented by Meredith's early creations. Thus, their further exploration will serve to reveal the significant departures from the conventional departmental form which have been deemed necessary to provide the arm's-length relationship best suited to each distinctive administrative mode.

The ORMB: The Adjudicative Regulatory Mode

If one sets aside the Board of Fish and Game Commissioners as an early experiment whose failure was signified by its absorption after 1907 into a department, the establishment of the ORMB in 1906 marks the inauguration of the first major non-departmental agency vested with regulatory powers. These provisions were to be replicated for subsequent non-departmental ventures, including Meredith's two other creations.

Although the three commissioners on the board who replaced the railway committee of the cabinet were to be appointed 'during pleasure' (not as protected a status as judges who hold their appointments 'during good behaviour'), the intention to confer a judicial status on the board was indicated by according it the powers of a court of record. Also paralleling arrangements for the judiciary, the salaries for the chairman, the two board members, and the secretary were established in the statute. Operational autonomy was provided by conferring on the commissioners the authority to appoint specialist advisers and appropriate staff, on approval of the lieutenant-governor-in-council, and to dismiss such staff at will. Signalling its antecedents in the railway committee of cabinet, the board reported directly to the governor-in-council. This provision was to have important repercussions in later years in that it anticipated the use of a 'political appeal' of board decisions to cabinet.

Another important precedent was created that affected the breadth of jurisdiction and general powers conferred on the board. Meredith's concern for hedging such discretion is revealed by the detailed provisions laid down in the act to govern the practice and procedures of the board. However, the act also included an early version of what has come to be termed a 'privative' clause, whereby decisions of the board are declared to be unreviewable by the courts, save on a point of law.

That this provision was taken to heart by the commissioners is revealed in their first annual report. Observing that they had drafted the rules and regulations covering their practice and procedures which were duly promulgated in the *Ontario Gazette,* the commissioners explained: 'The design of the Board was to make the rules so intelligible that with the aid of the forms, any mayor, reeve, or municipal clerk could, in ordinary, clear and concise language, prepare and launch an application.' Having broken down one of the barriers which would have existed if application had had to be made to a conventional law court, the commissioners went on to show how their proposed mode of procedure demolished a second barrier: 'One of the rules provides that no proceedings shall be defeated by any technical objection based upon defects in form, it being the policy of the Board that having the parties before it ... the proceedings should not be delayed or be made oppressive by mere technicalities.'

The unusual sensitivity of the commissioners to the breadth of their regulatory mandate also finds expression in their first report. Noting that the board had the power to act on its own motion or on request of the lieutenant-governor-in-council, the commissioners explained why they preferred citizens and local officials to initiate proceedings:

The Board has very responsible and drastic powers delegated to it by the Act, and for that reason should act on their [*sic*] own initiative with due caution ... one's sense of British justice revolts at the idea of a judicial tribunal acting as prosecutor, counsel and judge. Not only should justice be done by the Board, but the parties to any controversy should depart hence from the Board feeling that their cause had been fairly heard and decided. This could never be brought to pass if the Board initiated the proceedings, examined or cross-examined the witnesses and was therefore forced to exchange the zeal of the advocate for the impartiality of the judge.[4]

Perhaps it is only in the first fine youthful days of an agency, when first principles remain clear and unencumbered by accumulated decisions, that such frank and high-minded views as these are likely to be expressed formally and in writing. The passing years, with the addition of other regulatory agencies akin to the original ORMB, have not altered the validity of the commissioners' first assessments. However, the practices and subtle variations in the form and powers of subsequent non-departmental creations have clouded and confused the home truths so clearly expressed in the formative years of the ORMB. Over the years, the flexibility and informality of procedures, on which the first commissioners placed so much value, have also tended to be overrun by legal formalism.

Contributing to the subsequent beclouding of the intentions so clearly enunciated by the ORMB commissioners is a complicating feature in the original mandate of the ORMB itself. The valuable insights the commissioners had to offer concerning the proper exercise of their discretionary powers related primarily to only one element of their extensive mandate, – that which affected the municipalities, their territories or annexation of territory; their finances and debentures wherever lieutenant-governor-in-council approval was required; and the approval of public roads, bridges, streets, electric railways, waterworks and generally 'any other industry or concern commonly known as a public utility.'

These were to become the bread-and-butter regulatory business of the board, but as the inclusion of 'Railway' in its title implied, early priority was given to this aspect of its mandate. (Not until 1932 was the title changed to Ontario Municipal Board, in belated recognition that railways had long since ceased to be a major concern.) For railways, the instruments for implementing the regulatory mode differed from the court-like adjudicative/hearing processes considered necessary for handling the municipal side of its mandate. In effect, the board was replacing the cabinet committee for railway matters, and its concerns were with inspection to check on compliance with provisions governing fares and safety precautions. The board was even called upon to arbitrate labour disputes and mediate strikes and lockouts relating to railways. It was primarily for the exercise of this part of its mandate that the board was authorized to employ specialist advisers.

This combination of court-like responsibilities and more purely administrative activities has always been present; even the judiciary itself performs more than purely judicial functions when, for example, it administers estates. However, the vesting of judicial responsibilities in an administrative/regulatory tribunal such as the ORMB has been viewed askance by the legal profession in particular. It has also raised a more general issue of the right of the province to create courts of law in view of the constitutional provision in section 96 of the BNA Act conferring on the governor general the right to appoint 'the Judges of the Superior, District, and County Courts in each Province.'[5]

It is useful to trace the subsequent evolution of the ORMB to show how the conventional law courts have sought to maintain the final word on the judicial aspect of the board's work while, for its administrative aspects, continuous efforts have been made to pull these back into the orbit of a regular department. The history of the relations of the board with the Bureau of Municipal Affairs, created in 1918, aptly illustrates the efforts to resolve this problem of an agency with a complex mandate requiring both regulatory and administrative modes. At first, the Bureau of Municipal Affairs was treated as a subordinate arm of the ORMB. But at the height of the depression in 1935, with municipalities having to be put into trusteeship, a Department of Municipal Affairs replaced the bureau and assumed many of the administrative powers that had accumulated in the hands of the (now renamed) Ontario Municipal Board.

Perhaps no other representative of the regulatory agency amongst the entire mixed community of ABCs so amply demonstrates the problem of the hybrid organization struggling to preserve its mandate to exercise independently both administrative and semi-judicial powers. While having to keep in the good graces of the courts as the final arbiters of due process or natural justice, the board must at the same time struggle to buffer its operations from undue interference from the minister and cabinet. Because of its ultimate responsibility to the Assembly and because of the constitutional subserviency of the municipalities to the provincial government, the cabinet is tempted to be overly attentive. Thus the OMB has to tread a delicate line. On the one side are the courts, armed – despite the existence of a 'privative clause' – with the power to review the procedural propriety of the board's actions. On the other side is the cabinet with its authority to hear a 'political appeal' against the substance of the board's decisions. These ambiguities in the board's operating status enhance the opportunities for cabinet ministers to adjust their relations with the board. If public favour can be won by invoking their right to review and revise the board's decision, that course is open to them. Alternatively, the independence of the agency may be proclaimed as a reason for non-intervention and, presumably, as a reason for dodging responsibility.

Ontario Hydro: The Hands-On Operative Mode

The history of the OMB is a story of a hybrid regulatory agency seeking to find its proper place between the judiciary and the executive branch of government. The Hydro-Electric Power Commission of Ontario had to fight on only one front to establish its place in the organizational firmament. Its mandate as the monopoly wholesaler of electrical power to the municipalities did not involve the use of quasi-judicial regulatory powers highlighted in the OMB. Its entrepreneurial mandate was initially viewed as sufficiently different from that normally assigned a conventional government department that a separate legal corporate status was conferred. This legal distinctiveness enabled Ontario Hydro to be excluded from the progressively expanding reach of its compatriot OMB. In the early stages, however, it appeared to be threatened by a move to absorb it into the departmental fold as a department of power.

The major corporate predecessor of Hydro was the Temiskaming and Northern Ontario Railway which, though never seriously faced with a proposal to fold it into a department of railways, did remain throughout its formative years and beyond under the personal charge of the premier. This same intimate tie with the executive was clearly anticipated in the statutory provisions for the three commissioners who were to be placed in charge of the new HEPC. At least one of these was required to be a member of the Executive Council, with the option of appointing a second commissioner from the same source – an option that was immediately exercised with the appointment of Colonel John S. Hendrie to accompany the chairman, Adam Beck.

For all intents and purposes, this arrangement came close to placing HEPC under a committee of cabinet.[6] Under such circumstances it seems strange that there developed in the Whitney government a strong movement to transform the Hydro Commission into a department. Undoubtedly the presence of Beck stimulated this movement, to which Whitney himself appeared to lend such a willing ear that a measure to achieve the 'departmentation' of Hydro was on the verge of acceptance in 1911. The domineering Beck, with his independent support in the 'hydro municipalities' was opposed by a faction in Whitney's cabinet who were lukewarm to the monopoly powers conferred on Hydro. Chief amongst these opponents was Beck's fellow commissioner, Colonel John Hendrie, who, as the current gossip had it, was 'to harness Beck while Beck harnessed Niagara.'[7]

Colonel Hendrie's efforts to restrain Beck were unsuccessful. Although Whitney introduced a bill in February 1911 to make Hydro subject to the regulatory powers of the ORMB – a kind of warning shot across Beck's bow – the measure was not taken beyond second reading. However, in announcing the date of the provincial election, Whitney seized the occasion to propose a more radical containment move: 'In our opinion the time has come when, having regard to the public business under our system, the Hydro-Electric Power Commission should be discontinued and a new Department of Power created which would take charge of the great work, the head of which should be a cabinet minister.'

From the perspective of the municipalities, Whitney's proposal threatened to curtail their chief spokesman's power. In the view of the Liberal opposition under A.G. MacKay and in 1911 under a vigorous new leader, Newton Rowell, this threatened the entire people's power movement. Rowell viewed the commission as the trustee of this movement and a guardian of the interests of the municipalities. Moreover, echoing the views of Sir William Meredith, he opposed the proposal for a department of power because 'political patronage would creep into Hydro.' Rowell's concern, subsequently rephrased as 'the board as buffer' against such political intrusions, became a common refrain throughout the 1920s and 1930s. It was particularly strong at the federal level as successive crown corporations were established, for example, to manage a national railway system and later a national broadcasting system.

Rowell's opposition to the conversion of Hydro to a ministerial department, in view of the fact that two members of the commission were already in the cabinet, seems somewhat perverse. However, it is probable that the towering presence of Beck actually provided the 'buffer' that Rowell desired because Beck's power base lay outside the relatively hostile cabinet and rested with the municipalities. Perhaps the *Toronto Star*, no friend of the proposal to convert Hydro into a department, captured the essence of the claim to preserve the commission in a series of rhetorical questions. 'If he [Beck] becomes Minister of Power would his policy have to be submitted to a Board presided over, not by his own sympathetic self but by the premier? At present, on any point, he has to convince Mr. McNaught [the non-cabinet member of the Commission] that he is right. After the change would it be necessary for him to convince Mr. W.J. Hanna instead?' [Hanna, one of Beck's opponents in cabinet, was provincial secretary.] Then, with a flourish, the *Star* answered its own questions with a final question: 'Having power without a portfolio, is he [Beck] henceforth to have a portfolio without power?'

The re-election of the Whitney government in 1911 was viewed as a victory for public ownership of a province-wide electrical power transmission system, but it left unsettled the relative merits of a department versus a commission as the most appropriate delivery instrument. The proposed department of power had been scheduled to start at the end of May 1912, but in mid-January Beck announced the government's change of intent: until the rest of the municipalities had received service the commission was to remain intact. Thereafter, Beck was able to outmanoeuvre his cabinet colleagues and the department of power proposal lost its appeal. Even Howard Ferguson, at a later date, was prepared to concede that Hydro was an exceptional case that warranted its special structural status.[8]

After this near escape from absorption into the departmental fold, Ontario Hydro began to acquire more and more the accoutrements of managerial independence deemed necessary for its operating role. Hydro's original act had accorded independence with respect to hiring and firing by conferring on the commission the right to appoint such senior officials as the chief engineer, accountant, and secretary, as well as such other employees as deemed necessary. This independence persisted despite the post-First World War reforms that brought a central personnel agency for the public service into existence. Indeed, when a superannuation plan was approved in 1921 for the public service, Hydro employees remained on a separate plan inaugurated in 1919.

In contrast to the independence of the commission on personnel matters, initially a more restrictive financial management regime was imposed. Judging from the performance of the Public Accounts Committee of the legislature, the financial affairs of Hydro were viewed, like the accounts of any of the regular departments, as fair game for the committee's critical comments. In 1910 Beck had to defend expenditures for the purchase of automobiles and the expenses of the commission's solicitor, while in 1911 he confronted much more intensive probing with respect to various accounts and the tendering procedures of Hydro – the latter receiving particularly sharp scrutiny two years later by Newton Rowell. However, the real show-down occurred in the 1916 sessions of the committee when Beck clashed with James Clancy, the provincial auditor, over the discrepancies alleged in the respective accounts prepared by the commission and the auditor's office.

The exchange between two peppery protagonists illuminates the reasoning behind the proclaimed need for a governmental entrepreneurial activity to be freed of at least some of the central controls imposed on the financial management of departments. To the auditor's complaint that Hydro had retained its earnings to cover its own expenditures rather than turning them into the Consolidated Revenue Fund to be subsequently appropriated by the legislature (as with a department), Beck grandly replied: 'That might be alright, according to the Statute, but it is an impossible condition for operation from a business standpoint.' Further, when accused of using advances from the province 'without express authority of Statute,' a practice that, according to the auditor, had gone on 'for the last 6 or 7 years,' Beck deflected the attack by suggesting that the auditor must have his 'own reasons for not drawing the attention of the Government to it before.' Riposting this somewhat brazen rebuttal, Clancy rejoined that 'we did not get the accounts to enable us to do so,' the present year being the first time he had received full accounts from the commission! Faced with this accusation, Beck was reduced to a blustering effort to turn the burden of proof against Clancy: 'If you can convince me that you have not made any errors or mistakes in your books then we would have some reason for accepting your statements. We balance our books, and it is for you to prove that yours are correct.'

This highly unedifying, but most revealing, exchange continued in much the same vein, leaving any objective observer to conclude that Beck's high-handed management and accounting for Hydro's financial affairs was straining the comprehension of the mere mortals on the accounts committee. As if to underline such impression, the prolonged exchange between Clancy and Beck that raised fundamental questions about Hydro's accountability for overall policies as well as fiscal management took place with members of the committee for the most part playing the role of silent spectators. A succeeding question concerning the dismissal of a prison guard because he had helped with registration for an election drew the instant interest and active participation of the members.[9]

The Beck-Clancy clash resulted in a bill sponsored by the provincial treasurer, T.W. McGarry, designed, as the Conservative Toronto *Mail* suggested, to 'shorten its [the Government's] hold upon the Commission' by appointing a 'Hydro Comptroller' who was to sign all Hydro cheques. At the same time the measure recognized the merit of Beck's contention: 'If we are to carry Hydro and commercialize it and make it a business proposition we must have some latitude and the confidence of the municipalities and the government.'

McGarry's bill sought to do justice to Beck's concern by granting more financial autonomy with respect to operating expenditures. At the same time the government-appointed comptroller would provide the assurance required by the auditor that the accounts would be kept in acceptable form, with a proper system of internal control and audit. Beck managed to have the bill modified so that the financial comptroller became an appointee of Hydro itself, a change which found favour with the Liberal opposition because of their constant suspicion of excessive political interference with the commission. The Liberals, in fact, would have preferred a municipal auditor of the commission's accounts as well as a representative of the municipalities on the commission itself. Beck's victory for the financial autonomy of Hydro was followed more than a decade later in 1934 by empowering Hydro to borrow on its own account for capital purposes.[12]

Despite these signs of cumulative managerial autonomy, the original provisions for direct cabinet representation on the governing board of Hydro were to remain intact until 1973. The persistence of this arrangement reveals, as no other agency has, the ultimate difficulty of grafting such 'structural heretics' to a governmental system that operates in accordance with the doctrine of ministerial responsibility.

The WCB: The Distributive Regulatory Mode

The third important type of independent board whose creative muse was unmistakably Sir William Meredith was the Workmen's Compensation Board. This was to be the first exemplar of what might be termed the distributive or allocative regulatory mode. Interestingly, Meredith appears to have made no distinction between the boards designed for his three creations. In a revealing paragraph of his final report on employers' liability laws, where he is defending his proposed Workmen's Compensation Board, he equates it with his other two creations and adds the federal Board of Railway Commissioners. Admittedly, Meredith was seeking in this part of his report to defend the collegial nature of a board against the views of P.T. Sherman, a New York city counsellor-at-law who, in a lengthy submission to Meredith's royal commission, opposed the board form per se, because he contended it would lead to patronage. 'Whatever else may be doubtful as to the workings of the act,' Meredith wrote in rejoinder, 'there is no doubt, I think, that the members of the Board appointed by the Crown will impartially and according to the best of their ability discharge the important duties which will devolve upon them ... Whatever may be the experience of other countries the experience of Canada does not justify the view which Mr. Sherman entertains ... Whatever criticisms there may have been of the actions of these Boards [i.e., Ontario Hydro, ORMB, and the Dominion's Board of Railway Commissioners], no one, as far as I have heard, has ever charged or even suggested that any member of them has been actuated or influenced by partisan political considerations in any action that has been taken.'[10]

Meredith's defence of the board form of organization echoes the view that where certain matters need to be taken out of politics, the board effectively serves as a buffer. However, Meredith's treatment of boards as if they were all alike conceals the fact that boards vested with different mandates may require different administrative modes, which in turn require adaptations in the arm's-length status conferred on each.

On closer inspection, the statutory provisions Meredith proposed for each board suggest that the creator himself recognized this need to adapt the board form to the requirements of the mandate and the particular administrative mode required for implementing it. For the proposed Workmen's Compensation Board Meredith clearly endorsed this approach. The justification for the board, as Meredith saw it, was 'to get rid of the nuisance of litigation' and to have 'swift justice meted out to the great body of men.'[11]

What Meredith was proposing involved a radical alteration in the approach to the common law and its interpretation by the courts. The conventions of the common law up to this point had imposed on the courts the duty to uphold both private property rights and individual justice, at whatever cost to the litigants in time and financial means.

Increasingly, as the twentieth century opened, these judicial conventions were being diluted by socializing trends in which distributive justice tended to replace the corrective or punitive justice historically meted out by the courts. In the particular instance of workmen's compensation not only were these forces at play but there was the practical problem of the courts being unable to cope with the sheer volume of cases that could be anticipated.

All of these considerations are beautifully exemplified in the board's report on its first full year of operation in 1915:

The benefits of the new system of law to both workmen and employers are recognized and appreciated. Claims are expeditiously and inexpensively disposed of. Employers are immune from the expense and annoyance of litigation. The intricacies and hardships upon workmen and their families of the old doctrine of negligence, common employment and assumed risk are eliminated. The facts to be determined by the Board are usually few and simple. There is no longer need for payment of legal fees either by workmen or employers.[12]

No more succinct statement than this can be found to justify the creation of a board to perform functions hitherto exclusively the preserve of the judicial establishment. The displacement of costly, time-consuming 'judicial justice' by what one prominent legal scholar has aptly called trial and error and rough and ready administrative justice was not to be confined to this particular policy arena. But it has never found a better example than is provided by the Workmen's Compensation Board.[13]

The subsequent and far from untroubled history of the WCB gives reason to question the early assumption that the discretion conferred on the board was limited because the facts to be ascertained 'are usually few and simple.' Admittedly, in creating an insurance scheme for employers, the question of determining the payroll upon which each employer's assessment would be based was a matter of factual accounting. Somewhat less readily determined was the category for assessment purposes which over time could be firmed up by assembling accident statistics by industry, but which in the short term had to depend on the experience in other jurisdictions and the ratings already prepared by existing employers' liability companies. Because the amount of the assessment was directly related to the accident record, a purely administrative aspect of the Compensation Board's mandate was an early involvement in promoting accident prevention programs, largely by encouraging the formation of accident prevention societies. Here the board's efforts meshed with those of the factory inspectors who, since the 1890s, had been compiling accident statistics, arranged by type and by industry.

These activities of the board would ultimately be reduced to relatively routine determinations based on agreed factual data. However, the discretion conferred on the board to determine the type and extent of the injury and (more particularly) the disease incurred by the worker while in the workplace gave rise to a more elaborate bureaucracy. Seventy-five years after its formation the board now numbers some 3,500 employees. It is here that the board as a deciding tribunal faces its greatest tribulations and where, on occasion, 'offhand administrative justice' has had to submit to the more ponderous processes of judicial justice.

That Meredith recognized the judicial nature of the Compensation Board's mandate is apparent from the provisions of the act of 1914 that gave legal effect to his model bill. In all respects the provisions for appointment, tenure, and payment of salaries of the chairman and the two board members complied with those that applied to members of the judiciary: appointment by the lieutenant-governor-in-council with tenure during good behaviour (not at pleasure, as for civil servants proper); removal for cause; retirement at age seventy-five; and fixed statutory salaries. In addition, subject to cabinet approval of salaries, the Board was vested with the authority to appoint its own secretary, chief medical officer, and other employees, all of whom were to hold office at the pleasure of the board.

Short of declaring the board a court, in all other respects it was endowed with the trappings of the judiciary. However, to emphasize its independence of the judiciary, the legislation bluntly declared that the decisions of the board 'shall be final and conclusive and shall not be open to question and review in any court.' Once again the privative clause had been used and not for the last time. Nor was it the only agency so endowed that nonetheless was to find its decisions subjected to judicial review. The propriety of granting to an agency the right of so-called administrative finality remains a much disputed issue, particularly amongst the legal profession concerned lest the judiciary lose entirely its guardian capacity to ensure that justice is done and is seen to be done.

Comparing the two regulatory agencies attributable to Meredith, it is clear how the nature of the mandate affects the operation of each agency. The Ontario Municipal Board, as a regulatory agency, operates largely by means of public hearings and places little reliance on an expert staff of its own. In order to cope with the hearings, some of which may last for weeks, the board has been continuously enlarged from its initial three members to an indeterminate number of appointees at the discretion of the cabinet (numbering some three dozen in the 1980s).

The WCB, on the other hand, also began life with a board of three members but from the outset required a large administrative staff. Over the years, the relative weight of quasi-judicial discretionary work requiring the attention of the members of the board has become far less than the purely administrative aspects, that call for a staff several thousand strong.

The agencies, boards, and commissions that emerged during the first three decades of the twentieth century tended to fall into one or other of the categories represented by Meredith's models. The following chapter presents an extensive sample of these ABCs as a way of showing how the expansion of government responsibilities has encouraged much experimentation with organizational forms deemed to have the flexibility to cope with contemporary regulatory and hands-on administrative modes.

Expanding the Universe of Satellites

The Ontario Municipal Board, Ontario Hydro, and the Workmen's Compensation Board established the models for, and raised most of the problems encountered by, non-departmental agencies that were to proliferate in the second half of the twentieth century. It cannot be said that they exhausted all the permutations and combinations of structuring the arm's-length relationship, nor could they comprehend all the variations in species which have so frustrated contemporary attempts at systematic classification. In the terms of Roger Tory Peterson's classic bird-watchers' text, the ABCs all tend to fall into his category of 'Confusing Fall Warblers.' It would require a separate volume to provide a comprehensive guide to the extended array of non-departmental agencies built upon Sir William Meredith's exemplars. Sampling the most important specimens to emerge up to the start of the Second World War will serve to illustrate how the necessity of policy became the mother of administrative invention.

The Mining Commissioner as Adjudicative Agency

In the same year that witnessed the birth of the Municipal Board and Ontario Hydro, Frank Cochrane, Whitney's minister for the old Department of Crown Lands, now renamed the Department of Lands, Forests and Mines, pushed through the Assembly a major amendment to the Mining Act.[1] This measure was in response to the chaotic situation prevailing in New Ontario as a result of the fast-developing and virtually uncontrolled staking of mining claims. Since 1891 the Bureau of Mines had been concerned primarily with the collection of information. Such regulation as there was was handled by mining inspectors appointed by the lieutenant-governor-in-council in mining districts also set up by the same authority. Like the game wardens and fisheries overseers, the mining inspectors had been armed with powers of a justice of the peace. But like their scattered, ill-paid associates, they had been ineffectual.

For the regulation of mines and miners the solution was a hybrid structural response; a departmental inspectorate somewhat belatedly assumed the responsibility for ensuring that mining companies were complying with statutory safety requirements now laid out in elaborate detail, on the model of the factory inspectors. A more complicated arrangement was set in place to regulate mining itself. Faced with the need to implement a uniform policy of granting exploration licences and handling mining claims scattered throughout a forbiddingly broad terrain, the legislation of 1906 placed an officer of the department, a mining recorder, in each of the mining divisions established by cabinet order. While exploration licences were awarded to mining companies by the minister or deputy minister only, individuals or partnerships could be licensed by the recorder as well. The recorder was the office of first resort with respect to mining claims, periods within which claims had to be worked, and working permits. For these functions the recorder was vested with the powers of a justice of the peace and was authorized to appoint his own constables and peace officers.

In recognition of the considerable powers thereby granted to these regional officers of the department, the legislation made an unusual provision for a mining commissioner, who was to have the status of an officer of the High Court of Ontario. Part VIII of the act spelled out the power to subpoena and issue summons (as for a commissioner under the Public Inquiries Act); further, the commissioner's decisions on appeal from a recorder's decision were to 'be final and shall not be subject to appeal.' Where a matter had already been brought before a regular law court the case could be transferred to the commissioner. The apparently unqualified finality of the commissioner's decisions was constrained by providing for appeals to a divisional court. Moreover, laying the ground for a political appeal, the legislation provided for an appeal 'from any decisions of the Commissioner in respect to any ministerial duty of the Recorder to the Minister only, and the decision of the Minister shall be final and shall not be subject to appeal.'

Reporting on the positive outcome of the improved mining law of 1906, the Bureau of Mines made this assessment:

Under any conceivable system of mining law, disputes are bound to arise, and the richer the discoveries the keener are the disputes and the greater the number. The establishment of a special tribunal for the hearing and settlement of such disputes, with frequent sittings held at places most convenient for the parties, has made it possible to decide the great majority of the disputes within a short time of their occurrence. In some classes of cases the Commissioner's ruling is final, but in very important matters where valuable interests are involved, appeal may be taken to the Court of Appeal. The right of such appeal has not so far been largely availed of, and where exercised, the final decision has usually sustained the commissioner's judgment.[2]

The emphasis on convenience, expedition, and final disposition of many cases recalls the equally affirmative conclusions that were made a few years later with respect to the disposition of workers' compensation claims under the WCB. The fact that the mining commissioner was in essence a court of law in disguise was acknowledged outright in an amendment to the legislation in 1924, when the mining commissioner was replaced by a 'Judge of the Mining Court' and vested with all the appurtenances of judicial independence: tenure during good behaviour until age seventy-five and removable only on address of the Assembly to the lieutenant-governor. More than thirty years later, in 1956, the mining commissioner was reinstated. Clearly, as a separate entity within a department the commissioner no longer serves as the key instrument of mining policy he once was when New Ontario was the scene of frenzied feeding on the part of speculators and prospectors.

The Allocative Regulatory Boards for Minimum Wages and Mothers' Allowances

Two interesting organizational variants were added to the non-departmental mix in 1920 when E.C. Drury's United Farmers party was abruptly summoned to take the reins of government after its surprising defeat of the Conservatives in 1919: a Minimum Wage Board and a Mothers' Allowance Commission. These agencies were part of what Premier Drury later recalled, with questionable hyperbole, as 'such a program of social legislation as Ontario and indeed all of Canada and America had never seen, or perhaps thought possible.'[3] Indeed, Drury's predecessors were not immune to the philosophical and ethical precepts which were moving attitudes away from the hands-off negative state towards a more positive view of state involvement in 'redistributive justice.' Underlying the operation of the Minimum Wage Board was the concept of 'the right to live from one's work,' a concept that had surfaced at an industrial conference sponsored by the Dominion government in September 1919. Contrary to Drury's recollections, Quebec and the western provinces had passed legislation in line with the resolutions at the conference before Ontario acted.[4] In fact, an appointee of the Hearst government, Dr W.A. Riddell, laid claim to be the prime draughtsman for both new measures while serving as deputy minister of a Department of Labour.

The mandate of the board was to establish minimum wages for women and girls employed in various industrial undertakings. For the first time since the Factory Act had been amended in 1895 to make provision specifically for the appointment of a female inspector, the statute creating the Minimum Wage Board of five members called for the appointment of two women. No particular effort was made to hive the board off from the new Department of Labour, to whose minister its annual reports were submitted. The chairman was appointed during pleasure, the four members were given staggered terms, initially up to five years, which in itself might suggest that expectations were that the board's life would be finite. However, in its first annual report the board took particular care to show why its mandate could not be implemented quickly or once and for all. Observing that a 'flat rate law scarcely requires a Board' and, if applicable, 'could have been written into the Factory Act,' the report took pains to demonstrate that not only would wage orders have to be developed for each category of employment and varied by region, but that these would have to be monitored and annually adjusted or reaffirmed.

In exercising the discretion thus conferred, the board insisted that it was

fortunate in the nature of its task, which rests upon an economic and moral principle so simple and convincing that all admit its cogency. This principle is the right of the worker to live from her work. It asserts the value and dignity of human life within the industrial sphere. It does not fix wages, but sets levels below which wages may not fall. On this account, the Board though composed of members drawn from widely different classes of the community and possessing greatly divergent interests, has been able to act in constant harmony. (p. 14)

The most pressing need of the Minimum Wage Board was for information, first to develop a cost-of-living budget adapted to each industry and locale and the particular living conditions of the wage earner. In the early 1920s the absence of unions that could have provided such information meant that reliance had to be placed on widespread consultation, both with individuals and industries. That the orders issued by the board had 'behind them the general approval of those engaged in the industries to which they apply' was, in the board's view, attributable to its 'intimate and sympathetic study of the trades, in the informal and friendly discussions in conference.' The ensuing moral climate, the board proclaimed, 'wins and holds the support of the people of the trades, for the principle of "The right to live from one's work."'

The board's obvious interest in walking softly and wielding its discretionary order-making powers cautiously appeared to pay off. In its second year, it issued fourteen wage orders covering 53,000 female employees in confectionery and allied trades, paper box and allied industries, saleswomen in retail stores, telephone operators, textile and needle trades. By 1925 the board estimated that of the 1,451,772 females in Ontario (census of 1921), half were of working age (fifteen to fifty), 140,000 were gainfully employed, and 100,000 of these were working under wage orders of the board. In an interesting side statistic, which showed nearly 80 per cent of Ontario's females by age twenty were married, the board observed, 'we are one of the most married communities in the world,' their estimate being that between 10 to 20 per cent of the total workforce subject to board orders would be married women.[5]

When Mitchell Hepburn came to power his minister of labour, Arthur Roebuck, took the lead in sponsoring industrial codes for negotiated rates of pay and hours of labour.[6] The Industrial Standards Act of 1935 provided a diluted version of Roebuck's plan, borrowing the negotiating technique of conferences between employers and employees which had been used by the Minimum Wage Board. These conferences were to negotiate wages for male workers and were arranged at first by the minister of labour. In 1937 an Industry and Labour Board absorbed the old Minimum Wage Board and assumed control of the procedures. By 1963 the board was folded into an Employment Standards Branch of the Department of Labour. Despite the fact that the regulatory mandate now went well beyond the original Minimum Wage Board and extended equally to men and women, an independent board was no longer deemed necessary.

The evolution from independent agency to branch of a department also characterizes the history of the second agency, the Mothers' Allowance Commission, propelled into existence by the Drury government's social concerns. Following the example set by the Minimum Wage Board, statutory provision was made for the appointment of two women to the five-member board, all of whom uniquely received their commissions under the Great Seal of the province. Despite this apparent signal of independence (as for a royal commission), the staff of the agency were to be members of the civil service. This statutory provision seems not to have inhibited the aggressive advertisement by the commission for the seventeen 'Investigators' it immediately selected from over three hundred applicants and the one executive secretary selected from 125 respondents.[7]

Notable in a civil service that had historically been male-dominated, all of the investigators were women. However logical in view of the commission's title and mandate, in practice there was the question of whether the ladies had 'the right stuff.' An early report of the commission acknowledges the stiffness of the trial, while commending its appointees on their endurance: 'Sometimes a visit [of an investigator] entails a drive or horse back ride of thirty miles ... In the North, the Investigator has found it necessary to travel by hand car back into the mining districts. Train crews have let her ride miles on a freight train, having supper in the caboose and helping to wash the dishes [of course!].' Poor train service, where available at all, might mean a whole day for one visit which, if the claimant was away from home, might entail several such visits.

The paid staff of investigators was the first step in checking every claim before it could be submitted for commission approval. It was later instrumental in monitoring the beneficiaries, arranging housing, seeing to school attendance and family health, encouraging part-time employment of mothers – in short, a veritable social work consultancy role. 'This meant that for the first time an agent of Queen's Park was figuratively parachuted into the fringes of the province to inquire into basic social problems, an expansion of governmental influence that went relatively unnoticed at the time.'[8]

While the operative core of the commission resided in this unique all-female staff of investigators, the members of the commission itself, as well as its impressive tail of local boards, exemplified another feature of the times: all members of the commission and of the local boards were unpaid. Indeed, like the Childrens' Aid Societies to which the commission had occasion to refer mothers deemed unfit for allowances, the administration of mothers' allowances was a remarkable venture in volunteerism. For example, a not untypical board is to be found in Kingston. The wife of the principal of Queen's University, Mrs Bruce Taylor, chaired a board whose secretary was Professor W.A. Mackintosh, accompanied by a city alderman and two women members. The average annual cost of each of the ninety-six local boards that had been brought together by the end of the second year's operation came to $27.30. Nor was their role a perfunctory one, for they approved all local applications for referral to the investigators, who in turn passed on their assessments to the full commission. Though commission members were also unpaid, they had occasion to meet in the formative years as many as nineteen days in a single month. By the second year, full commission meetings had been reduced to about three per month and there were only twenty-four sessions over the two-year period of 1927–8.[9]

The discretion of the commission to determine the amounts of allowances and those entitled to them was extended in its second year to cover children as well as mothers. Looking back from our inflated contemporary expectations of the welfare state, the administrative apparatus for dispensing what amounted to forty dollars a month for a city dweller with two children appears to be excessively elaborate. The arrangement by which, until 1936, the municipalities paid half the allowances obviously necessitated the input from volunteer local boards. Despite the apparent niggardliness of the allocations, the independence of the commission was shown by according its allocative decisions the same kind of administrative finality and the same immunity from court review that was provided for such agencies as the OMB and the WCB. There was also the same flexibility to reconsider any of its decisions, 'to rescind, alter or amend any order, direction or decision previously made.'

The reason for what may appear to be an excessive concern for protecting the independence of the commission becomes clear from the reproduction in the first report of the commission of a letter sent by Premier Drury to an applicant in response to her appeal to him to use his influence on her behalf. Here is a striking instance of the previously encountered notion of the 'board as buffer,' particularly when many individual distributive decisions have to be taken.

I would beg to remind you [Drury wrote] that the Government or any member of it has not the power to say who shall or shall not receive allowances under the Mothers Allowances Act ... I think when you consider the matter, that you will see that it is quite proper that it should be so. Governments are, after all, dependent upon the good will of the people and are always under the temptation to do things that would bring them popular support, either in the mass or individually ... It would become almost inevitably a means for the exercise of patronage or favouritism. For that reason, the Mothers Allowances Act provides for the Administration of the Act by a Commission, which is, properly, I think, as independent of the Government or any other influence, as the Judges on the Bench.'

Drury's view was echoed by his successor, Howard Ferguson, who a few years later when old age pension legislation required provincial collaboration with the federal government, used the Mothers' Allowances Commission in 1929 as the model for administering old age pensions.[10]

It is a measure of our growing acceptance of the welfare state that it is no longer considered necessary to place allocative decision makers in agencies vested with the arm's-length relationship accorded the Minimum Wage and Mothers' Allowances boards. In these instances at least, the functions once served by an independent tribunal have been folded into a section of a parent department, the only remnant of concern for the arm's-length principle being displayed by an administrative tribunal, set up *within* the department.

The Liquor Control Board: Combining Regulation and Operation

We come now to one of the most politically contentious of all policy arenas for government, the regulation of the sale of liquor. The early involvement of government, as previously noted, was through local boards of licence commissioners appointed by the lieutenant-governor-in-council, as were the provincially paid inspectors operating under their supervision. The creation in 1906 of a Licence Branch attached to the Office of Attorney General signalled the beginning of a new regulatory regime. In addition to controlling the local patronage appointments of licence commissioners and inspectors, the centre now became involved in the monitoring of the local authorities, standardizing their accounts, and auditing the revenue and expenditures from the Licence Fund. The receipts from this fund, as had long been the practice, were divided between the provincial treasurer and each municipal authority, after paying all the costs of administration.

At that point, the arrangement appeared to portend the fate of earlier satellites – namely, ultimate absorption into the ministerial fold. However, with the next centralizing move taken in 1915 by an act to 'improve the administration of the Liquor Licence Laws,' the movement towards departmental absorption was checked. Instead, a single provincial board of five commissioners displaced the local boards, whose powers to determine the licence year and time of issuance of dispensing licences were assumed by the new Board of Liquor Licence Commissioners. The board was also empowered to reconsider any matter dealt with by it and could rescind, alter, or amend any decision, order, or resolution. This was a significant discretion in light of the further transfer to the board of the minister's powers to make regulations with respect to the liquor trade. However, the board's exercise of such powers was subject to confirmation by the lieutenant-governor-in-council, as were the appointment of inspectors, the secretary, and all other 'officers, clerks and servants' deemed necessary. Expenses were no longer to be paid out of the Licence Fund but appropriated out of the Consolidated Revenue Fund. This enactment was the prelude to passage of the Ontario Temperance Act of 1916, which deployed this new administrative organization to implement what was to become, under Dominion regulation, a policy of total prohibition.

Policy respecting the control of liquor dispensing and consumption became one of the most contentious issues upon which elections turned during the last years of the Hearst regime, the short-lived United Farmers' government, and the two terms of the Ferguson government.[11] Throughout, the Liquor Licence Board was in the eye of the storm, contending with small success against the hypocrisy of the times that, for example, converted the medical profession and the pharmacists into virtual 'bar-tenders' dispensing generous libations in the form of pre-scriptions for 'medicinal purposes.' The board's efforts to fulfil its mandate under the rabid prohibitionist direction of W.E. Raney, attorney general in the Drury government, succeeded only in drying up the middle, while bootlegging and other blatant defiance of the regulations kept the province very wet around its edges.

In 1927, under the wily and patient Ferguson, an uneasy compromise between the wets and the dries was struck with new legislation. A new Liquor Control Board, with up to three members, retained all the regula-tory powers of its predecessor, including a new privative clause that rendered its decisions final and unreviewable. But Part II of the act provided for the creation of government stores whose earnings would be retained by the board to pay all expenses before the net proceeds were paid into the Treasury. It was this move to involve the government in the retailing of liquor that accounted for the statutory provision conferring the status of a 'body corporate' on the board, an 'emanation of the Crown' which, nevertheless, was capable of suing and being sued in its own right, like any incorporated business.

The combination in one agency of extensive discretionary regulatory powers with the monopolistic management of sales outlets was intro-duced presumably as the most satisfactory method of controlling a societal problem that had bedevilled provincial politics almost since confederation. The rationale for a board as buffer now was reaffirmed in even stronger terms by the new Liquor Control Board. Indeed, the concept took on new meaning for, from Premier Ferguson's perspec-tive, the LCBO buffered *him* as well as serving its ostensible purpose of protecting the agency from undue interference from the political level.[12]

One may speculate that the decision to combine regulation and opera-tion of the sale and distribution of liquor in Ontario may have had much to do with a previously mentioned policy paradox. On the one hand, regulation in the name of social control is designed to keep consumption rigorously restricted (the sop to the dries). On the other hand, through the very instruments of control (originally fees, fines, and licences but ultimately through direct operation of retail outlets) the government coffers willy-nilly stand to be generously enriched *despite* regulatory interventions.

In the highly volatile and divided mood of the twenties, no government could risk the charge that its approach to the liquor trade was based on such crass considerations as the revenue return resulting from its regulatory policy. Yet Premier Ferguson was as aware as the next man that in other provinces government control of sales was in effect a taxing device that happily produced enough additional revenue to help balance their budgets. In Ontario, which continued to show deficits that Ferguson could no longer attribute to the alleged profligacy and incompetence of the preceding United Farmers' government, the confirmation of the LCBO in its new combined role of regulator and monopolist retailer fortuitously produced the additional revenue to cover the budget deficit. Thus, adoption of a policy of combining the old regulatory powers with new entrepreneurial powers in a single independent agency sufficiently obfuscated matters that both wets and moderates were placated and the government could claim a hands-off purity while listening to the cash registers' merry ring.[13]

The incompatibility of combining regulatory and operative responsibilities in one agency remained unacknowledged during Hepburn's regime and was not recognized until 1944.[14] In that year the licensing and operative functions were confided to separate agencies.

Agriculture: The Special Case of Marketing Boards

The department that proved most receptive to the deployment of semi-independent satellites in the decade of the 1930s was Agriculture. By about 1910 Agriculture was beginning to assume a more *dirigiste* approach to the various clientele associations upon which it had depended. Departmental divisions were created to mirror these groups, the educational role of the Farmers' Associations was pre-empted by employing its own agricultural representatives, and inspection, as an instrument of the regulatory administrative mode, remained in the department proper.

In addition to these developments, reliance also came to be placed on satellite organizations to cope with two policy initiatives emerging in the aftermath of the First World War. As early as 1915, a resolution in the Assembly decried the decline in agriculture. It called for fresh governmental initiatives to address particularly two needs: for financing through rural credits and low interest loans, and for cooperation in the marketing of products.[15]

The organizational response to the call for financial assistance was the emergence of the 'body corporate,' modelled on private banking and financial institutions but with a rather limited arm's-length relationship to the minister of agriculture and the Provincial Treasurer's Office. The first timid step was taken in 1919 when the government contracted with the Canadian Bankers' Association to guarantee the loans of its member banks to individual farmers. Prompted by the advent of Drury's United Farmers' government, a bolder step was taken in 1921 with the creation of an Agricultural Development Board. This three-member board appointed by the lieutenant-governor-in-council was set up to handle short-term farm loans from a fund of up to $500,000 created by the provincial treasurer's purchase of bonds. Clearly, the board operated at far from an arm's length with respect to the total funds available. However, the further provision of a Farm Loan Association to consider and recommend on individual loan applications was an interesting reversion to the self-help enabling mode which had been so characteristic of the department's early relations with its clientele.

The precedent once established was used again to provide loan assistance to marketing cooperatives in 1932 and again in 1952, when the Ontario Junior Farmers Establishment Loan Corporation was created. In each instance, the provision for the provincial treasurer to assign staff to these corporate entities effectively signalled the reluctance to place them at an arm's-length relationship consistent with their formal legal status as 'corporations.' Towards the close of the Second World War and later, greater independence was accorded such corporate ventures as the Ontario Stock Yards Board in 1944 and the Ontario Food Terminal Board in 1946.

It has been Agriculture's experimentation with another type of non-departmental entity, the regulatory marketing board, which has most clearly reflected the emphasis on what we have termed the enabling administrative approach to the clientele of the department. In 1931, with little opposition, the Ontario Marketing Board was inaugurated, to be promptly followed by the Live Stock and Livestock Products Board in 1932 and a Milk Control Board in 1934.[16] Thus were born the agencies destined to administer a supply management policy for the products deemed to be the most vulnerable to the presumed depredations of the free market. Their detailed examination lies beyond the scope of this brief survey, but several features deserve mention.

The basic structure consists of a central agency, a marketing board representative of the producer interests, and a 'neutral' chairman to oversee a regulatory process that is, in effect, in the hands of separate marketing boards for each product. Each board is initiated by a particular group of producers and approved by the lieutenant-governor-in-council on recommendation of the central board. Over the years some dozen or so marketing boards have been licensed by the central agency (with government approval). The several boards are empowered to determine prices, establish quotas, and generally control the marketing of products that cover the gamut: asparagus, beans, chickens, eggs, flue-cured tobacco, grapes, pork, rutebaga, soya beans, tender fruit, turkeys, vegetables, and wheat.

The regulation of the production and distribution of milk and milk products has been conducted since 1934 under a separate Milk Control Board, renamed the Milk Commission in 1965. Under its aegis a Milk Marketing Board has been delegated the power to determine the terms and conditions of sale for raw milk, milk pricing to processors by classes of end use, and market sharing by producers through quota systems. Equivalent powers have also been assigned to a Cream Producers Marketing Board. In both instances, elaborate provision is made for election of members to the board from the regions into which the respective producers' constituencies have been divided. Provision is also made for board consultation on policy questions with county and district milk committees and advisory committees of those engaged in the transportation as well as the production of the products.

In short, the complex administrative machinery for regulating marketing would appear to be an institutionalization of the historical reliance on the enabling mode which characterized the first fifty years of the Department of Agriculture's existence. The arrangements also expose a paradox that is associated with their clientele orientation: how to provide for the protection of the public interest – in this instance, the consumers' interest in a fair and reasonable price – when the interests represented on the board are dedicated to reducing the competitive pressures that would adversely affect their client producers' income. This conundrum is bound to emerge wherever there is a strong clientele orientation of the regulatory agency, as in the case of marketing. The question also has salience for the regulation of labour relations through a board, a development that occurred in the wake of the Second World War and lies beyond our immediate purview.

Such regulation through a public authority is presumed to be conducted under the rubric of the public interest. But where the interests on the regulatory board are representative of those being regulated, there is unusual responsibility imposed on the chairman to mediate the more clearly articulated interests of the parties represented and the more amorphous but nonetheless important concept of the public interest. In the case of the agricultural marketing boards, the fact that the chair tends to be drawn from the staff of the department (or in the case of the Milk Commission consists entirely of civil servants) amounts to the perpetuation of the practice which the department adopted when it first created divisions to be mirror images of its clientele associations.

It was this issue concerning the appropriate protection for the public interest that engaged Mr Justice Dalton C. Wells in his royal commission report on milk in 1947. He took no exception to the sensible measures designed to level the playing field for unorganized, dispersed producers faced by more powerful distributors of products that cannot be stored for any length of time. However, as the commissioner pointed out, the resulting dilution of competitive pressures left the price of milk unaffected. All that regulation achieved was competition in services – 'the most wasteful form of competition.' Exacerbating the problem, according to the commissioner, was the subjective nature of price-setting in the public interest, where there was an inadequate statistical base and too small an investigative staff for the task. Thus, *faute de mieux*, the regulatory board's role was reduced to giving perfunctory approval to agreements reached between producers and distributors, thereby reaffirming the initial clientele bias in the task of defining the public interest.[17]

The problem of securing a more rounded version of the public interest, not only for the marketing of agricultural products but in the many other public policy arenas for which the regulatory administrative mode has been invoked, remains one of the most intractable challenges facing public administrators. Attempts to solve the problem account, in no small measure, for the continued expansion of the contemporary universe of agencies, boards, and commissions.

10

Regulation and Reform of the Public Service

In tracing the evolution of the organizations and administrative modes developed in response to the growing demands placed on governments, there has been occasion to take note of the kind of person drawn to the senior ranks of the bureaucracy. But thus far there has been little reference to the problem of regulating and controlling staff with the objective of achieving a career public service, which is the true insignia of a maturing bureaucracy. It is with this issue and the larger issue of the accountability of public servants that this and the next two chapters are concerned.

Once again it is necessary to return to the BNA Act of 1867 for guidance on where to find the legal authority to regulate and reform the civil service. In the first 'whereas' clause introducing the act, the uniting provinces express their desire to be federally united 'with a Constitution similar in Principle to that of the United Kingdom.' This innocent phraseology has provided a major source of tension between the executive and legislature over who should have authority to regulate and reform the administrative branch of government. Thus Ontario inherited the scheme whereby the political executive is deemed capable of governing only so long as it can retain the support of a majority in the Legislative Assembly of elected members – an Assembly to which the members of the executive also belong. In such a system of fused powers, whenever matters concerned with the organization, staffing, and financing of the public service arise, uneasy tension is generally created over conflicting claims to jurisdiction: the responsible ministry claiming a collective authority to deal with such matters, even as the Assembly invokes the doctrine of parliamentary supremacy to validate its claims to manage the public service.

In Britain this tension was first expressed in two centuries of struggle between the executive officers of the crown and the monarch over control of a civil list that covered both the expenses of the royal household and of the public services proper. As the latter came to be disentangled from the personal expenses of the monarch, the political executive claimed the right to control these services of the crown. By the time Victoria became queen in 1837 the executive had won its battle. But almost immediately it had to confront the demands of an increasingly assertive and representative legislative branch to hold it to account for the mode and manner of its expenditures on the public service.

The colonies of British North America entered the fray at this second stage. However, the tension between executive and legislature was even more accentuated in the colonies because local legislatures were having to conduct their struggle with an absentee executive in Whitehall which claimed authority over them by virtue of the colonies' subordinate status. Perhaps because of this sense of subordination, the colonial legislature, at least in the Province of Canada, fought the harder to gain control over its local public service and the associated patronage potential. When in 1857 the legislature of the Province of Canada approved a civil service act, it asserted a legal right to regulate the civil service which the British Parliament had been unable to acquire and which, indeed, it has never attained. This unique achievement is probably best explained by the legislature's drive for self-government and the consequent need to assert local control over what had hitherto been the patronage preserve of an executive controlled from Whitehall and Westminster. Whatever the reasons for this departure from British practices, the measure of 1857 established an enduring precedent which was adopted by the new Dominion in 1868 when it re-enacted the Civil Service Act of 1857, followed exactly a decade later by Ontario's passage of its own legislation.[1]

The British preference for dealing with the public service by means of order-in-council or ministerial regulation may be viewed as their way of resolving the question of who should control the public service – coming down quite clearly in favour of the executive branch. The decision by the colony and subsequently by Ontario to proceed by way of a comprehensive statute would seem to weigh the answer in favour of the legislature. The Assembly's formal imprimatur has always been sought by the executive in order to bring major departmental organizations into being. But that practice has nothing to do with requirements laid down in the Public Service Act; it must derive from the general power residing in the legislature, long characterized as parliamentary control of the purse.

In reality, the presence of a public service act has had very little impact on the political executive's claim to managerial pre-eminence over the public service. Indeed, that claim appeared to be spelled out in section 134 of the BNA Act wherein the five named executive officers, acting collectively through the lieutenant-governor-in-council, were assigned the right 'to prescribe the Duties of those Officers, and of the several Departments over which they shall preside or to which they shall belong, and of the Officers and Clerks thereof ...' On the other hand, reflecting the tension built into the British system of responsible parliamentary government, the opening phrase of the same section made such conferral of powers on the executive provisional – that is, 'until the Legislature of Ontario ... otherwise provides.'

The First Reform Measure: The Act of 1878

In fact, it was ten years after the confederation settlement before the provincial legislature got around to 'otherwise providing' with its enactment of the civil service measure of 1878. This act, similar to its predecessor of 1857, established a legislative foundation for regulation of the civil service, which constituted a departure from the British bias towards outright executive control. This bias was revealed, for example, when in 1870 the major administrative reform involving the introduction of open competitive examinations for entry to the British civil service was confirmed by an order-in-council. This same procedure had been used in 1855 to introduce a Civil Service Commission which was to administer the scheme.[2]

The provincial enactment of 1878 was not, however, as great a break with the British tradition of executive dominance as its continued presence on the statute books might lead one to suppose. That it did little to resolve the latent tension between legislature and executive over civil service matters is revealed by the interventions of individual members of the Legislative Assembly even before debate on the measure of 1878 occurred.

Throughout the early years the executive proved surprisingly responsive to individual requests for returns detailing the names, numbers, salaries, workload, even religious affiliation, of civil servants. That most of these were published was not only an indication of the executive's openness but also a boon to the administrative historian which, sad to say, was not as willingly vouchsafed after the turn of the century. On other civil service matters, however, the executive proved far less cooperative. When, for example, in February 1874 D'Arcy Boulton argued in the Assembly that 'some proper system should be at once devised, whereby the salaries paid under authority of this Legislature ... shall be placed on a proper basis and the present inequalities adjusted and the present injustices remedied,' the government maintained a stony resistance.[3] Curiously, the arguments for and against Assembly control turned on the same principle – namely, the right to control the purse strings. From the Assembly's perspective, this right enabled its members to control the government; from the vantage point of the executive, the right to introduce all money bills entitled it to preserve the initiative in all matters affecting the administrative branch. This built-in tension, persisting to this day, serves to underline the contradictions within a system where the political executive is fused with the legislature.

These ambiguities of the parliamentary-cabinet system of government, together with what was to become the normal resolution in favour of a dominant executive, were illustrated by another set-to that also occurred in 1874. A motion from the opposition benches sponsored by Matthew Crooks Cameron sought to empower the Public Accounts Committee 'to inquire into the circumstances attending the resignation, removal or dismissal of any public officer or servant of the Government, to whom any gratuity may have been awarded and paid, where such gratuity forms an item on the public expenditure.'

Premier Mowat's response clearly reflected what was to become the standard position of the executive in warding off what for them were undue intrusions of the legislature into administrative matters, even when couched as Cameron had contrived to do in terms of parliamentary control of the purse. 'The appointment and removal of public officers and servants,' Mowat's amendment stated, 'are matters which by constitutional rule are within the exclusive authority of the Executive Government, having the confidence of this House, and do not fall within the sphere of the Public Accounts Committee.' Nevertheless, Mowat's amendment did go on to admit the case for ultimate parliamentary control by asserting 'if there should be a case for impeaching the exercise of the discretion of the Government in such a matter, the proper course is for the case to be brought before this House, on a special motion referring thereto, so that the House may deal with the case as the circumstances may seem to the House to require.'[4]

Mowat's somewhat double-edged views were sustained by his majority in the Assembly. The skirmish proved to be a preamble to the head-on encounter between the opposing views concerning control of the administrative branch that was precipitated by the introduction of the first comprehensive act respecting the public service of Ontario in 1878 (41 Vic. c. 2). At first glance this act appears to accord the legislature unusual influence over the most detailed terms and conditions of public service, an important qualification being that the measure touched only those officers and clerks working in the departmental services located at the seat of government in Toronto.

Apart from the restricted application of the act, the opposition were quick to point out that the legislation was riddled with references to the lieutenant-governor-in-council making the real decisions with respect to a wide range of specified matters. These included an impressive list: classifying civil servants within the two divisions provided; specifying the salaries in the special division (though the salary scales for the ordinary division were precisely set out in the legislation); approving all appointments, promotions, and exceptions to an established probationary period; appointing examiners for the conduct of pass examinations where required; approving any assignment of extra duties; sub-dividing any department into branches and sub-departments; approving all disciplinary measures, including the dismissal of any deputy head, officer, or clerk; awarding gratuities; regulating hours of attendance or other conditions of service.

Overall, it would appear that only in the case of the classification/pay plan was the final word left with the legislature, presumably in recognition of its constitutional role in voting the appropriations to cover the executive's estimates of expenditures. In this important respect the plans for the size and salaries of the permanent establishment at headquarters had to be submitted for legislative approval, and any subsequent departures therefrom were permitted only with the legislature's adoption of a separate item in the estimates.[5]

In its itemization of executive responsibilities vis-à-vis the public service, for such a small service and at such an early date, the act reveals a comprehensive conception of the essentials of the management tasks within government. Indeed, with surprisingly few additions and some up-dating of terminology demanded by today's management gurus, this early itemized agenda still serves to define the field of what in the current vernacular is termed 'human resource management.'

The lion's share of authority to deal with this large range of public management tasks was clearly vested in the executive and this was the issue which attracted the most attention in the debate on the bill.[6] In defence of executive dominance, Mowat and his colleagues produced an ingenious twist to the argument in favour of regulation by order-in-council. According to Mowat,

there were two branches of Government – one administrative and the other legislative. The Bill, instead of providing for the heads of Departments making changes, provided for an Order in Council, so that all members of the Government should know of, and take part in, the changes. This was in order to increase safety, and to make sure that every appointment made should be done deliberately, and not to be the act merely of one member of the Government but of all members.

In short, collective exercise of discretionary managerial powers would serve as a better check on abuse than if such authority were to be entrusted to individual ministers acting on their own.

Clearly, the opposition's concern for the inroads the new act would make on the legislature's prerogatives was not eased by Mowat's formulation. His comments illuminate the practice of collective log-rolling that must have characterized early cabinet meetings, concerned as they often must have been with highly parochial affairs, where it was important to play the game of 'I'll scratch your back, if you'll scratch mine.' One can only assume, then, that when Mowat spoke of the procedure of collective decision making 'increasing safety,' he had in mind less the protection of some higher public interest or the interest of the Assembly but more likely the necessity of preserving cabinet solidarity through collective decisions, even extending to the minutiae of dividing the loaves and fishes of patronage appointments.

Mowat's colleague, Arthur S. Hardy, while introducing the public service bill, showed that he had done impressive homework in assessing movements of administrative reform in neighbouring Quebec, at the Dominion level, and also abroad in the United States and Great Britain. He used this background information to reinforce Mowat's assurance about the greater protection afforded by collective decision making. But he also carried the argument a step further. In England, he contended, there was no statute whatever governing appointments to the civil service, all being made by order-in-council alone. In Ontario, on the contrary, 'we made them in a much more open fashion,' in that the orders-in-council could be called for by the House at any time. This last concession to the ultimate supremacy of the legislature Hardy claimed to have provided by introducing a late amendment to the bill which required that all orders-in-council issued under authority of the enactment would have to be tabled in the House and thereby open to public comment. The version of the bill which finally found its way onto the statute books reveals no signs of Hardy's alleged amendment. Even if such a provision had been incorporated in the act, the government's protestations that its presence somehow validated the claim to collective executive control of the public service offered no solace to the opposition members proclaiming the higher rights of the Assembly as the only way in which they could get to share in the patronage appointments process.

The debate over the public service bill of 1878, in seeking to rationalize collective control of the administrative branch, asserted a feature of cabinet government as practised at both the Dominion and provincial levels which differs markedly from its British prototype. In Canada there has always been this preference for collective decision making, expressed through governor/lieutenant-governor-in-council, whereas in Britain legislation more often entrusts decisions to the individual minister rather than the collective ministry.[7]

The Public Service Act went into effect on 1 January 1879 and thereafter drew little opposition fire. Nor were there many indications of a desire to continue contesting the official position that the political executive in its collective capacity was effectively responsible for managing all aspects of the public service. Several factors may have been responsible for this apparent acquiescence, not the least being the limited application of the act, confined as it was to the departmental staff at the seat of government and to a number of offices associated with the administration of justice.

No doubt a second reason for the acceptance of the act was the long, unbroken hold on government by the Liberals – thirty-two years all told, of which the first twenty-four were dominated by Sir Oliver Mowat. Such political stability did not lend itself, at least amongst the small corps of public servants employed at the seat of government, to the 'changing of the guard' which characterized the state of affairs amongst Ontario's southern neighbours and which came to be viewed by political leaders on this side of the border as a peculiarly Yankee practice. Certainly the record as revealed by C.R.W. Biggar, Mowat's early biographer, convincingly demonstrates the security of tenure enjoyed by the staff at headquarters. When Mowat resigned the premiership in July 1896, no less than thirty-seven out of sixty-four officers who had been appointed before he came to power in November 1872 were still in place. Of the remaining twenty-seven, only one had been dismissed, twenty had died in service, and six had resigned or been pensioned off.[8]

A third stabilizing factor was the slow growth in the number of departments to which the act of 1878 applied and the correspondingly limited additions to the staff at headquarters, even after the Conservatives under Whitney began their first long run at governing. Judging from the continued presence of many senior headquarters officials after 1905, the practice of carrying over appointees of the previous regime survived its most severe test.

While these factors contributed to the apparent acquiescence to the act of 1878, it is important to recall that much of the service lay beyond the reach of the act. In the field or outside service (not covered by the act), particularly the highly dispersed 'working departments' of Crown Lands and Public Works and the staff of the scattered institutions coming under the eagle eye of the inspector of prisons and charities, the opportunities for patronage were legion. The opposition, leaning on the major leverage provided them – the opportunity to state 'grievances before supply' – constantly moved resolutions at the supply stage in order to call attention to alleged malpractices and patronage proclivities.

The Public Accounts Committee of the Assembly was the other forum for assertion of the legislators' dissatisfaction with the executive's management of the public service. Throughout the early years it provided a platform to which the opposition resorted frequently, often rancorously. An annual stream of witnesses paraded before the committee, focusing particularly on the record of the 'public institutions' – a motley group that comprised organizations as varied as the Agricultural College, the penitentiaries, lunatic asylums, reformatories, old age homes, and schools for the deaf and the blind. The opportunities for patronage in making the numerous appointments – often of a rather menial nature, it is true – as well as the charges of graft in their maintenance and provisioning were regular fare for a voracious Public Accounts Committee. Its records provide little evidence to sustain a very positive view of the high level of public morality at that time.[9]

Another large public service domain that fell outside the central regulatory powers contained in the act of 1878 was that occupied by the municipalities. However, beginning in the 1880s, the province began to invade this terrain, either by taking over responsibilities hitherto in municipal hands or by regulating them more strictly from the centre. These changes affected a wide range of officials, including sheriffs, marriage licensers, police magistrates, officials of the York registry, of the Toronto Police Court, and of Land Titles Offices. Such offices and their appropriate status were still the subjects of inquiry by a royal commission as late as 1922.[10]

Perhaps the most conspicuous effort to extend the writ of the centre over the periphery of local officials or employees engaged in the administration of justice occurred in conjunction with the regulation of the sale and distribution of liquor. By the 1880s the numerous appointments to local regulatory boards and their attendant host of inspectors had all become patronage plums of the cabinet. After 1906 the province progressively tightened its hold on the system to the point that in 1915 all pretence at local control was dropped in favour of a single regulatory board. Despite this centralization, the evidence before the Public Accounts Committee in 1922 revealed that the regulatory regime had corrupted and suborned officials, even as it had fostered widespread hypocrisy in the efforts at evasion.[11] Such evidence makes it easier to grasp the importance of the connection between the prohibition/temperance movement and the administrative reform movement that emerged in full flood during the first two decades of the twentieth century. It was this renewed movement for civil service reform that posed afresh the question of who should control the public service and challenged anew the presumption of executive domination over the administrative branch.

The Call for a Merit System

Although administrative reform was in the air prior to the advent of the Conservative government in 1905, the end of the thirty-four-year Liberal rule provided the occasion for the revival of the old struggle between the executive and the legislature for control of the public service. While in opposition, Whitney had sounded the customary note of righteous outrage in a motion of 1899 deploring 'Ministers of the Crown encouraging electors to believe they will receive material favours and advantages provided they return supporters of the Government to this House.'[12] In 1905 and 1906, from the different vantage point of the front benches, Whitney's enthusiasm for reform had so cooled that he adamantly refused every request of the opposition to publish lists of dismissals from the civil service on grounds of alleged partisanship. A year later, in 1907, petitions from the respective boards of trade in Orillia, Paris, and Waterloo were tabled in the Assembly, calling for the public service to be put on a non-partisan basis – an indication that nothing had changed.[13]

Despite these rumblings of discontent, an amendment to the Public Service Act in 1909 subtly reaffirmed the patronage practices of the day by making possible the appointment of 'extra clerks' on certificate of the head of the department, an appointment that could then be renewed every six months ad infinitum. Such open inroads of the patronage system on the public service simply fed the mounting tide of concern. Matters came to a head in the 1912 session of the Assembly under the aggressive, articulate Newton Rowell who had recently assumed the leadership of the Liberal opposition. On 2 April, Rowell moved:

That in the judgement of this House the spoils and patronage systems are inimical to the highest efficiency of the public service and to the best interests of the country; that the public interests demand the immediate creation of a non-partisan Civil Service Commission with ample powers, and that all appointments and promotions in the public service shall be by merit after competitive examinations except in those cases where the conditions of the public service render this impracticable.[14]

Rowell's motion contained all the essential ingredients of administrative reform then abroad in the United States and recently urged on the Dominion government by a royal commission in 1907–8: advocacy of efficiency as the primary goal; denigration of contemporary patronage practices as inimical to the attainment of the goal; promotion of the merit principle and of open competitive examinations as the means of achieving efficiency; and an independent commission to administer and monitor such a scheme. In general terms, this was the agenda of the administrative reformers which for the next decade was to be urged on a reluctant government.

The gist of Rowell's 1912 motion was reintroduced in 1913, 1914, and 1916, and then again in 1917.[15] Each motion was defeated. The government's defence was embodied in Whitney's lengthy amendment to counter Rowell's motion when first introduced in 1912:

That this House congratulates the people of the province on the fact that under the administration of public affairs by the present Government no such system as the Spoils System has any place; recognizes the difficulties which would surround the operation of a system of so-called civil service [i.e., merit] over a small number of officials, and that it would be wholly unwise and practically impossible to bring under such a system the various officials in the service of the province, including such officials as Registrars of deeds, Sheriffs and County Crown attorneys; this House recognizes the fact that success in a competitive examination is in no way a guarantee of preeminent or ordinary fitness for Government service, and this House also recognizes the wisdom and fairness with which the Government has dealt with appointments and promotions in the Government Service.[16]

This lengthy root-and-branch dismissal of the reformers' program would have been familiar to mid-nineteenth-century supporters of the Trevelyan-Northcote Report of 1853, which had promoted the merit principle, open competitive examinations, and an independent commission as the means of reforming the British Home Civil Service. The headline with which the *Globe* of 2 April 1912 greeted Whitney's amending motion was a deft and incisive rendering:

> Government Hands Itself a Bouquet
> Congratulates People on Fine Administration
> Keeps Patronage System.

The mood of the legislature that encouraged this first dismissal of the administrative reformers' proposals was conveyed by the remarks attributed to W.J. Johnston, MLA for West Hastings, who considered Rowell's motion 'the joke of the session.' And when Whitney claimed to have been pestered by office-seekers, unidentified voices from the back benches shouted 'we don't mind.'

When the motion for a non-partisan civil service commission was reintroduced for the fourth time in 1917, the government found yet another objection: 'The creation of a Commission in the present time of war would be particularly inopportune, both on account of the expense and the multiplication of officials involved and the barrier that would be imposed thereby to returned soldiers receiving appointments in the public service.'

The explanation for the government's stubborn resistance to the gathering tide of administrative reform proposals goes back to the debate over the first public service act of 1878. Lurking in the background to all the arguments deployed by Whitney and by his successor, Sir William Hearst, was the concern to preserve the executive's claim to dominant control over the administrative branch, despite the Assembly's proclaimed stake in this enterprise as symbolized in the 1878 act. But the authority of the executive branch, whose virtue Whitney and Hearst extolled and swore to defend, extended only to the inside service. Out in the field was a much larger group for whom, as Hearst was bluntly to declaim, 'I have yet to find a better system than that of appointment recommended by the local member for the constituency where the appointment is to be made who appreciates the situation better than any one else, who knows the qualifications of the man for the position and who is responsible to the Government, which in turn is responsible to the Legislature and the people.'[17]

Hearst's high-sounding encomium to what might be characterized as a 'trickle-down,' version of democratic selection was basically flawed. Unless the sitting member belonged to the governing party, there was little chance of one's views on appointment being solicited since, by Hearst's formula, the magic chain of responsibility would be broken were the government to appoint on the basis of a recommendation from anyone other than a party member.

Creation of the Office of Civil Service Commissioner

After such a prolonged and vigorous refusal to accept any part or parcel of the reformers' agenda, the Hearst government's abrupt decision in 1918 to amend the Public Service Act and to appoint a civil service commissioner warrants further investigation. Certainly, the government could not remain blind to the fact that administrative reform was in the air, not merely in Ontario but nation-wide. Indeed, through organizations such as the Civil Service Assembly of the United States and Canada, the reform movement linked hands with the scientific management movement and gathered momentum. Despite the government's disclaimer concerning the inappropriateness of tackling reform while the country was at war, it was the wartime situation that had created an atmosphere favourable to reform.

At the Dominion level, for example, pressed by reformers who saw patronage as a supreme social evil and by business interests who sought 'efficiency in government,' Prime Minister Borden had called for a new Civil Service Act.[18] Adding strength to his convictions, Newton Rowell, the ardent advocate of civil service reform in Ontario, was now a strong lieutenant in Borden's Union government. And working behind the scenes was the redoubtable Adam Shortt, unquestionably the most important architect of the measures which were designed to address the administrative reformers' agenda both at the national level and in several provinces. Even before his appointment to the Civil Service Commission of Canada, which had been created in 1908 on the recommendation of a royal commission into the public service, Dr Shortt had been at the forefront of the reform movement. He appears to have lost some of his influence with Borden as his term wore on. As a result, he had less to do with the final form of the Dominion's revised Civil Service Act of 1918 than one might have expected. On the other hand, between December 1916 and February 1918 he prepared and helped with the adoption of civil service legislation for the provinces of British Columbia and Manitoba.[19] His interventions in both instances indicate that his preference for a single civil service commissioner influenced Ontario's decision.

Through its premier, British Columbia was the first to seek help, probably because of the favourable opinion formed of Shortt as a result of a study of B.C. Electric Railways which he had undertaken in 1916 and was to complete early in 1917. Significantly, it was the Canadian Society of Forestry Engineers and H.R. MacMillan, a leading industrialist and spokesman for the B.C. Forest Service, who indicated the most interest in the successful outcome of Dr Shortt's intervention. In the event, Dr Shortt's contribution went well beyond mere advice, for 13 March 1917 found him in Victoria, writing home to 'Dear Beth': 'busy night and day getting the final details of the Civil Service Bill worked out with the Premier and the Law Department' and preparing answers to questions for the premier in the legislature.

Manitoba was the second province to request Dr Shortt to 'render similar assistance' in mid-January of 1918. Clearly, the model established for British Columbia was imported directly by Shortt, for by 29 January he was writing home to explain that he had spent the day going over the civil service bill with the caucus. There, he 'carried things so well' that, in a most unusual expression of confidence and quite a constitutional departure, as Shortt was quick to observe, 'they want me to meet the whole House' to assist the government in defending the bill!

Dr Shortt's influence was less direct in Ontario, but nonetheless important. It is clear from his correspondence that leaders of the reform movement relied on him for both information and inspiration. One of these, G.A. Warburton of the Toronto YMCA, was the recipient in early January 1918 of a lengthy letter in which Shortt responded not only to Warburton's request for information on the subject of patronage but also to the notion of a citizen's group to lobby on behalf of the reform movement. Shortt's response is worth quoting at length because of the light it throws on the perceptions of one who, as a civil service commissioner in Ottawa for a decade, had had the opportunity to see how deeply entrenched patronage was and what persistent effort would be required to effect change.

Commending Warburton on the proposed line of action to stimulate reform, Shortt suggested that the proposal conformed to what had been a successful procedure in Britain and the United States:

In these countries reforms were accomplished and in the latter are still being followed up by associations of public spirited citizens, and above all vigourously [sic] supported by that element among the members of Parliament of Provincial Legislatures and City Councils, as also through executive bodies who are in favour of the elimination of the patronage evil, but who naturally find it difficult to take an active stand in such matters in the face of an apathetic public opinion on the one hand, and a very active and persistent pressure of sectional and private interest on the other.

Shortt's comment on the best strategy for achieving reform is a reminder that the administrative reform movement was never a matter of a clearly identifiable pressure group single-mindedly pursuing its objectives. Rather, more like a moral cause, it was to be championed by right-minded citizens, organized in a somewhat ad hoc fashion to fight the good fight. Sustenance for such evanescent groups was to be found in their leaders' associations with more established groups that could be counted on to incorporate civil service reform into their own concerns. Thus, for example, Warburton's position with the YMCA provided a base for his leadership in rounding up a citizens' support group for the cause. Contributing in a similar fashion was the Citizens Research Institute of Canada organized by Toronto businessmen who, in turn, created a Civil Service Research Centre.

Shortt's letter to Warburton went on to indicate the difficulties of sustaining a popular movement when confronted by entrenched opposing interests:

My experience of nine years as a Commissioner of the Civil Service has revealed to me two aspects of the subject unappreciated before, first the extent to which the country and its service suffers from the patronage evil and secondly the fact that a considerable majority of Cabinet Ministers and members of Parliament would gladly see the whole system abolished if the general public would actively support them in this important reform. It is an erroneous idea that as a rule Ministers and members profit by patronage or are its active supporters. The greater part of the patronage prevails and much the worst part of it is exercised by the local political organizations of both parties, which, because they are instrumental in securing the nominations for the members claim to be all powerful in securing the election of the successful candidates, demand that the members and through them the Minister shall secure positions in the Civil Service and contracts and other economic favours for the persons whom they nominate to them. The members and Ministers are themselves, to a very large extent, only the servants and often the severely browbeaten servants of organizations from whose thraldom they would most willingly be free, if the independent electors would encourage them to strike for freedom with any hope of permanently maintaining it.

Shortt concluded his letter, after further explanation of how civil service reform associations operated in the United States, with this deft summation: 'It is of course essential that any system of Civil Service Reform be sound in principle and workable in practice, allowing all necessary freedom to those who are working for efficiency and the recognition of merit in their department, while affording effectual and practicable checks on the conduct of those whose chief object it is to support and manipulate a patronage system.'

Certainly at the federal level, experience was to show that Shortt's call for maintenance of a precarious balance between overhead control and autonomy for departmental managers was an ongoing exercise. The early reformers' insistence on central control to defeat the patronage mongers created a lingering bias against freeing up the departments. To the present day an apparently endless quest by many inquisitors has never succeeded in finding a permanent equilibrium between the claims for overhead control of the public service and the equally legitimate need of departmental administrators to be accountable for managing their respective agencies.

The legacy of the reform movement at the federal level has been the creation of strong overhead controls which it has been the object of successive investigations to ameliorate in favour of liberating departments to manage their own affairs. In Ontario the legacy has rather been the reverse – in other words, an initially weak set of central controls confronted by relatively autonomous executive departments that over the course of time have been harnessed by progressively strengthened central agencies.

Returning to the reform situation in Ontario, it is clear that Shortt's letter fairly represented the situation with which reformers would have to contend in that province. However, Shortt's pessimism on the likelihood of an apathetic public rousing itself to the action he deemed necessary was soon dispelled by one of his associates, the University of Toronto historian Professor G.M. Wrong. In a quickly scrawled note dated 25 January, Wrong wrote: 'By the way I found the officials at the Legislative Library on the look out for the Reports on Patronage [presumably a reference to such documents as the report of the royal commission on the Dominion civil service in 1908 and the famous one-man commission headed by Sir George Murray on the Organization of the Government of Canada in 1912] but having difficulty about finding them. Is this not a hint that they are going to bring in a Bill for Ontario?' Shortt responded in mid-February, claiming that he was more optimistic about the likelihood of reform in Ontario than in the federal civil service, where 'some spectacular patronage appointments' in the Post Office and Customs had been made. This situation called for what Warburton was in the process of creating in Toronto, 'an independent Civil Service Association with a permanent Secretary' to follow up on all government actions.

Professor Wrong took a direct hand in ensuring the desired outcome, for he wrote a series of four articles for the *Globe* in February and, along with Warburton and the influential editor of the Toronto *News*, John Willison, busied himself with forming a Civil Service Association. In this connection, Wrong wrote to Shortt on 20 February, explaining that 'Willison and I are arranging a dinner for forty or fifty representative people and the Secretary of the U.S. Association is coming and will make a public speech here. We are going to have a permanent Secretary and the salary is already secured. I wonder whether you would be free to come?'[20]

All this behind-the-scenes activity, and the example set by both British Columbia and Manitoba, apparently sufficed to overcome the resistance of the Hearst government to administrative reform. An even more powerful impetus intimately associated with the reform cause was the movement to 'abolish the bar,' greater attention being attached to the latter than the former. Significantly, Newton Rowell figured prominently as Liberal leader in both causes. The connection between the two movements was perhaps most eloquently stated on 16 March 1916 by a leading reformer, Samuel Carter, the MLA for Wellington South, when he launched his attack on the patronage system. He argued that there was no liberty of the citizen as long as appointments were restricted to supporters of the party in power. This system prevails, he contended, because 'so far as I can see, for the last twenty-five years the machine of about 100 men on each side in every riding, linked up with the liquor traffic, has dominated politics ... When we get rid of the liquor traffic there is some prospect of real solid government by the people and for the people.'[21]

The confluence of the two movements produced sufficient pressure to induce the attorney general, Isaac Benson Lucas, to introduce first reading of a bill 'to Provide for the Better Regulation of the Public Service' on 11 February 1918. Lucas professed to have used the federal legislation as a model. His bill was a somewhat pale reflection of that legislation, which had extended its reach to incorporate the hitherto excluded outside service. Lucas wisely neglected to call attention to this major difference, thereby guaranteeing the perpetuation of the restricted coverage provided by the 1878 Public Service Act. Thus, the entire sprawling field services of the departments and agencies were excluded, remaining prey to the same old nefarious practices which the reformers had targeted for elimination or at least amelioration. On another vital difference between the two reform measures Lucas was quite frank: the federal legislation provided for the open competitive examination principle – a key element of the merit system of appointment and promotion – but Ontario, he claimed, had settled more realistically for 'qualifying examinations.'

Another major difference separated the two measures: the provision for a collegial body (commission) to administer the merit regime at the federal level as contrasted with a single civil service commissioner for Ontario. In this particular, Ontario had clearly been guided by Shortt's model enactments for British Columbia and Manitoba, which provided for single commissioners. No doubt, Shortt's preference for one-man oversight was based on his unhappy experience in Ottawa working on a two-man Civil Service Commission of co-equals where difficulty in securing agreement led to endless delays. It was precisely this problem that induced the federal government to adopt a three-member commission with a named chairman; quite possibly it was this decision that induced Shortt to convince Borden to create an altogether new and more congenial position for him as chairman of a Board of Historical Records.

Many years were to pass before Shortt's one-man commissioner solution was dropped by all three provinces in favour of the collegial agency, but at the outset in Ontario Shortt's recipe found little favour with the opposition.[22] Their antagonism was roused by the fact that the new measure, in reaffirming the role of the political executive in regulating the civil service, revived the old debate between the executive and legislature which enactment of the original act of 1878 had precipitated. Nearly all of the matters of importance to administrative reformers – particularly a scheme of classification of the public service, a salary plan, and a pension plan – were reserved for the attention and advice expected to be provided by the new post of civil service commissioner. As in 1878, the opposition were quick to point to the heavy reliance on executive decree rather than legislation to determine all the key matters affecting the public service: as William Proudfoot put it, 'too much order in council business.'[23] The fact that such executive decisions were now to be informed by the advice from the new office of civil service commissioner failed to dispel the criticism, particularly when his office was located cheek by jowl within the office of the premier.

Howard Ferguson, in responding to the opposition's complaints, made no bones about the intentions of the new act and the significance of locating the commissioner in the premier's office. The Executive Council, he contended, had to take responsibility for the civil service and 'it was therefore impossible to make the Commissioner independent of the Cabinet.' When one adds Ferguson's belief that the federal government's recent adoption of the open competitive principle 'has been proven a failure' and Attorney General Lucas's contention that the spoils system was foreign to Ontario ('all previous Governments' appointments having been kept on and given loyal service'), one appreciates that the government's response to the pressures for reform was cautious in the extreme.[24]

Perhaps the most striking epitaph to mark the conclusion of this allegedly positive response of the government to the administrative reformers came in an answer to a question posed by the Liberal MLA, H.H. Dewart. According to the workings of this bill, he inquired, do all applicants for positions under the government have to be nominated by the party in power? The government's response, as reported in the Toronto *Globe*: 'The Attorney General merely smiled.' A year later, in April 1919, Premier Hearst confirmed the Delphic message of that smile by admitting that 'not many from the other side' managed to slip through the party nomination process and acquire entitlement to be considered for certification by the civil service commissioner.[25]

Howard Ferguson made even clearer his government's perception of what its reform measure of 1918 really meant and how little it was intended to erode the executive's power over the civil service. On 11 March 1920, while Premier Drury listened from his unfamiliar seat on the front benches, Ferguson sought to instruct him on what he conceived to be the proper tradition. 'I am a firm believer in a fair, proper patronage by men who are conducting the affairs of the province properly, I do not believe in the spoils system by the prostitution of public business for party purposes. But the Ministers must have some say in the selection of men who surround them in their work. Any other selection is giving Ministers an opportunity to dodge responsibility.' This being so, Ferguson went on, 'If a bill is introduced to institute what is known as a Civil Service Commission, where appointments will be made regardless of what the Minister thinks, I propose to oppose it strenuously. There should be some restrictions.'[26]

Ferguson's comments are interesting not only for the light they throw on the motives of his own party in approving creation of the Office of Civil Service Commissioner in 1918 but also for the distinction he drew between spoils (a bad thing) and patronage (a good thing). Patronage, in the view of many politicians, especially when in power, was the perfectly proper exercise of personal discretion to choose your own trusted advisers and not to leave selection to an 'irresponsible' (because independent) commission. As Whitney, the pragmatist, had earlier observed, 'The advice of a Deputy Minister of a department is of far more consequence as to the efficiency and promotion of an official than all the examinations you can record in the space of fifty years.' Premier Hearst, in making the same point while testifying to the nonpartisan nature of the process, drew attention to the fact that the three chief officers in the department for which he was responsible (and on whose advice for appointments and promotions he was presumed to rely) were themselves appointees of the former government.[27] In his view, this was what distinguished the proper exercise of patronage from a spoils system which, if it had been in effect, would have resulted in a wholesale turning out of the previous government's appointees.

While these high-minded views applied to the corps of officials employed at the seat of government, the same could not be said for the much more numerous members of the unprotected outside service, where turnover at a period of a shift in party power was a standard practice. In short, leading politicians in Ontario at this period differentiated between a spoils system which they professed to abhor (yet was widely practised in the field) and a patronage system which they viewed as a legitimate exercise of a politically responsible executive's prerogative to choose those who would be working closely with them at headquarters.[28]

However self-serving the protestations of those upholding their version of the patronage system, the arguments of Whitney, Hearst, and Ferguson did reflect the traditional bias in favour of executive control of the administrative branch. It therefore comes as no surprise that the lot of Dr J.M. McCutcheon, appointed as the first civil service commissioner in 1918, was not 'an 'appy one.' Indeed, his office was under pressure from both the government and the opposition. The government was uneasy about extending discretionary powers to its new appointee, in view of its concern not to let control stray too far from the hands of the political executive. The opposition, for its part, was unhappy with an act that provided for a lone commissioner instead of a collegial body, the more so because of the enormous range of discretionary powers conferred on the commissioner to be implemented by order-in-council.

The preference of administrative reformers for a collective rather than a one-man form of decision making as applied to public service matters derived from a perception that only an agency representing all the vested interests could be counted on to provide the necessary objective, non-partisan forum. The concept of such a politically neutralized commission was much in vogue in the United States. There, however, the method of achieving such a commission was a representative 'bi-partisan' body. While reformers in Ontario did not endorse this solution per se, in certain quarters proposals for a 'representative' commission went to extremes in the search for a method to ensure that members from all parties had an equal opportunity to nominate candidates for civil service appointments.

Undoubtedly the most extreme formulation of the 'representative commission' proposal was presented to the Assembly by Hartley Dewart, the Liberal leader, on 21 January 1921. Reinforcing his attack on the 'one-man power' of the civil service commissioner, he complained that 'a man utterly devoid of business training and experience ... was placed in sole charge of highly-skilled and experienced servants of the public.' Then, getting down to the real objection to the one-man power, Dewart lamented the failure of Premier Drury to implement a promise of the previous session to give information to leaders of all parties concerning vacancies in the public service, 'so that all would have the right of nomination.' To promote such opportunities, Dewart then produced an extraordinary proposal 'to press for legislation which would establish a real commission, on which each of the four parties in the House would be represented, on which the Civil Service Association would have its own representative and of which the Premier might act as Chairman.'[29]

There has surely never been a more extravagant formulation of the notion that to achieve a non-partisan agency one needs to have representation of all affected parties. How such a conglomerate could have made decisions, let alone provided that business training which Dewart found wanting in Dr McCutcheon, must remain a mystery.

Suggestive, however, of the populist ideas prevailing in the United Farmers groups and Independent Labour Party members that sustained Drury's government of the day, a proposal going even beyond Dewart's conception of a representative commission was apparently canvassed in 1921. The proposal was to name 'a committee of ten or twelve citizens in each constituency for the purpose of advising the Government in connection with appointments of [sic] the Civil Service.' A motion for tabling the correspondence relating to this proposal was debated on 3 February 1921 before being withdrawn.[30]

In the light of proposals for some form of collective decision making to be applied to civil service appointments, one can only express relief that Premier Drury decided to stick with the one-man arrangement which he had inherited. Equally important, he decided to stand by the original appointee, Dr McCutcheon, whom he had found 'to be actuated by zeal for the welfare of the Province.' Drury confirmed this intention in response to a direct question on 12 May 1922: 'Is it the intention of the Prime Minister to implement his promise to appoint a Civil Service Commission on which the different parties in the House would be represented and to replace the Commissioner, J.M. McCutcheon and make Mr McCutcheon Secretary to the Commission?' Drury's evasive reply, 'No decision has been reached,' was reiterated in 1923.[31] It was not until 1947 that legislation was introduced authorizing the creation of a commission of not more than three members. This provision was not invoked until 1957, although from 1953 on the commissioner was designated chairman.

It is fair to conclude from the discussions of administrative reform in the decade beginning in 1912 that there was much posturing and a good deal of lip-service paid to the precepts of the reformers. However, enthusiasm for changing the old ways tended to diminish once seated on the government benches. Administrative reform, particularly when it involved an assertion of legislators' rights to participate in the regulation and control of the civil service (and most particularly appointments), tended to be diluted because of its declared incompatibility with the entrenched principles of responsible cabinet government, with its bias in favour of the executive.

The United Farmers' government under Drury might have been expected to be somewhat more hospitable to modifications in the cabinet system in order to provide the broader participatory opportunities desired by the more extreme advocates of administrative reform. However, the inexperience that led to debilitating scandals, and the constant tension between elected members of the Farmers' party and strident extra-parliamentary groups led by J.J. Morrison, all combined to frustrate any dramatic changes in past practices. Moreover, the populist proposals for reform of the Office of Civil Service Commissioner were either too idealistic or simply too naive to gain any chance of acceptance. Thus the promises held out for the cause of administrative reform by the passage of the act of 1918 appeared to have withered on the vine in the early twenties.

11

Implementing the Administrative Reform Agenda

The act of 1918 for the better regulation of the public service took the cause of administrative reform as far as those in responsible political office were prepared to go in the early 1920s. Indeed, the government that introduced the legislation held a very restricted view of the application of the act and particularly of the status and powers conferred on the Office of Civil Service Commissioner. In this less than hospitable climate, J.M. McCutcheon, the man vested with the responsibility for implementing the new legislation, commenced operations. Located as a unit within the Office of the Prime Minister and President of Council, McCutcheon was assisted for the next two years by a permanent staff of one clerk-stenographer, Miss Vera Glenney, and a small staff of temporaries. Unlike her superior, Miss Glenney was to survive the overthrow of the Conservative government by Mitchell Hepburn in 1934, and would herself become a civil service commissioner in 1957. Even for the more enlightened postwar years of the 1950s, Vera Glenney's progression through the ranks to become a senior civil servant was an exceptional achievement for a female employee. Indeed, her accomplishment was sufficiently unique that it warranted special mention in the speech from the throne in 1958.

McCutcheon was not a newcomer to the public service.[1] After graduating from Queen's University, he began a career as a teacher of English and subsequently served the Department of Education as an inspector. In 1914 he was appointed secretary to the Workmen's Compensation Board. His appointment in September 1918 to the office of civil service commissioner was to place him in charge of an equally innovative and, at that time, politically somewhat more exposed agency.

Setting the Reform Agenda

The Public Service Act of 1918 set out a comprehensive legislative framework for managing the public service. Even more than its predecessor of 1878, the act of 1918 made clear the dominant role of the lieutenant-governor-in-council in dealing with a lengthy list of specific responsibilities associated with the overhead control of the bureaucracy. The major difference was that under the new legislation the executive was to be assisted in its tasks by the new civil service commissioner. The list of matters of central importance to the management of the civil service on which the commissioner was authorized to undertake investigations, make recommendations, or take action on his own initiative was all-inclusive: organization and business methods; grading and classification of positions; rules for dealing with office discipline and promotion; a scheme of superannuation; promoting the coordination of work with a view to greater economy and efficiency (a bow to the scientific management movement); examining and reporting on every nomination for appointment to any position; and, generally, the conduct of any inquiry proposed by the executive.

The government may have hoped that this extensive shopping list of management tasks – in several important areas going well beyond the already impressive mandate in the 1878 legislation – would reduce the new appointee to a state of helpless apathy. If so, the government sponsors must have been taken aback by the alacrity and informed enthusiasm with which Dr McCutcheon tackled his responsibilities. Indeed, such a surmise is reinforced by the subsequent consignment to archival oblivion of the commissioner's annual reports. After enjoying five years of publication in the *Sessional Papers*, they abruptly ceased to be as publicly available during the next twenty-five years. Presumably reports were made for tabling in the Assembly, as the legislation required, but once they were no longer printed, they might just as well have entered a black hole. However, the historian must be grateful for small mercies, and the failure of governments to suppress publication of the first few reports of the commissioner must be counted as one of these blessings.

These early reports provide a remarkably comprehensive picture of the reformist ethos of the day, even as they demonstrate what enormous room for improvement lay before succeeding governments for years to come. It was surely the gap between prevailing practices and the reformists' ideals that induced an embarrassed government to put as low a profile as possible on the commissioner's reports. Despite these dark speculations about the real intent of the government that had sponsored the legislation of 1918, it must be said that both the terms of the act itself and the manner in which McCutcheon set about implementing them revealed a complete familiarity with the doctrines of the scientific management movement which were being promoted vigorously in the United States at all levels of government. Conjoined with these forces, and a dominant theme in the reformers' book for Ontario, was what might be called the 'patronage to proficiency' movement, an amalgam of the ethical or moralistic views of those opposing the evils of patronage and liquor.

In the United States the scientific management movement developed out of the time and motion studies first undertaken in the private sector but rapidly extended to 'big government' that had been rendered bigger by the First World War.[2] The more ethically driven movement to eliminate the spoils system in government was a natural outcome of the postwar drive to reform local and state government in the United States by introducing strong mayors and/or city managers and strong state governors. Only by creating a strong executive, the reformers felt, could one offset the nefarious influences of the political machines and bosses that allegedly dominated the legislative branches of the states and the elective councils of municipalities.

In Canada the concepts and concerns of the scientific management movement were well known, partly through the mediation of the Civil Service Assembly of the United States and Canada. This cross-border association, in this area as well as such policy areas as factory inspection, institutional care, and public health, represented the constant organized interchange of ideas and practices that has so characterized the relations between the two countries. The transmission of scientific management concepts was effected by the earliest types of management consultancy firms, notably in the case of Canada by the firm of Arthur Young and Company who specialized in reorganization and classification studies. Ontario found inspiration from the same source and, as McCutcheon's reports made clear, effectively established the administrative reform agenda for the province.[3]

The parallel theme given equal weight in McCutcheon's reports was the notion of merit as the principle guiding the selection, appointment, and promotion of personnel in the public service. Although this had long been a theme of administrative reformers in the United States as well, Ontario reformers did not feel the need to take lessons from their counterparts to the south in seeking cures for their own patronage problems. Indeed, Ontario's politicians sought to distance themselves from the American spoils system in order to proclaim the virtues of the judicious exercise of executive discretion which they characterized as patronage. In fairness, the stability of the staff at headquarters tended to confirm this view. But in the wider arena of the outside service it was clear that patronage as practised in Ontario was as antithetical to the principle of selection on grounds of merit as was the maligned American spoils system. The more the outside service grew and called upon skills and training extending well beyond the lowly clerical order of tasks, the more urgent it became to achieve the reformers' goals of efficiency and economy.

The early published reports of McCutcheon trumpet the reformist agenda sponsored by the scientific management school and the anti-patronage protagonists. Through his single-minded, courageously outspoken pursuit of the ideals preached within the two types of reformist groups, Dr McCutcheon was so much in advance of his political over-lords that he failed to ingratiate himself with them. But the public service of Ontario has reason to be deeply indebted to McCutcheon for firmly establishing and disseminating the agenda of issues to which public service managers, right up to the present day, have had to address themselves. For all the naïveté that is the customary accompaniment of any missionary movement, one must hand the accolade to McCutcheon. His proselytizing set the public service of Ontario on a path of modernization along which it became all the more necessary to travel as the province moved into the large-scale administrative state of the second half of the century.

Arguably, then, the first few years after the end of the First World War constituted the period during which the agenda for modernizing the organization and management of Ontario's civil service was clearly articulated, even if it was implemented but hesitantly and with snail-like pace. The key promoter was McCutcheon, who used his reports as his chief educational instrument. Since these published reports encapsulate the concepts of public service management, not only as conceived at the time but essentially for the time to come, their contents warrant fuller attention.

The Central Planks of the Reformers' Agenda

Although the first annual report covered a mere seven weeks of operation, ending on 31 October 1918, it highlighted three of the key planks of the administrative reformers' platform. 'It is anticipated,' the report stated, 'that a classification of the Service, based on the duties and responsibilities of the employees, will be undertaken in due course.' From this, would spring 'the standardization of salaries and the application of improved methods of organization and administration,' which were equally important to the cause of administrative reform goals of efficiency and economy. The third major project to which the commissioner attached high priority was the need to introduce a superannuation system that would be in the best interests of both government and employees in that it would 'insure permanency in the personnel of the Service, ... keep open the avenues of promotion, and ... provide an adequate retiring allowance on account of old age or incapacity.'[4]

In the commissioner's second report, the first to cover a full year of operation, McCutcheon added a fourth and all-inclusive theme, 'the application of the merit system to employment problems.' In what was, given the prevailing official perceptions, far from unnecessary pedantry, McCutcheon the teacher took over to expose the advantages of the merit system 'concerned with the selection and the maintenance of an efficient personnel and with the application of sound and scientific employment principles.' Its adoption, he continued,

would result in the displacement of the patronage system with all its attendant evils ... and would permit the Government to select public employees of as-certained fitness, demonstrated in competition, from the best material in the Province. Its uniform application to employment problems would insure effi-ciency and economy in the Public Service and eliminate irregularities and anomalies ... I strongly recommend its adoption and uniform application in making appointments to the Service, in determining promotions, transfers, and salary increases, and in all other employment problems. The principle of merit is one of the keystones to the arch of progress. It has long been amply demon-strated, in both public and private employment that the merit system provides the remedy for waste, inefficiency, and lax methods and supplies a sound basis for the administration of public affairs.[5]

In such ringing phrases, the first civil service commissioner, sounding like a barker at a fair extolling the benefits of a favourite curative elixir, set out to sell his tonic to an apathetic political system. Contrasting his eloquent plea with Howard Ferguson's put-down of virtually the entire program espoused by McCutcheon, it is easy to see why the government lost little time in putting a damper on his reports and why, in the after-math of Mitchell Hepburn's sweep to power, his reward for a fifteen-year dedication to office was to read of his 'resignation' in the daily newspaper.[6]

Before either of these blows fell, McCutcheon determinedly and elo-quently pieced together the administrative reform agenda, a task that was no less important for all the hurdles it would still have to surmount in the future. Thus, in repeating his exhortation on behalf of the merit principle in his fourth annual report for the year ending 31 October 1921, McCutch-eon called attention to another facet of public personnel administration that some years later was to become a significant responsibility.

The growing demands of modern government, with its changing activities and enlarging functions, require a well-equipped and efficient body of employees who are prepared to invest themselves in the work of the state. There is a greater need than ever before in the administration of public affairs for high-grade intelligent service and for a high degree of business efficiency. The time is not far distant *when great attention will be given the problem of training employees for public service.*[7]

That Commissioner McCutcheon was well in advance of his time may be confirmed by observing that twenty or more years later, in 1944, the third item in the terms of reference assigned the newly established Joint Advisory Council representing management and the Civil Service Association was 'the development of a career service, including methods for training members of the civil service.'

Equally percipient and in advance of its time was McCutcheon's plea for instituting employee performance records in order to make possible a promotion system based on merit. He could have been under no illusions concerning the prospects for an early introduction of such a system for, in the last report to be published, he was still trying to convince deputy heads of departments to impose a minimal monthly reporting system for employee attendance. Pursuant to his legislative mandate, in 1921 the commissioner had succeeded in getting cabinet approval for regulations governing attendance at Toronto head offices. The hours were from 9 a.m. to 5 p.m., with an hour and a half out for lunch and a 9 a.m. to noon session on Saturday. The qualified success with enforcing this regulation is apparent from the commissioner's observation: 'Some improvements in the attendance have resulted ... but if it were strictly and uniformly enforced and properly observed ... considerable economy would accrue, the dispatch of public business would be greatly facilitated, and one of the greatest obstacles to efficiency in the Public Service would be removed.'[8]

Despite the obvious resistance to embracing even such basic regulations as those applied to attendance, McCutcheon continued to urge 'upon the administrative officers of each department the desirability of making a start in the systematic recording of the efficiency of employees. The adoption of some plan will eliminate guess work and doubt [euphemism for favouritism?] when promotions and salary advances are under consideration. A beginning might be made by keeping a record of daily attendance, punctuality, vacation and sick leave, and at least some approximate record of the quality and quantity of routine work, and of the willingness, industry and initiative of each employee.'

Lest one think the commissioner's fixation on record-keeping a somewhat pedestrian concern, it is useful to remember that the absence of such records could frustrate each and every one of his grand designs in the scientific management mode. For example, a prerequisite for the superannuation plan, high on the commissioner's list of priorities, was a system that recorded appointments and continuity in service. 'It is, therefore, highly desirable,' wrote McCutcheon, 'that all appointments to the permanent staff should be approved by Order-in-Council and that all leaves of absence, due to illness or other cause, should be made in compliance with the provisions of the Ontario Public Service Act.' In that regard, the necessity for securing commissioner certification of all new appointments to the civil service (under terms of the 1918 act) provided an opportunity for the creation of one central source of statistical information concerning the bare bones of civil service employment. At the same time, it should be added, the commissioner gained a leverage which he might not otherwise have been able to apply: without his certificate employees would not be able to receive such benefits as the pension or leave entitlements; therefore there was every reason to secure the imprimatur of the commissioner and not try to bypass him.

Presumably this task of compiling statistics would have been the main preoccupation of Vera Glenney and a permanent staff of only four persons when McCutcheon's regime came to an end in 1934. As with so many of the commissioner's initiatives, long after his departure his campaign for proper records and employee performance ratings was being continued by his successor, C.J. Foster. In Foster's report for 1946–7, for example, there is this plaintive reiteration of the old plea: 'the need in some departments for more centralized control of staff records and more supervision of personnel procedures generally. A considerable time of the Commissioner's staff is spent in details of personnel administration ... The conclusion also cannot be escaped that in some departments a lack of properly trained personnel officers has been responsible for a certain laxity in applying the regulations of the service.'

A persistent criticism of the scientific management movement, made in retrospect rather than at the time of its ascendancy, was that it was too mechanistic and lacked concern for the human factor. In McCutcheon's favour it must be said that his dedication to the efficiency and economy precepts did not blind him to the importance of the human element. This awareness was possibly fostered by his training as a humanist (as a teacher he had taken the lead in inducing his students to put on Shakespeare plays, for instance). His previous experience as secretary of the Workmen's Compensation Board would also have sensitized him sufficiently to present the following definition of personnel administration in his fourth annual report: 'The direction and co-ordination of the human relations of any organization with the view of getting maximum production with a minimum of effort and friction and with a *proper regard for the well-being of the workers.*'[9] This statement surely has a less manipulative ring to it than such contemporary appellations as 'human resource management.'

Proper regard for the well-being of the workers necessitated the putting in place of a superannuation plan. It also included a conception of the state as model employer which to this day has remained a debated and debatable principle of salary-setting for government employees. From the outset, McCutcheon's review of the classification and pay arrangements in the civil service revealed serious inequities which, if permitted to continue, would have a debilitating impact on employee morale. 'The survey of the Service,' he reported after his first full year of operation, 'in connection with the work of classification has convinced me that further increases are amply justified in a great many classes of positions.' In the following year's report he observed, 'the standardization of salaries should be adequate, fair and equitable.' Then, in a most revealing couple of sentences, he went on to assert: 'If the State is to be a model employer in every respect, as it undoubtedly should be, there should be no discrepancy in salaries as between public and private employment. The public has the same right to be protected against excessive salaries as the employees have to receive adequate salaries.'

In phrasing this conception of the state as model employer McCutcheon would undoubtedly have been aware of the antipathy of Premier Drury's farmer supporters to what might appear to be preferred treatment for the white-collar employees in the civil service. This antipathy was forcefully expressed when Drury promoted the civil service superannuation plan. In any event, the tricky balance called for in this formulation of the model employer principle has never been easy to achieve. The introduction well after McCutcheon's time of collective negotiation between management and civil service unions of salary and other service conditions has not made achieving this objective any easier.

Dr McCutcheon could not be faulted for neglecting this later intervenor in public service management any more than he should be criticized for failing to anticipate such contemporary issues as fair employment practices, or (given the community attitude towards women in the workforce that persisted even beyond his time) for women's pay equity. Even without these more contemporary concerns, McCutcheon faced a formidable and somewhat lonely task of trying to put in place a set of precepts and practices for public service management that remain as relevant today as they were in his time. Some account of his early struggles to implement the major elements of administrative reform, together with a brief projection of their subsequent development, modification, and even rejection is now in order.

Superannuation

The first item on McCutcheon's reform agenda, to be implemented by legislation in 1920, was a superannuation plan. A probable reason for the higher receptivity to this plank in the administrative reform program was pointed out in the commissioner's first report. 'There appears to be a growing tendency at present,' he wrote, 'on the part of Governments, the larger urban municipalities, financial institutions and industrial organizations, to adopt superannuation systems.' In fact, as early as 1880 a bill had been introduced 'to enable the officers of the Public Service to provide retiring allowances.' But the bill did not get past first reading.[10] It is doubtful, in any event, that the proposed measure would have been much of an advance on the provisions incorporated into the Public Service Act of 1878. There a gratuity was to be awarded for civil servants dying in office or retired on grounds of poor health or old age. Even this vague, completely discretionary arrangement proved too generous; in 1898 amending legislation ruled out the payment of gratuities to any employees appointed after 1 January of that year, and a major consolidation of the Public Service Act in 1913 left this situation untouched. Thus, when in 1920 the legislature approved a measure concerning the superannuation and retiring allowances of civil servants, an important forward step was taken.

Accustomed as we have become today to the virtually universal presence of pension plans in the public sector, we might be prone to play down the importance of this measure. It was sufficiently novel in the view of the rural supporters of Drury's government to compel them to denounce it as class legislation – an undesirable cossetting of urban, white-collar workers. On the other hand, the Labour members upon whose support the Farmers' government also depended were favourably disposed.[11] McCutcheon, recognizing how essential the plan was to achieving other elements of his reform package, played a prominent part in establishing the terms of the plan and thereafter supervising its administration. E.C. Drury, in recalling his personal preparation of the plan, wrote of 'the help of Dr. J.M. McCutcheon, Superintendent of the Civil Service and of the President of the Civil Service Association.' Sharing McCutcheon's view concerning its necessity, Drury went on to observe:

There was then no provision for the superannuation of members of the Civil Service, and as a result many old persons were retained long after their usefulness had passed. There was, moreover, a general feeling of insecurity through the whole service for the majority of civil servants did not receive salaries high enough to enable them to provide for old age. The act we fashioned ... which is still in force, was modelled largely on the superannuation arrangements for ministers of the Presbyterian Church.'[12]

The first feature of the plan was its surprisingly broad coverage, based on a generous definition of 'eligible employee,' which was extended to the staff of the Assembly as well as that of the provincial auditor. Even the initial exclusion of so-called temporaries began to be lifted in 1922, probably because of the intense pressure put on the civil service commissioner to issue certificates approving the transfer of temporaries to permanent status. The fact that temporaries were declared admissible may tell us something about the looseness of nomenclature, given that ten years of continuous service was a minimal requirement to qualify for a pension! Not that McCutcheon would have been inclined to quibble, for it was this very provision of the pension plan, calling for his certificate, that gave him a powerful leverage in pushing for other and much less welcome elements of his reformist agenda.[13]

It must also be observed that a comprehensive pension plan was very much in the interest of the political executive intent on maintaining an oversight of its agencies – particularly as the use of semi-autonomous agencies began to expand. One of the methods by which such independent status can be symbolized is to confer on the agency the right to act as its own employer, as in the case of the Hydro-Electric Power Commission. Consistent with the logic of special status, Hydro was authorized to create its own pension plan in 1919, to which the staff of local utility commissions, created under the Public Utilities Act, were permitted to subscribe.

The special status conferred on Hydro has been the exception. But the 1922 act amending the Superannuation Act of 1920 made provision for the permanent staffs of any board or commission to be included in the public service plan by order-in-council. With singularly few exceptions, even when agencies have been authorized to be their own employer, governments have nonetheless tended to place their staffs under the plan created for the departmental civil servants.

While this examination of the relationship between independence (as an employer in one's own right) and a pension plan may appear to be a diversion, it reinforces the theme with which we began: the significance of a comprehensive pension plan for central control over the bureaucracy. At a minimum, the plan required the maintenance of central records – a kind of window on a scattered, ill-defined public service which an office such as McCutcheon's sorely needed. In addition, McCutcheon was provided some real clout as he sought to implement other elements of his reform program.

Another benefit of the superannuation plan was the establishment of a retirement age. Admittedly, the original plan calling for retirement at age seventy, with the possibility of continuing beyond that age on a year-by-year basis by mutual consent, was extraordinarily generous. Save for such preferred officials as members of the judiciary and Senate, this initial cut-off age has since been greatly reduced. However, a glance at the first two reports of the board set up to administer the plan reveals why such generous arrangements seemed necessary and why the age of retirement was not lowered to sixty-five until 1933, along with more stringent constraints on year-by-year extensions.

After holding eighteen meetings, the Superannuation Board had recommended or accepted the retirement of exactly one hundred employees, of whom seventy-five were over the maximum age of seventy. Indeed, a large number were in their eighties, prominent among these being a ninety-year-old caretaker of the Queen Victoria Park Commission and a ninety-five-year-old sheriff for the counties of Prescott and Russell. Even with this picture of a public service grown long in the tooth, the board could not find it in its heart to force the retirement of another hundred employees who had also surpassed the statutory limit of three score years and ten. Obviously the time was long past for a pension scheme that would enable such old retainers to afford to retire with some sense of security. As the board concluded, after its examination of such cases, lacking a pension plan, 'the public service becomes a charitable institution.'[14]

Viewed in the most objective managerial terms, then, superannuation was a way of clearing out dead wood, but in a humane way. More positively, such a plan would open up opportunities for promotion that had been closed and admit of the appointment of fresh candidates. These attributes of a superannuation plan were not lost on McCutcheon; they were consistent with his dearest ambition to attain a true merit system and, by extension, the creation of a permanent career civil service that would attract the brightest and best. The pension plan was, of course, necessary for such a merit system but not sufficient by itself to achieve this objective – a goal, in truth, that has proven as elusive as the search for the Holy Grail.

A third feature of the superannuation plan is worth examining. In making provision for a contributory fund made up from percentage

deductions from employees' salaries and equal contributions from the
public purse, the act of 1920 represented the model for the future, both
for the public and the private sector. The complex changes made in its
detailed provisions almost annually since its inception need not detain
us. What was of immediate interest was the composition of the Superannuation Board that was established to administer the plan. It appears that
the government, although unprepared to create a civil service commission and particularly a fully representative collegial body recommended
by some reformers, was quite willing to have the representative formula
applied to the composition of the pension board. Dewart's model had
called for a commission chaired by the premier and members drawn
from all four parties then in the legislature, as well as a representative
of the employees, with the ubiquitous McCutcheon as secretary. This
was precisely the formula used to compose the membership of the
Superannuation Board.

The subsequent evolution of the board and the provisions for administering the superannuation fund illustrate the capacity of the executive
branch to reassert its historic hold on all matters pertaining to the management of the public service. Four years after its creation, the board's
membership was reduced to just three, the only reference to the formula
featured in the original act being that one member be 'a representative
of and employed in the Ontario Civil Service.' In practice, the original
representatives of the political parties in the legislature continued on
into the early 1930s, the only immediate effect being that the premier
no longer chaired the board. However, as long as the civil service
commissioner served as secretary and as long as his office was located
within the office of the prime minister, the close executive supervision
of the superannuation plan was preserved. No doubt such executive
influence was enhanced by the formal transfer of responsibility for the
fund itself to the provincial treasurer in 1931.

In the early 1930s, with the elimination from the board of the representative MLAs of all parties, the process of transforming the administration of the pension plan into a routinized 'internal' concern of management proceeded. The overarching presence of the civil service commissioner that existed from the beginning was progressively extended
as the commissioner moved from being secretary to the position of
member and finally ex officio chairman of the board. Successive amendments to the superannuation legislation left undisturbed the original
provision for employee representation on the board. However, by the
1980s administration of the pension plan no longer appeared to require
the same high-profile involvement of either the central personnel agency
or the staff association representatives. In short, superannuation as a key

element in the administrative reformers' program, initially involving supervision by an unusual combination of representatives of the executive, the legislature, and employees, has become thoroughly incorporated within the executive branch and the board's function itself a routine element of central management.

Classification

Turning now to classification of the public service, it will be recalled that McCutcheon gave it high priority because it constituted the very foundation of the platform of the scientific management school. Like the pension plan that was first to be put in place, a classification plan of sorts also had its historical antecedents in the Public Service Act of 1878. This measure provided a detailed classification-cum-pay plan that was to prevail until a new classification was introduced in the 1920s.

Although the original approach to classification differed markedly from its successor, it was clearly inspired by the same perception that classification was the foundation upon which all other significant elements of the administrative reformers' program could be built. Thus, the act of 1878 reflects this basic understanding, for it begins with a classification plan which in turn becomes the basis for a pay plan, and from there describes an appointment process, followed by a promotions scheme, each of which hangs on the classification plan.[15]

Forty years later, McCutcheon's first full year report confirmed this same conception of the classification plan as basic to all other reforms. In his words, obviously borrowed from the lexicon of the position-classification experts of the day, such a plan was designed

to remove inequalities and anomalies; to establish standards on which to base definite lines of promotion; to standardize salaries and to establish improved methods of providing for increases; to establish a standard title and to specify the work requirements for every class of position in the Public Service; to provide, for the information of the general public and employees in the Public Service, a convenient summary of the various positions in the Service, the qualifications necessary for appointment thereto, the compensation paid, and the promotions that may be anticipated.

In McCutcheon's view, the conditions of Ontario's public service demonstrated a desperate need for the immediate application of this basic tool of management. In a more general sense, the changes recommended (and pursued to this day) reflected a turning away from a pattern of civil service organization that had been much influenced by policies and practices developed in Britain. Instead, the proposals were inspired by an emergent philosophy whose advocates were largely in the United States.

The alleged scientific quality of the principles of administration, and the notion that such principles were equally applicable to large organizations regardless of whether they were governmental or private, seemed to give a special cachet to the message which was carried across the border and promoted in the meetings of such bodies as the Civil Service Assembly of the United States and Canada. (It was surely not pure coincidence that in the first budgets of the civil service commissioner there appeared an item to cover an annual subscription fee to the Assembly.) Also advancing the cause were growing numbers of outside specialists and advisers who were not averse to playing a missionary role when acceptance of their message expanded the market for their particular services. The management consultancy fraternity came into being at this time and has never looked back, nor since wanted for governmental clients.

Since their classification plan was considered such a prerequisite to the proper management of the public service, it is useful to take brief note of the scheme which was to be displaced and which had served as the basis for organizing and regulating Ontario's public servants.

The essence of the classification scheme of 1878 was a simple separation into two groups: a special division that was to include all those offices 'which require for their exercise some skill usually acquired only in some professional or other pursuit, different from the Civil Service'; an ordinary division to include all others – namely, 'Deputy Heads of departments, Officers or Chief Clerks, Clerks, and Probationary Clerks.' The special division was to be divided into two classes of officers and clerks, the salaries for both classes to be set by order-in-council and approved by the legislature. The ordinary division had a more elaborate breakdown into four classes of clerks with statutorily assigned salaries, fixed annual increments, and a requirement for minimum years of service before being eligible for promotion to the next class. Deputy heads were listed by their departments and were to receive such salaries 'as may be assigned to them by the Legislature.' Officers and/or chief clerks were to have their salaries set by order-in-council and voted by the legislature. Finally, the act required the lieutenant-governor-in-council to determine the establishment of personnel required in each category, fit the existing staff into the several divisions and classes, and then submit the entire scheme to the legislature for its approval.

Viewed as a classification plan, the schemata of the 1878 act was distinctly lacking in criteria upon which to make the decisions affecting the placement of each public servant. The act implies that work in the public service – as was held to be true at the same period for the British civil service – could be regarded as demanding either 'intellectual' or 'mechanical' (i.e., routine) capabilities. The exceptions were to be found, as the act proclaimed, wherever professional skills were required – as, for example, an architect or engineer for public works, or someone with a lower-order technical skill such as a land surveyor. For these, the dispensation of 1878 provided the two classes in the special division. Every other job was deemed to fall within the ordinary division. But here no criteria were provided for placing employees in their appropriate classes, despite the elaboration of categories. The criterion for promotion, as a result, was based on the dubious but safely non-discretionary assumption that one improved with age. This theory was reflected in the provision for automatic annual increments and the requirement that before promotion could be contemplated, a minimal period of service had to be put in.

As a plan from which to develop a logical scheme of recruitment, the classification was totally unsatisfactory. Lacking proper job descriptions, how could one determine what qualities to look for? Under these constraints, the act had to settle for the requirements that a candidate submit evidence 'as to his age, health and moral character,' along with a somewhat guarded reference to 'such examination, but without competition' as the lieutenant-governor-in-council might direct for candidates seeking admission into the ordinary division.

As a basis for a compensation plan the classification appeared to be more satisfactory, particularly from the perspective of the Assembly with its interest in controlling the public purse. In this respect, the act either set out the graded salaries and increments, or else required legislative endorsement of any proposals for change of salaries or new salaries submitted by the executive. The provision, finally, for legislative approval of the overall establishment that the executive was required to prepare in light of the classification scheme represented the high-water mark for legislative influence over public service management. Even so, the classification plan for which it was given a formal right of approval failed the legislature in two respects.

First, even as a pay plan the classification scheme was faulty because it could not be applied equitably. Without a description of the work to be done in each position it was impossible to guarantee – as administrative reformers were soon prone to point out – the principle of equal pay for equal work. In short, the door was open for completely subjective salary determination which could occur within the vague contours of the classification plan and without much prospect of possible favouritism being brought to light in the legislature.

The second weakness of the plan of 1878 was that the legislation applied only to the 125 officers and clerks operating at the seat of government. As the public service grew, especially after the turn of the century, the number of civil servants in the outside service not covered by the classification plan grew proportionately. Thus, by the time McCutcheon started to agitate for a new plan, he had to contend with the problem of more complete coverage as well as seek remedies for the demonstrable flaws of the old classification scheme.

What McCutcheon had in mind was fundamentally different from the 1878 plan. As revealed by the title attached to the plans then being promoted by firms of efficiency experts, the 'position' was the basic cell upon which the comprehensive classification grid was built. Exponents of such schemes stressed the fact that what was being classified was not the person holding the job but the characteristics of the job itself.[16] The individual would be slotted into the grid after the various tasks had been assessed, categorized in accordance with their general nature (e.g., scientific, technical, administrative, clerical, and so on) and then graded according to the degree of difficulty of the work, the formal professional requirements, and the degree of responsibility (e.g., routine, whether supervised, or supervising the work of others). Only then, having objectively determined the requirements of the positions and the numbers required in each category, was it possible to turn to the human element and fit existing staff into their appropriate niches. The result, as the classification experts were fond of saying, was that there would no longer be square pegs in round holes. And because one now had a clear description of each category of tasks and the skills/knowledge required to fulfil it, the recruitment process could be similarly rationalized. Examinations for public service employment could now be geared to the job descriptions and the candidates themselves would have a clearer sense of what qualifications they would need in order to apply realistically for positions. For those already in the public service, the classification plan could provide a map of the career path open to them by the promotional ladders provided within the graded classes of positions.

With all these positive attributes, it is not surprising that McCutcheon visualized the installation of a position-classification plan as the centrepiece of his administrative reform agenda. Unfortunately, his aspirations did not meet with the same early success of his superannuation plan. His failure is only partly attributable to the natural resistance to jettisoning the much more relaxed scheme of the past for the seemingly squeaky-clean, scientifically objective replacement. More important was the complexity of the procedure involved in making such a complete turnabout – one which was to involve far more public servants than the relatively small group at headquarters.

McCutcheon's expectations for success, and perhaps even his initial enthusiasm for a position-classification plan, must have been cooled as he observed the veritable turmoil his federal counterpart, the newly empowered Civil Service Commission, was experiencing as it sought to make good on its mandate to classify the entire war-swollen Dominion civil service. The American firm of Arthur Young and Company had been brought in by the Civil Service Commission because of their expertise in developing and installing position-classification plans.

When the work was completed, the federal civil service had its classification plan, replete with nearly 1,700 classes which within a decade or so had more than doubled in number. The Civil Service Commission was so caught up in nursing and policing the plan that it claimed to have neither the time nor the resources to fulfil what the efficiency experts believed to be a vital preliminary to classification. In their view, nothing short of a major reorganization of the departmental system would suffice in order to prune the underbrush that years of neglect and the exigencies of war had allowed to flourish. Logically, for the efficiency experts, before classifying jobs, every effort should be directed to eliminating the redundant ones. Many years were to pass, in fact, before the Dominion commission was able to turn to structural reform of the kind visualized in the 1920s.

Meanwhile McCutcheon in Ontario was apparently undeterred by what was transpiring in Ottawa, if one is to judge from the eloquent pleas for action on a classification plan that were contained in his first three annual reports. These pleas were in response to the duty conferred on him by the act of 1918 'to report to the Lieutenant Governor in Council such changes as he may deem proper in any department with a view to systematizing the work of the department and the grading and classification of the civil servants employed therein.' Unlike his federal counterpart, McCutcheon was not directly mandated to undertake a full-sale classification; that was not to come until long after he left office. Presumably, however, he could use the procedure selected by the federal commission to contract with outside experts to perform the task. According to the act of 1918 the lieutenant-governor-in-council could 'authorize the employment by the Commissioner of expert and special assistance from time to time as may be deemed necessary in the discharge of the duties of the Commissioner.'

McCutcheon's intention to move on the matter was signalled in his first report, produced after only six weeks in office. There he anticipated 'that a classification of the Service, based on the duties and responsibilities of the employees will be undertaken in due course.' Unlike the efficiency experts on whose ideas he was drawing, he seemed to believe that classification had to precede 'the application of improved methods of organization and administration' rather than the other way around. Did he also stray from another of their axioms when he spoke of classifying *employees* rather than the *positions*?

McCutcheon's second annual report in 1919 promised the classification study would be available for legislative approval early in 1920. The Assembly's *Journals* duly record that the Report on Classification was tabled on 18 March. But there it died, apparently without debate and certainly without any formal approval being given. Since the report was never printed, without the evidence from the commissioner's own annual reports to confirm its existence one would be inclined to doubt that it had ever been prepared. Adding to the aura of mystery surrounding its preparation is McCutcheon's purported use of the firm of Griffenhagen and Associates – the same team of experts then deployed on a number of studies of the federal departments – to prepare the plan.[17] Although the public accounts of the day are detailed to the last penny, nowhere do they show an expenditure for preparation of such a plan. (There is a remote possibility that its costs are buried in an unusually large 'contingency' allocation of over $5,000, but none of it is earmarked.) Nor can one possibly assume that the commissioner was able to do the survey unassisted, provided as he was at the time with one permanent clerk and a handful of temporary typists.

The mystery of the provenance of the Classification Report is matched by the miraculous way in which McCutcheon claimed to be able to use it for its intended purposes, even though the legislature had failed to approve it. In his annual report for 1921 McCutcheon stated that when salaries were adjusted by order-in-council in 1920 and thereafter confirmed in the estimates for 1921 and 1922, the scales were in conformity with those presented in the aborted classification plan. Moreover, as of July 1920, he claimed that all appointments, promotions, transfers, and salary increases had also been based on the plan. In short, the other elements of sound personnel administration presumed to be dependent on the existence of a position-classification plan had in effect been achieved, despite the failure of the plan itself to gain formal legislative approval.

In retrospect, McCutcheon was probably fortunate to have lost the main battle over formal acceptance of the classification plan and still achieve a reasonably peaceful settlement of the issue of salaries which was so closely dependent on such a plan. It was precisely this issue that plagued the efforts to implement the comprehensive plan that had been prepared for the Dominion civil service. There, in pursuit of the objective classification of positions, as opposed to persons, the consultants had underrated the impact of inflation on salaries paid to civil servants and this error had translated into pay scales associated with the new classifications which were deemed to be too low. This discrepancy became visible only when the time came to slot incumbent civil servants into their new niches. The ensuing uproar was directed against the classification plan and the outside firm of experts who had perpetrated this outrage. The massive program of assessing departmental organizations was abandoned, along with the experts engaged on it. For its part, the Civil Service Commission immediately instituted damage control procedures in order to ameliorate the adverse impact on the civil service. Over the long haul it inherited a complex and unpopular classification plan whose upkeep and maintenance was to preoccupy the commission in its 'guardian' role almost to the exclusion of other elements of the extremely comprehensive mandate as *the* central personnel agency which it had acquired in 1918–19.[18]

In short, the Achilles heel of the position-classification scheme, so fully exposed in the tribulations of the Canadian Civil Service Commission, has been the assumption that it is the position and not the person which is the object of assessment. Such an assumption falters when confronted by the reality that, after all is said and done, there are human beings already in the positions who have firm convictions about the true nature of the work they perform. Thus, no matter how dispassionately derived, formal job descriptions inevitably collide with these personal, but none the less real, evaluations. When, in addition, the salary scales attached to the classifications were found to be out of line with postwar inflationary conditions, it was a recipe for constant agitation to change the plan. The experience of the federal government in the 1920s taught at least one lesson about the new mode of classification: the preparation and installation was just a beginning; its administration would require constant and expert vigilance on the part of some central authority.

The stormy reception of a classification plan at the federal level may have had a hand in the negative response in Ontario to McCutcheon's similar design. His apparent satisfaction at achieving the side benefits of a set of salary scales and new appointments and promotions in accordance with the classifications may have been McCutcheon's way of putting the best face on his failure to get formal legislative approval for the plan. In any case, he seemed to have been able to avoid the problems faced by his federal counterpart as it sought to break in the new classification regimen.

This appearance of relative quiet on the Ontario front as contrasted with the turmoil at the federal level might give rise to the supposition that McCutcheon was able to get ahead with his reform agenda precisely because his classification plan failed to achieve the saliency of the federal scheme and become a target for seething dissatisfaction. On the other hand, the quiescence of the Ontario civil service is more likely to be explained by the perfunctory role assigned the commissioner as contrasted with the extraordinary range of powers formally assigned to a federal commission quite unprepared at the outset to handle such a mandate. The limited and essentially advisory mandate prescribed for Ontario's commissioner by the act of 1918, by contrast, was made explicit by the niggardly resources put at McCutcheon's disposal and the placement of his small office directly under the premier's supervision.

The subsequent attempts to incorporate a classification plan into the public service and the problematic role of a central agency in this endeavour were clearly brought to a head by the enormous growth in governmental activities characterizing the years following the Second World War and can be traced here only in the broadest terms. The first forward step was taken in October 1927 when by order-in-council, a classification plan akin to that which had been allowed to die in the legislature in 1920 was reintroduced.[19] However, in the light of the experience of the federal Civil Service Commission, Ontario's commissioner lacked one crucial authority – the power to police and develop the plan. Lacking such authority, there were no service-wide standards for classification, reliance had to be placed on civil servants' own evaluation of their jobs, and the age-old problem of pay inequities persisted. Like the federal plan, Ontario's classification plan showed the same signs of luxuriant growth, matching the more than three thousand federal classified positions with well over eight hundred of its own by the 1940s.

This situation was to prevail until 1945, when the commissioner at last received the statutory right to undertake, without the help of outside experts, a full-scale overhaul of the classification plan. This effort to go it alone was far from successful. The work, one expert claimed, 'was largely done in a piecemeal fashion by an "evolving" committee of public officials who could not give full time to their tasks. The result was a considerable amount of haggling and bargaining. No outside assistance was secured ... No appeal procedure was provided.'[20] Thus when the schedule of new classes began to emerge in 1947, it left so much to be desired that ten years later the Gordon Committee on the Organization of Government in Ontario had to field numerous complaints concerning the continuing inequities and inadequacies of the plan. The response was to initiate another comprehensive review, this time conducted by the outside firm of Stevenson and Kellogg but with the assistance of staff drawn from the departments and the (by now) Civil Service Commission, as well as representatives of the Civil Service Association of Ontario. In the midst of this review, the Public Service Act was amended in 1961–2, vesting the commission with the authority (subject to lieutenant-governor-in-council approval) to make regulations for prescribing methods of evaluating, classifying, and reclassifying positions, and for prescribing classifications for positions, including qualifications, duties, and salaries.

That such an explicit spelling out of a mandate for the Civil Service Commission occurred more than forty years after McCutcheon had first prescribed it speaks volumes for the casualness, the desultory nature of supervision, the reliance on subjective assessments, and the consequent need for frequent massive overhauls that characterized the attitude towards the use of one of the basic tools of modern management. Moreover, the new-found authority of the Civil Service Commission was not to be exercised unchallenged, for in the same legislation provision was made for a classification rating committee of three members, one of whom had to be appointed from outside the civil service, to adjudicate disputed classification decisions.

The Merit System

Consideration of the efforts to implement what McCutcheon termed 'the keystone to the arch of progress' – the merit system – provides the most suitable method of ringing down the curtain on the impact of the reform movement on the management of Ontario's public service. Ideally, as McCutcheon interpreted the reformers' proposals, the merit principle involved 'the application of sound and scientific employment principles' by an independent central agency vested with the authority, on a competitive basis, to recruit, examine, and certify candidates' eligibility for civil service places whose job descriptions and pay schedules had already been mapped out by a classification/pay plan. The installation of the merit *principle* involved a complex of institutions and procedures that in their full deployment could be referred to as the merit *system*. As the Glassco Royal Commission on Government Organization was to observe presciently in the 1960s, the prevailing tendency at the federal level to treat the two terms as synonymous concealed the possibility that the system itself might evolve in ways that would be counterproductive for the principle.[21] Alternatively, as Ontario's experience would suggest, a tepid enthusiasm for the merit principle had much to do with the deficiencies of the structural and procedural devices which were ostensibly created as the means for giving flesh to the principle.

The one-man office of commissioner created in 1918 can be seen as betokening the lukewarm attitude of its creators. First, the independence of the office was suspect; the legislation, in contrast to the special provisions made for a number of other non-departmental agencies, provided no extra security for the commissioner through special tenure or a fixed lengthy term. This situation was to persist even after the collegial principle was formally provided for in 1947: when finally acted upon in 1957, the addition of Miss Glenney from the staff of the commission and a departmental deputy minister as part-time commissioners scarcely represented a strengthening of the independence of the commission. The subsequent twists and turns in its status reflect a steady erosion of the original conception of the functions that the administrative reformers thought appropriate for a central agency. How these functions were initially conceived and what role the civil service commissioner came to play in their performance as guardian of the merit principle must be briefly addressed as a way of explaining the state of comparatively benign neglect into which the contemporary commission appears to have subsided.

Extensive as were the managerial matters assigned the commissioner, their exercise was subject largely to cabinet review or concurrence, which meant that the commissioner's powers were essentially advisory. In the realm where merit was to apply – that is, for appointments to the public service – the fatal restriction was that the duty of the commissioner was 'to examine and report upon every *nomination* for appointment to any position in a department' (my emphasis). The commissioner's discretion, once confronted by a nominee, was to certify in writing 'that such appointment is necessary and that the salary attached to the position does not exceed a fair and reasonable remuneration for the service required,' and 'that the person to be appointed is duly qualified for the position to which he is to be appointed.' The means by which the commissioner was to ascertain the duly qualified status were discreetly left in limbo. Curiously, only for certain named officials connected with the administration of justice – registrars of deeds, registrar and deputy registrar of the Supreme Court, sheriffs, crown attorneys, and the like – was the commissioner to ascertain whether the 'applicant or nominee possesses the necessary qualifications as to character, education and ability for the discharge of the duties of the office.'

As a final reminder of the limited capacity of the commissioner to implement the merit principle, the act of 1918 made a distinction between 'department' (involving only 'employees at the seat of government in Toronto') and 'public service' (involving employees 'at the nomination of the Crown, as representing the Province of Ontario, wherever held or performed'). The commissioner's limited right to certify candidates applied only to the first departmental group, while the far more numerous body in the public service group continued to remain under the free-wheeling patronage proclivities of the past, save for a limited number of those enjoying salaries exceeding $1,000 whose appointments would have to be certified by the commissioner.

Even this restricted mandate was subject to erosion by specific exclusions. Notably, appointments to the field services of Highways and Game and Fisheries were left in departmental hands. The Highways Act of 1919 authorized the minister to appoint, where work was performed outside the seat of government, 'such officers, clerks, servants and labourers, fix salaries and give directions as to appropriations against which to be charged.' The Game and Fisheries Act of 1927 went a step further by conferring similar authority on the deputy minister (subject to approval of the minister), but added to the determination of remuneration the discretion to dismiss any appointee. When to these specific exclusions is added the general authority conferred on ministers to make temporary appointments to their departments, have them annually renewed and automatically certified by the commissioner, the constricted conception of the merit principle is plain to see.[22]

When Mitchell Hepburn succeeded the long Conservative regime in 1934, this vulnerability of the merit principle was amply revealed. Hepburn, of course, had campaigned with more than the usual rhetoric directed at an overblown bureaucracy, promising that 'the exodus of supernumeraries from Queen's Park would dwarf the annual Orange parade.'[23] The first officials to go were those whose appointments had been in the most blatant defiance of the merit principle. These were promptly replaced, relying on the same partisan considerations. As Mitch bluntly explained, 'there are enough efficient Liberals around to do the job.' For the more extended task of ripping out 'the deadwood' in the bureaucracy, Hepburn enlisted his new civil service commissioner, Charles J. Foster, to keep score. By his account, 'between 11 July 1934 and 18 April 1935, 1067 employees of all kinds had resigned or been discharged and 839 were hired.'[24]

Incomplete returns presented to the legislature revealed that most of the dismissals occurred in the outside service among the more menial grades. Among the lesser lights involved in the administration of justice, for example, where appointments were held at pleasure, a clean sweep was made, 492 new justices of the peace and twelve crown prosecutors being appointed. In the recently established Securities Commission, George Drew (later to be Hepburn's nemesis) was replaced as director along with the rest of the staff. The Liquor Commission lost 481 employees and regained 265 Hepburn appointees. Eight district medical officers were fired; all local old age pensions boards, except those in the larger centres, were abolished. These were just scattered indications of what was a much more pervasive housecleaning, if one is to judge from the large number of questions seeking similar replies for other areas of the public service, most of which remained unanswered.[25]

Among all these dismissals, it is important to note, the practice of respecting the most senior appointments continued to prevail. Only six of the twenty most senior officials were replaced. Clearly, however, the slender defences for the merit principle which McCutcheon had sought to erect provided no barrier to the inexorable tidal wave of patronage released by Hepburn's victory and to which McCutcheon himself succumbed.

Charles J. Foster, McCutcheon's successor, was one of the senior officials carried over from the previous regime, having been secretary to George Henry. He entered Hepburn's office at first also as private secretary and promptly became commissioner. Trusted by Hepburn, he showed less disposition than his predecessor to tilt against the political windmills in his efforts to press the claims of the merit principle.[26] Perhaps because of a more complaisant approach to his office, Foster served both Liberal and Conservative governments, continuing until June of 1958. His last year was spent as chairman of a three-person Civil Service Commission for which statutory provision had been made in 1947. Possibly this reluctant acknowledgment of the value of a collegial body for handling the quasi-judicial role of defender of the merit principle – something the early administrative reformers had deemed essential – was attributable to Foster's own bias in favour of a one-person agency. He somewhat facetiously described his role 'as personnel director I apply the rules and regulations and as Commissioner I recommend policies to the Government. After many years of discussion with myself I am on the way to achieving a certain degree of unanimity. This I believe is not always true of multiple commissions.'

The collegial commission had little more success than the one-man agency in embodying the merit principle in the systems and procedures governing recruitment, appointment, and promotion. This is clear from subsequent developments that belong to the contemporary period lying beyond the immediate reach of this study. It is sufficient to note that shortly after the Conservatives regained power, the speech from the throne in 1944 was declaiming in a special paragraph relating to the civil service that 'The first step has already been taken to establish a system of appointment by merit through the application of uniform tests in certain classes of appointments.'[27] The modesty of this step can be ascertained by examining the reports of the commissioner which show the examinations confined largely to headquarters' personnel in the clerical and stenographic ranks where wartime shortages had dictated the use of 'open registers' of candidates who had qualified in a series of continuing competitive examinations.[28] Over ten years later, a response to the opposition leader Donald MacDonald's query about methods of recruiting for the public service indicated little had changed: 'The Departments recruit the staff they need. They are assisted to a considerable extent by the Civil Service Commission which also establishes the required qualifications for appointment.'[29]

In effect, the growth in the size of the bureaucracy and in the requirements for specialist attainments arising from the postwar social and economic demands placed on government was forcing a rethinking of the precepts underlying the reformists' zeal for the merit principle.

12

Financial Management and Public Service Accountability

The agenda of the civil service reformers focused on questions of organization and personnel as they related to the attainment of the primary administrative goals of economy and efficiency. Surprisingly, their concerns left largely unattended the other basic ingredient for public administration – that is, the management of material resources, primarily the raising, spending, and accounting for the moneys spent on public objectives. Even more than the management of public service personnel, the raising and spending of money within a parliamentary-cabinet system of responsible government has been considered to be the purview of a political executive vested contingently with authority to govern so long as it could retain the confidence of the legislature. Thus the executive's disposition of public money has been subject to the formal imprimatur of the legislature, the granting of supply being viewed as the ultimate constitutional victory of the legislature over the monarch and his advisers. Indeed, as we have seen in considering the debates between the executive and legislature over the right to manage the public service, it was the claim to be the ultimate controller of the purse strings that was used by the legislature to justify its mostly futile assertion of the right to have a direct say in the management of the public service.

The passage of time has resulted, as Fred F. Schindeler has shown in his classic study, *Responsible Government in Ontario*, in the strengthening of party control over the legislature by an increasingly dominant executive.[1] Its initiatives in developing expenditure plans, expressed in the form of appropriations for various services, are presented on a take it or leave it basis to the legislature – in short, treated as a matter of 'confidence' on which the executive is prepared to stake its claim to continue in office. Whatever claims the legislature once might have been able to make to influence money-raising and expenditure decisions – the supply side of the equation, so to speak – has been weakened over time. Correspondingly, increasing attention has had to be directed to strengthening the right of the legislature to monitor the ways in which the executive has delivered on its promissory notes as formulated in the various appropriations for public purposes – the accounting side.

In light of these observations, it is apparent that the evolution of the management of public moneys must be traced by pursuing two themes. One might be characterized as having external dimensions associated with the concept of parliamentary supremacy; the other has internal dimensions associated with the concept of fiscal probity and efficiency.[2] The external facet involves the historical constitutional right of the legislature to control the purse. In particular, the legislature has a monitoring role, holding the executive to account for expenditures which it has initiated and for which legislative approval has been formally granted by means of appropriations subdivided into estimates. The internal aspect involves the examination of the means by which government organizes to handle the revenue accruing to it from various sources. Involved also are the procedures for allocating, dispensing, and accounting for the appropriations which the legislature has placed at the executive's disposal – in short, financial management in its more down-to-earth technical sense. Within the bureaucracy, the mounting claims on contemporary governments, expressed in public expenditure budgets vastly greater than in earlier times, have necessitated the creation of specialized agencies and complex procedures that have compounded for the legislature its always present problem of maintaining its external oversight role.

For purposes of exposition, it will be useful to pursue this distinction between the external and internal dimensions of the control and management of the public purse. Unfortunately, the early approach to managing public moneys in Ontario did not conform to this neat dichotomy. On the contrary, the external and internal threads were so intertwined that the central thrust of this chapter of necessity will be concerned with exposing how, over a long period of time, a separation was achieved and why such separation has been so important to the preservation of at least a modicum of the legislature's traditional constitutional role. Moreover, more than the usual liberties will have to be taken with the time frame chosen for this study in order to track the long-drawn-out transformations to their contemporary resting place. Since Schindeler has written definitively about the developments up to the late 1960s and others have continued his story into more recent decades,[3] here the focus will remain on their less well-known antecedents, depicting the contemporary outcome only with the broadest of brush strokes.

Internal Financial Controls

Revenue Management. Beginning with the internal arrangements for handling revenues, it must be noted that more than one hundred years had to pass before responsibility for revenue collection was concentrated in one agency, a Department of Revenue, in 1968. In the immediate post-confederation period, however, the Treasurer's Office was by no means the only agency responsible for collecting and accounting for the revenues due the province. As a royal commission reporting on the finances of the province indicated in 1900, the 'territorial revenues' collected by Crown Lands between 1867 and 1899, representing in total one-third of all provincial receipts and exceeded only by the Dominion subsidy, was completely subject to the independent accounting procedures in Crown Lands, without reference to the treasurer. As the commission explained, because of the heritage of statutory charges against these revenues (for example, receipts from the sale of lands set aside to help pay for the common schools), much of this money never reached the Consolidated Revenue Fund through the provincial treasurer but remained to be accounted for by Crown Lands.[4] The decentralized nature of revenue collection was further exemplified by departments other than the treasurer's retaining responsibility for collecting sundry revenues such as those from the Jury Fund, liquor licences, and municipal payments. Each of these, after paying their costs of collection, required subdivision between the province and the local authorities by an 'inspector' or other official not necessarily or even usually located in the Treasurer's Office.[5]

The dispersed nature of early financial management was revealed by S.C. Wood, who described for the legislature's Public Accounts Committee in 1888 the system he had inherited when he had become provincial treasurer in June 1877. The 'then Auditor [William Cayley], owing to weight of advancing years resigned. We had then been some eleven years since confederation. In the last part of 1867 or the first part of the year 1868, and also in 1868–9 part of the Public Accounts were kept in Ottawa and part here, owing to the Crown Lands and some other departments not being transferred.' During the eleven years some $13 million had been expended and imperfectly audited, not because of want of ability or integrity, but because it had never been ascertained whether the cash book, along with cheques outstanding, balanced with the accounts in the banks.[6] Wood's own attempt to introduce a more orderly system of taking monthly balances, so that he and his colleagues would know 'what cheques were out and what amounts paid,' was frustrated by the arrangement whereby Crown Lands accounted for and audited its own receipts and expenditures. The same situation prevailed for the administration of the finances of the Agricultural College and the various public institutions under the inspector, little or no examination of these accounts being conducted by the Treasurer's Office – nor, indeed, by the auditor, who remained for many years a subordinate appendage to that Office.

It required the belated disclosure in 1888 of a series of defalcations extending over a decade to force the government to face the need to introduce a more orderly and more centralized method of accounting for revenues. In 1889 the provincial treasurer, A.M. Ross, explained to the legislature's Public Accounts Committee the measures he had taken to improve the system – locking stable doors well after the event. His description is worth extended quotation because a dozen years later it was commended by three prominent members of the financial and banking community making up a royal commission whose mandate in part was to comment on the financial methods and accounts of the province.[7]

I think all will agree that it is wrong in principle that the accountant who keeps the books should handle the money ... I took authority at the last session of the Ontario legislature to appoint that officer [a cashier or receiving officer] who should receive all the moneys payable to the Province from the different departments ... The system in paying moneys is this: Every department is furnished with a requisition book in which there is a duplicate form of application to the cashier to receive a certain sum of money named on the form of application. One of these duplicates is kept by the cashier. The other, with the cashier's acknowledgement that he has received the sum named therein, is returned to the department. The department is required at least once a week to transmit the duplicate to the auditor. The department still retains the counterfoil held by the cashier. In this way the payments by the department are checked by the auditor and also the receipts of the cashier. The cashier deposits the money in the banks under the direction of the Assistant Treasurer [i.e., the deputy minister].

Ross was obliged to admit that the ever-recalcitrant Crown Lands Department had only partly been drawn into his system. The widely dispersed and substantial expenditures on colonization roads (a great source of local patronage) continued to be covered by warrants accounted for within the department, without reference to the Treasury and, indeed, beyond the ken of the provincial auditor.[8] The latter official took a remarkably cavalier attitude to the grey areas; he forthrightly and without apparent embarrassment repeatedly informed the Public

Accounts Committee that he knew nothing about any accounts lying outside the Treasurer's Office.[9]

On the revenue side, the Treasurer's Office gradually began to reflect in its staffing the accretion of responsibilities that were associated with the province's need to take advantage of its constitutional authority to impose direct taxes. The first of these was the Succession Duties Tax approved in 1892. It left little imprint on the Office until Frank Ford was appointed solicitor in charge of a separate branch. Interestingly, his predecessor, Alfred McDougall, was the cause of another scandal involving a substantial defalcation. This lapse had apparently occurred in defiance of the accounting and monitoring procedures which the treasurer had introduced in 1888 and whose virtues had been extolled by the royal commission on finance in 1900.[10]

From the turn of the century on, the Succession Duties Branch was the only growth centre in an otherwise moribund department. After the First World War an Amusement Tax was added, accounting for a miscellany of modest revenue collectors, such as an inspector of theatres. By 1926 these developments had converted J.T. White, the long-time solicitor of the Succession Duties Branch, into the controller of revenue. The creation of this position was undoubtedly attributable to Treasurer William H. Price's discovery, reported in his budget speech of 1924, that 'although half a century has passed since Confederation, there has been no real audit of the receipts in this Province.' Price then announced his campaign to institute a more rigorous check to correct the laxity of officials in departments outside the Parliament Buildings. Included in this scrutiny was his own Amusement Tax division, where he had found the clerks 'sitting around knitting and reading books' while some of the cash received 'was sticking out of the files when we came in – five-dollar and ten-dollar bills, and cheques there for months.' By 1926 the treasurer was reporting that 'Since the audits have been under way, every department seems to have realized the importance of keeping a closer eye on the revenue.'[11]

This concern to audit the revenue collectors throughout the service was well taken for, as Controller White explained to the Public Accounts Committee in 1930, his office did not collect all the tax revenues and others collected and returned their own earnings to the treasurer quite independent of him.[12] However, an increasing proportion of the province's revenues came to be collected by the Treasurer's Office. With the arrival in the early 1960s of one of the most lucrative direct taxes, the retail sales tax, the incumbent controller of revenue, H.H. Walker, was made an associate deputy minister in the Treasurer's Office.

Walker's promotion was the prelude to the creation in 1968 of a Department of Revenue over which he presided as deputy minister and to which was assigned no less than thirteen acts representing the cumulated ingenuity of successive governments in maximizing their direct taxing powers. This consolidation was brought about as a result of the recommendations of the Smith Committee on Taxation set up by Ontario. The committee's report called for 'a Department of Provincial Revenue responsible for the administration of all revenue statutes now administered by the Treasury Department under the Comptroller of Revenue' which would also include other revenue statutes assigned to boards and commissions where the primary purpose was revenue collection as opposed, say, to regulation.[13]

Expenditure Management. The centralization of responsibility for collecting or monitoring the revenues that entered into the province's Consolidated Revenue Fund took a century to find formal expression in a department separate from that of the Treasury. Almost as slow in its evolution was the role of the Treasury as the centre for preparing the expenditure budget of the province and accounting for expenditures. It is upon the efficacy of the internal procedures used to achieve these objectives that the external control by the legislature of the public purse so heavily depends.

Internally, the expenditure budget is built from the estimates of anticipated needs of the departments and agencies for the forthcoming fiscal year. Based upon the estimates, a supply bill is prepared for legislative approval, subdivided into appropriations or votes. It is upon the basis of the appropriations that money is released to the spending departments. This process ensures that the departmental requisitions for money fall within the prescribed terms of the appropriation and that there are sufficient unexpended funds in each vote to cover the claim. This particular activity which, for many years, was characterized as an auditing function, only gradually came to be recognized for what it really was, a comptrol function for which internal management was responsible. It should not to be confused, as for so long it tended to be, with the external independent audit of the public accounts.

It would appear that in the early years after confederation the Treasurer's Office played little more than a post office role in putting together the estimates prepared by the individual departments. Ten years after confederation the provincial treasurer described his system thus to the Public Accounts Committee:

My duties in connection with the estimates commenced in the Session of 1873, and was [sic] continued through the Sessions of 1874, 1875, 1876 and 1877; but in connection with my duties as Treasurer in explaining the different appropriations as paid for from the House, I am not personally responsible for any other appropriation than those required by the Treasury department. The Provincial Treasurer is not required in any sense to take the initiative in furnishing the data of any Department but his own. My system was to notify, previous to the Session, each particular Department to send in its estimates of the sums required by that particular Department at the ensuing Session.[14]

Casually permissive as this procedure appeared to be, it was at least an improvement on a pre-confederation practice against which the then active Public Accounts Committee of the Assembly inveighed and was successful in changing. That practice consisted of presenting 'estimates' to cover expenditures *already made*; at least the post-confederation practice acknowledged the propriety of presenting *future* expenditure plans as a means of giving formal expression to the concept of legislative control of the process.

These somewhat free-and-easy and uncoordinated procedures for putting together the province's expenditure budget do not seem to have changed very much until mid-way into the twentieth century. Had such activity come to be located in the Treasurer's Office it would have registered as a highly visible increase in staff and a significant upgrading of the existing band of clerks and bookkeepers. Nor were these to be found in the audit section originally attached to the Treasurer's Office, even after the act of 1886 formally created the Office of Provincial Auditor.

The legislation of 1886 also introduced a Treasury Board composed of three members of the Executive Council. The unstated purpose of this unique statutory committee of cabinet was undoubtedly to check any tendencies the new Audit Office might display in administering the rules and orders affecting the 'conduct of business' and the guidelines for the form of the accounts. The board was to be the final arbiter between the auditor and the spending departments should differences between them arise. Moreover, since the rules and orders according to which the auditor operated were all subject to Treasury Board approval, it was clear that the auditor was viewed as part of the executive branch and not the 'officer of Parliament' that even then some claimed him to be.

In this legislation of 1886 and in its subsequent amendments through to and beyond the Second World War, there is no indication that the administrative arrangements for assembling the expenditure budget from the departmental submission of estimates had been much altered. Indeed, as late as the early 1950s the continuing informality of the process and the reliance of the treasurer on whatever expertise he could find and trust was captured in the centennial history of the Audit Office. Citing the influence of Harvey Cotnam, who assumed the position of provincial auditor in 1938 as the first chartered accountant to be thus appointed, we receive this picture of provincial budget-making in the late 1940s: 'Mr Frost consulted with the Auditor while he was Treasurer, he grew really dependent on Mr. Cotnam ... The Provincial Auditor would be up 2 or 3 nights preparing the budget speech for Mr. Frost ... He attended every Treasury Board meeting and sat in on a lot of Cabinet meetings.'[15]

Apart from the interesting questions this story poses about the independence of the Audit Office, the foregoing vignette discloses the persistence of the informal methods historically employed for developing and assembling the expenditure budget. Formal acknowledgment of the impracticality of continuing to use such methods for the expansive budgets of the post-1945 world awaited passage in 1954 of an act 'to Provide for the Financial Administration of the Government of Ontario and for the Organization of the Treasury Department.' This measure was really the first organic act to acknowledge the existence of a department whose legal base to this point had rested on the provision in the BNA Act for the Office of Provincial Treasurer. Even the enactment of 1886 that provided for the Treasury Board as a committee of the Executive Council was entitled an act for 'the Better Auditing of the Public Accounts,' and had no reference to the organization of the Treasurer's Office.

With the Financial Administration Act of 1954, the provincial treasurer was effectively placed in charge of preparing the budget by being confirmed as chairman of an enlarged Treasury Board with his deputy head serving as secretary to the board. Equally important, the informal 'budget committee,' composed of senior officials who for the previous few years had assisted in this task, was now recognized in law to consist of officers drawn from both the Treasury Department and other departments designated by the lieutenant-governor-in-council. Thus Treasury Board was able to fulfil its mandate to 'examine, advise upon and compile annual and supplementary estimates.'

Internal Comptrol versus External Audit

The control of and accounting for public expenditures are essential elements of financial management, having both an internal and an external dimension. It was in this area that confusion persisted between what in simplest terms can be referred to as pre-control and post-control of expenditures. In early days and for a surprisingly long time into the twentieth century, the word 'audit' was applied to both activities, and even today is retained in the terms pre-audit and post-audit. The legislation which created the provincial auditor in 1886, therefore, was ostensibly concerned with the better *auditing* of the accounts. In fact, it was much more dedicated to improving the mechanisms and procedures for checking and double-checking expenditures *before* they were made – not as we would interpret audit today as a checking *after* the event. Pre-control of expenditures was to be achieved by having the separate office of the auditor keep its own set of expenditure accounts as a check on individual departmental accounts.

In fact, long before the Provincial Auditor's Office was given a separate statutory identity, an order-in-council of 1869 had authorized the appointment of an auditor, and the statement of his functions clearly demonstrated the contemporary perception of audit as a pre-control device. As the preamble stated: 'the proper auditing of the accounts, and of the individual disbursements connected with all branches of the Public Service in Ontario is essential, not less as regards that vigilant supervision of the conduct of all persons engaged in or entrusted with the disbursements of the public revenue ... than in the ever recurring dread that their acts and doings will be subject to the closest surveillance.'[16]

The auditor's responsibility for maintaining accounts of all moneys paid in to the treasurer and to the departments was matched by his responsibilities for checking on expenditures. 'Every cheque made out in the name of the party entitled' was to be countersigned by the auditor, as were the much-favoured advances by way of accountable warrants assigned to the departmental clerks for contingencies. If complexity of procedures were a test of effectiveness of a system for preventing fiscal transgression, the system described to the Public Accounts Committee by William Cayley would have to be viewed as fool-proof.[17] A departmental requisition for funds would come to the auditor, who would certify that 'Funds for Service' were available and return it to the department. The requisition so endorsed would go to the Executive Council for the issuance of a warrant by the clerk of council, thence to the accountant in the Treasurer's Office for a cheque to be made out, then back to the auditor for countersignature and notation in his books, and finally, back to the accountant to go to the payee – if he was still alive!

Accompanying what was essentially a comptrol function was the monthly check-up on the transactions to date, described by Cayley thus:

At the close of each month, I go to Mr. Harris' [the accountant and chief officer in the Treasury] Department accompanied by my clerk and we go over the cash books, calling out each item. I then take the Bank Pass Cash Book and we call over the entries there, then verify the entries in the Cash Book with the Bank Pass Book deposit slips. I add up the Cash Book and, if correct, I initial it. The Bank Pass Book is also added up and, if correct, my work is done.

Despite the appearance of having stopped every loophole, the frailty of the system became apparent with the revelations of a decade-long fraud. The detailed inquest undertaken by the Public Accounts Committee began in 1885 and triggered passage of the Audit Act of 1886. Nor did the formal creation of a separate office make any immediate improvement. In 1888, in response to the questioning of William Meredith, the opposition leader, Auditor Sproule admitted that he did not know how the departments or the Treasury operated before cheques came to the Audit Office or after they left it. Meredith: 'Even after twenty years?' Sproule: 'No official knowledge ... It was the system I inherited and I did not query it.'[18]

The bureaucratic inertia so clearly reflected in Sproule's approach to the system used for control of expenditures was also displayed by the provincial treasurer, S.C. Wood, to help explain away the defalcations then under scrutiny. Admitting that the system of bookkeeping could be improved, he then added defensively, 'but when you have a staff that have been following a system for a long time they have got to run in that groove, and it is very difficult to make a change.'[19] The treasurer did little to ease anxiety about the security of the system of double-checks when he admitted that the number of cheques requiring his signature had increased to such a point that he had had to introduce a stamped signature, and 'speaking of that, I may say that the signing of cheques is really a farce. It is no protection to the public in the world.'[20]

How prophetic Wood's comments were about the resistance to systems change was revealed in 1971 in the description given by the Committee on Government Productivity of the procedures still used for paying accounts and which proposed reforms were designed to improve. In terms not far removed from those used by William Cayley ninety years before, the committee claimed that their recommendations would reduce the time required for processing accounts 'by eliminating the movement of requisitions and cheques back and forth from departments to Provincial Auditor to the Government Accountant's Division and back to the Provincial Auditor and then back again to the Government Accountant's Division.'[21]

One cannot resist noting that the problem of signing cheques, even after their numbers became overwhelming, continued to be handled with that same cavalier disregard for the proprieties that Treasurer Wood had evinced in the late 1880s. According to the commemorative history of the Audit Office, when Chester Walters investigated the Audit Office in the 1930s he found that the now more than 300,000 cheques a year were still being signed by hand, the person delegated to perform the countersigning for the auditor allegedly being chosen because his name, F.H. Lee, contained the fewest letters.[22]

The solution of the Committee on Government Productivity to the time-wasting procedures they found to be still in place was a simple one: transfer the pre-control (pre-audit) function from the provincial auditor to departmental financial officers. But in view of the unequal capacities of departmental personnel to handle the task immediately, the committee recommended shifting responsibility to the comptroller of accounts in the Treasury, who would then determine when each department was qualified to take over and maintain centrally imposed standards. This transfer would then leave the provincial auditor free to concentrate on post-audit which, in the committee's view 'should address itself to the examination of the suitability of financial accounting systems, to maintaining the required control of expenditure and to ensure the legality of transactions.'

Belated Arrival of Independent External Audit

Why did it take more than a century to attain this reform? The answer is surely to be found in the undue reliance placed on two sets of internal checks before expenditures were made as the means of ensuring both internal probity and external accountability. It is clear from the moment an auditor was created *within* the Treasurer's Office in 1869 that the check on expenditure was to be an internal one; two sets of accounts were to be kept by two separate officials, that of the auditor's to be used as the check against the integrity of the accountant in the Treasurer's Office. The merits of such a system were thrown into question by the discovery in the 1880s that the two sets of accounts did not conform, that it took over a decade for the defalcations to be revealed and, such was the sorry state of bookkeeping in the departments and central offices of the accountant and auditor, that no one could determine which set of accounts was correct.

One might have anticipated that the Audit Act of 1886 would have sought to address the problems thrown up by this evidence. In fact, the system of internal pre-control was left intact. The new Office of Provincial Auditor was empowered to keep running accounts of departmental expenditures against authorized appropriations and to disallow payments where appropriations had been exhausted or where no legal authority existed. The significant advance effected by the act was that the process of separating the Audit Office from the Treasurer's Office was begun, the appointment of the provincial auditor being 'during good behaviour,' removable for cause by the lieutenant-governor-in-council on an address of the legislature, and with a salary fixed by statute.

There are intimations here of the transformation of the position of auditor from an officer of the executive branch to an officer of parliament, but the complete transformation was not to occur until the Audit Act of 1977. The legislation of 1886 was a harbinger of this change primarily because of the special independent status conferred on the Office but also because the auditor was now to report to the legislature whenever his decisions were overruled by the Treasury Board created by the same legislation. Although the functions vested in the Office were described as 'auditing' functions, they were essentially all exercised as pre-control functions all executive in nature, and bound to bring the auditor on collision course with the spending departments and, in the end, all subject to the fiat of the Executive Council, as exercised by Treasury Board.

Despite the obvious intent to affirm an independent status for the auditor so that he might better serve the needs of the Assembly, even members of the legislature did little to advance the transition of the auditor from a servant of the executive branch to an officer of parliament. As early as 1869, for example, the Public Accounts Committee proclaimed that they 'did not recognize a detailed audit as within the functions of the Committee of Public Accounts ... The House will therefore understand that the only detailed investigation of accounts in the nature of an audit, now established, is the departmental examination and control in the Treasurer's Office.' In a succeeding report the committee commended that system for 'securing due responsible executive authority for all expenditure', in 'affording exact and complete record of financial transactions' and in providing an audit.[23]

Confusion over the role of the auditor continued after the transformation of status conferred by the act of 1886. The minutes of the Public Accounts Committee for 1892 illuminate the nature of this confusion in the persons of Charles Sproule, the provincial auditor, and his inquisitor, James Clancy, a Conservative member of the opposition who was, ironically, to succeed Sproule in 1905 when the latter was transferred to the position of deputy provincial treasurer. In the course of questioning Sproule, Clancy asked rhetorically: 'But your duty as an officer is entirely independent of the government, as you are an officer of this House?' To which Sproule replied: 'Certainly, and if I thought anything was improper I would oppose it and find against it.'

Despite this response, it is clear from Sproule's subsequent replies that he was merely giving lip service to this concept of his office, being too bound by his own experience to view it in any other light than that of an appendage of the executive. After all, he had entered service as a bookkeeper in the Treasurer's Office. Even when formally separated, he worked in adjoining offices to the accountant (an arrangement continued long after the move to the new Parliament Buildings in 1893) and finally was to shift to the deputy treasurer's office in 1905 without raising an eyebrow.

Observing Sproule's performances before the Public Accounts Committee – and they were by no means regular and never impressive – it is clear that he was never at ease when called upon to proffer comments on the actions of the executive from his position as the officer of the legislature he professed to be. His pained reply to James Clancy's persistent questioning in 1892 typifies his subsequent behaviour. 'I tried to explain that for you,' he remarked testily, 'but I cannot get at it exactly. I am not accustomed to giving evidence before a public committee.'[24]

What he could not explain to Clancy's satisfaction went to the very heart of the independent auditor's function – the ability to cry foul when the executive was proposing an unauthorized payment. In this instance, Sproule was unwilling to call out the executive for making a particular expenditure because it was done under the comfortably vague umbrella of one block appropriation for 'Public Institutions' authorized by the legislature. As long as the specific expenditures fell within the bulk vote, Sproule claimed, 'I do not pay particular attention to them.' Further weakening any prospect of his acting the genuine role of legislative watchdog were Sproule's added words: 'I think I should explain to the committee ... that it is the general custom for Ministers or Departments to say "We give these details to the House merely for information and not to be strictly adhered to".'[25]

In striking contrast to Sproule's cautious approach is that of James Clancy. But Clancy's leverage on the executive branch and on behalf of the legislature in his proclaimed role as watch-dog was not based on the audit function proper, but on the comptrol of expenditures which was essentially a responsibility of the executive and could only be exercised by the 'independent' auditor subject to the executive's override.

The continuing contradictions built into his office were brought home four years after Clancy's appointment when the Audit Act was amended in 1909. The government contended that the amendments were designed to strengthen the auditor, while the opposition argued that they were designed to rein in Clancy's growing proclivity to exercise his independent role of whistle-blower on behalf of the legislature.[26] On the government's side, it could be said that by authorizing the auditor to prepare a report separate from the public accounts, his independent hand had been strengthened. However, the opposition were also correct in pointing out that this separate report had to be submitted through the treasurer to the legislature, its form was dictated by Treasury Board, and its contents could merely draw the legislature's attention to those cases where the auditor, in the exercise of his comptrol functions of disputing or withholding expenditure claims, had been overruled by, or obliged to countersign warrants authorized by, the Treasury Board.

Throughout his period in office Clancy used his annual report as the platform from which to conduct an increasingly bitter guerrilla war against departments and Treasury Board. He could only deploy his one real weapon – the power to refuse to countersign expenditure claims. For Clancy, every battle was a matter of high principle. But he was often driven to using the most picayune cases, involving such earth-shaking issues as the payment to a part-time stenographer which he withheld on the ground that the government had no legal right to employ a 'part time worker.' As revealed by the centennial history of the Audit Office, citing this particular case amongst others as one of far too many battles fought by Clancy, such indiscriminate zeal made him so unpopular that it reputedly gave impetus to the early passage of the Superannuation Act of 1920 as a means of hastening the departure of this awkward gadfly.

Despite Clancy's energetic efforts to give his office a high public profile, the fundamental weakness of the provincial auditor acting in his independent role on behalf of the legislature remained unaltered. In his customary blunt style, Howard Ferguson stated the situation, as seen from the government's perspective, in the course of castigating the opposition for seeking independently to get information directly from the auditor before the Public Accounts Committee in 1915. Directing his remarks to Newton Rowell, the Liberal leader, Ferguson declaimed: 'When my honourable friend pretends to say that the Auditor is bound to prepare a statement for any member of the Legislature he is stating something that is entirely erroneous. The Auditor has no business to do anything of the sort. The Auditor is subject to the Treasury Board.'[27]

For the next thirty-five years Ferguson's bald assertion of executive dominance over the Audit Office remained uncontested or at least unexamined. In 1949, reflecting the renewed interest in standardizing governmental accounting procedures to which a Dominion-provincial committee of financial officers had been devoting their attention since

1946, the province's Public Accounts Committee returned to the subject of the role of the auditor, with particular reference to the compilation of the public accounts. Stimulated by the informed probing of J.G. Brown, a member who was a chartered accountant, the committee mounted a critique of the statutory provisions that effectively made the auditor a servant of the Treasury Board. Of particular concern was the wording of the act which could be and (as Ferguson's comments implied) was interpreted to this effect. Provincial Auditor Cotnam's assurance that he had never been overruled and that, despite the wording in the act, had never experienced executive interference did not satisfy the committee. Nor did Treasurer Frost's similar assurance from the executive's standpoint. Indeed, recalling the intimacy with which these two individuals worked in preparation of the budget, it would have been surprising if they would have acknowledged any differences between them, so cosy was the relationship. Despite these reassurances, Brown successfully persisted in calling for recommendations from the committee, many of which were incorporated in 1950 into the first really significant amendment to the Audit Act since its first passage in 1886.[28]

In order to respond to the Public Accounts Committee's concern about the dominance of the treasurer, the formula for tendering the public accounts to the legislature was amended. Since 1906 the auditor had been authorized to prepare and deliver the public accounts to the treasurer for tabling in the Assembly. This directive was rephrased to provide for direct delivery to the lieutenant-governor-in-council.

This modest reform failed to get at the real source of the problem that had plagued the system from the beginning and which was not to be fully resolved until 1972. The problem revolved around the simple question: whose accounts were they – the provincial treasurer's or the auditor's? The question arose because of the system of maintaining two separate sets of accounts to be used as a check against one another and therefore treated as the means by which mismanagement of public funds could be detected. When the two accounts failed to corroborate each other, the question remained whether the treasurer's or the auditor's accounts should be regarded as the 'official' public accounts. The formulation in the Audit Act of 1906 that the auditor was 'to prepare' (later amended to 'direct the preparation of') the public accounts would appear to have settled the issue in favour of the auditor, even though he had to tender the accounts through the Treasurer's Office. This legal provision remained unchanged until 1972, when an act creating a Ministry of Treasury, Economic and Intergovernmental Affairs provided that the public accounts for 1971–2 and for subsequent years were to be prepared under the direction of the treasurer and delivered to the lieutenant-governor-in-council for tabling in the Assembly.[29]

The lay observer may be forgiven for asking why it took so long to arrive at this logical solution. Surely, as long as the public accounts were of the auditor's making, when it came to auditing them on behalf of the legislature, he was in the compromising position of having, as it were, to audit himself. This contradiction was created as a result of his prior involvement as comptroller in countersigning the executive's financial transactions. To be sure, after 1909, the auditor was empowered to make a report of his own, separate from the public accounts, to go to the legislature. However, this could consist only of an assemblage of correspondence generated by his confrontations with the departments and overrulings by Treasury Board – and even these were in a form prescribed by Treasury Board. And, with auditors of a more co-operative attitude towards the executive than James Clancy's regime proved to be, the stage was set for a prolonged period in which the Audit Office much preferred to work things out with the departments behind the scenes. Walter Bagehot's formula for the exercise of monarchical powers – the right to advise, consult and warn – was much to be preferred to blowing the whistle publicly in the annual report to the legislature. Harvey Cotnam, reflecting on the pre-audit approach of the Audit Office in his day, perfectly expressed this philosophy: 'We always thought, on balance, we were accomplishing a lot ... in putting the place to rights without a lot of publicity that a [modern] audit report gets. The departments didn't want bad publicity and they were receptive to my suggestions and it made one think twice about changing the method of reporting.'[30]

The transfer of responsibility for preparing and presenting the public accounts to the Treasury in 1972 was the signal for the final elimination of the attachment of the Audit Office to the executive branch and the corresponding affirmation of the status of the auditor as, unequivocally, 'an officer of the Assembly.'[31] This decision was taken in the major revision of the Audit Act in 1977 – a little over one hundred years after the inauguration of the Office of Provincial Auditor. The formal trappings of independence conferred in the 1886 legislation were retained and further embellished by having the auditor report to the speaker of the legislature and subjecting his appointment power to the Assembly's Board of Internal Economy, although keeping his staff under the superannuation plan for the public service.

The matters on which the auditor could report were also greatly extended, going beyond those recommended in 1970 by the Committee on Government Productivity – that is, on the suitability of financial accounting systems, control of expenditures in conformity with legislative votes, and legality of transactions. Reflecting the recommendations of an influential committee created on the initiative of the federal auditor general, the auditor could now go beyond any comments regarding the exercise of 'due regard to economy or efficiency' to make observations on the use of systems to measure 'effectiveness of programs.' The auditor and his expert staff were directed to work with the Public Accounts Committee in developing its agenda, its procedure for considering the public accounts and generally to undertake any special referrals made by members of the committee. The contrast between the official perception of the status and functions of the auditor represented in the act of 1977 and those typified by the comments of Howard Ferguson some fifty years before suggests the nature of the sea change finally undergone by the Audit Office.

It has been the purpose of the last portion of this chapter to seek explanations as to why it took so long to achieve these changes and, most particularly, why the status of the auditor as *the* agent of the legislature dedicated to providing an external counterweight to the internal financial management practices of the executive was not fully endorsed until nearly a century after it was first adumbrated in the act of 1886. Perhaps because of the belated nature of this evolution in the face of vastly expanded expenditures which have revolutionized the internal administrative means for handling public moneys, the calls made upon the auditor by the legislature in the name of keeping the bureaucracy accountable may be placing burdens on 'their' expert which some might consider to be either excessive or inappropriate. That debate can be said to arise, as has this tangled story of the evolution of the independent auditor, out of the confrontation between executive and legislature which is an inevitable consequence of operating within a parliamentary system of fused powers.

Epilogue: Beyond the Formative Years

More than 125 years separate the primitive public service of the newly created Province of Ontario from its contemporary highly developed counterpart. This study has traced the first seventy-five years of an evolution which we have characterized as a gradual shift from an arm's-length to a hands-on approach to the administration of public affairs. The arm's-length approach featured a disposition on the part of government to take advantage of instruments already in place to provide the basic services then expected of governments. In the private sector these instruments – most notably in the case of the Department of Agriculture – were found amongst the associations and societies, many brought into existence well before confederation, that were to be engaged in providing to relevant user groups services of an educational and promotional nature. In the public sector there was the firmly entrenched system of municipal government inherited from pre-confederation Upper Canada to which the province could turn, for the provision of basic law and order services.

The practical consequences of emphasizing what we have here termed the facilitative administrative mode were that over the first three decades the initially minuscule group of public servants increased very slowly and the original constitutional provision for five Offices (combined with the early addition of Education) sufficed to meet all needs. The smallness and relative stability of this early public service might well be taken as evidence for the view that the laissez-faire philosophy purportedly flourishing in the Victorian Age was indeed alive and well in post-confederation Ontario. Certainly, in comparison with the overloaded agenda of today's governments, the early responsibilities assumed by government pale into an insignificance that is matched by the embryonic bureaucracy of the period. And yet, the arm's-length mode tended to conceal the extent of the government's early involvement. As an example, there is the striking statistic of one-fifth of the province's budget spent on the institutionalizing and care of lunatics, the social misfits and outcasts, the poor, dispossessed and disabled, which barely registered on the administrative landscape as a single inspector and a staff of two or three clerks.

More important, in the early 1880s, the initial reliance on municipal authorities to deal, for example, with public health and social problems arising out of growing industrialization and urbanization, began to give way to provincial initiatives and institutions capable of coping with matters that could no longer be confined to parochial boundaries. Even here, however, the impact on the public service was minimized by the creation of tiny satellite agencies, relying primarily on inspection, each of which performed herculean tasks with lilliputian resources. Indeed, the early public service was amazingly well served by the people attracted to its senior ranks, some of whom were dedicated amateurs but many of whom came from the then dominant professions of law, medicine, and engineering.

Within the restricted perimeter determining the late nineteenth-century view of the appropriate reach of the state, it is surprising how much was done by so few. Moreover, in a day-to-day administrative realm that relied so heavily on paper records as a means of meeting the substantive policy concern to provide information and inducements for its varied clienteles as well as for rendering account, the office equipment available for such tasks belonged to the era of the quill pen. Richard III might offer his kingdom for a horse, the nineteenth-century bureaucrat might similarly have cried out for a typewriter, even a fountain pen or, more ambitiously, a telephone or an automobile.

Nor can one overlook the importance of new office technologies and new means of communication and transportation in encouraging the assumption of new public services which could not otherwise have been contemplated. Of equal importance, in this context, was the impact which the introduction of certain of these facilities, such as the typewriter, had on the composition of the workforce. Unfortunately, the association of female workers with the machine reinforced their subordinate role in the civil service hierarchy. In this respect, however, the public sector employer differed not at all from employers in the private sector. Indeed, it is unlikely that private sector employers have done as well as the provincial government in opening up senior positions to women. As a result of practising what it has preached through Fair Employment Practices legislation, roughly one-half the government's appointments in the early 1990s to the ranks of deputy and assistant deputy minister positions are held by women.

With the Whitney government in 1905 we find ourselves on the launching stage for the second thirty-five-year period of civil service development. It was in this period that practically all of the main elements of a rationalized bureaucracy, considered by the influential sociologist Max Weber to be the criterion of modern statehood, emerged along with their attendant problems, differing from today's fully matured bureaucracy only in their more modest size and scope.

Growth of Departmental Building Blocks

Beginning with the expanding universe of public service organizations, we find that the consolidation and integration of functions into coherent departments which commenced in Whitney's time continued unabated into the post–Second World War period. Such developments consorted well with the Weberian concept of a rationalized bureaucracy. They were also consistent with the precepts of the scientific management movement of the early 1900s, which sought to determine the most efficient methods of classifying and combining units of work and fitting workers into prescribed positions corresponding to their training and abilities as ascertained by tests administered by a politically neutralized examining agency.

Thus, by the close of the 1920s the number of ministerial portfolios had doubled, while in the next decade there were only two additions, for a total of fourteen ministerial departments. This process of growth in the number of departments has continued unabated into present times, the departmental roster having once again doubled since the Second World War. What was different about the postwar additions was that many of the newcomers were not spin-offs from previously established entities but in many instances reflected governmental recognition of new policy arenas whose saliency on the public agenda was now to be marked by the award of departmental status. For example, in the two decades extending from the outbreak of war, six new departments were added, four of which (Planning and Development, Travel and Publicity, Economics, and Energy Resources) represented new initiatives; only Correctional Services and Transport could be said to have had antecedents, the former having been long incubated in the Office of Provincial Secretary and the latter being an enlarged version of the Department of Highways.

The characterization of the next decade as the restless sixties is singularly appropriate when applied to departmental building. The shuffling and shifting of names and functions of many departments that occurred in this period was a measure of the struggle to allocate work units rationally in a time of rapid growth and when many policy domains seemed to be so inextricably entwined as to defy neat or permanent compartmentation. When the dust settled at the end of the decade, the roster of departments had grown only by three – Revenue, University Affairs, and Consumer and Commercial Affairs. Of these, perhaps only University Affairs represented a fresh initiative. It evolved in response to the spate of new post-secondary educational institutions for which the government assumed either a direct involvement or a formula-based financial commitment. The Department of Revenue simply splintered from the Provincial Treasurer, and responsibilities assigned to Finance and Commercial Affairs in large measure merely absorbed the functions that had been accumulating over the years, particularly in the Offices of the Attorney General and of the Provincial Secretary.

The decade of the 1970s opened with a bold organizational experiment in response to recommendations of the Ontario Committee on Government Productivity. In line with its proposals, secretariats of a departmental rank and cabinet status were established to coordinate the now renamed ministries, grouped according to the broad policy categories of social development, resource development, and justice policy.[1] This organizational venture, whose impact on the morale and working habits of the public service still awaits a study by some astute participant-observer, was abandoned in the mid-1980s when the long Conservative regime was broken, although without dropping the ministry concept. While the original acceptance of the recommendations of the Government Productivity Committee produced new departments to lengthen the roster, there were accompanying consolidations achieved by the omnibus Government Re-Organization Act of 1971–2 that offset the additions.

The process of departmental formation since seems to have settled for a departmental roster of some twenty-six to twenty-eight ministerial departments, approximately double the number at the outbreak of the Second World War, which in turn represented a doubling of the departments with which the province began. Current interest in stabilizing the growth of cabinet portfolios may be promoting the use of a structural model which proved helpful in the earlier years. Then, a satellite entity loosely attached to a minister to administer a newly identified policy area was a favoured method. Legal 'departmental' recognition might be given but without a separate minister of its own. A modern equivalent has been used for skills development. The normal current organizational means of recognizing such new policy concerns as women's issues, francophone affairs, or Native affairs, is achieved by identifying a 'minister responsible for ...' and providing a modest administrative structure headed by a senior official of less than deputy minister rank.

Reinforcing the Top Command

The use of such expedients to stabilize the growth of ministerial departments is, of course, related to the practical problems that emerge from trying to operate a cabinet whose membership becomes unduly large. Even in the days when the number of departments to be represented in cabinet was such that the cabinet remained manageable, concern was invariably expressed each time a new department was added. Such concern, however, tended to focus on the added cost rather than the anticipated adverse impact on the operation of the cabinet. Guided by such economizing considerations, governments sought to placate critics by creating omnibus departments that housed several quite unrelated 'departments' under two or more deputy heads. Contemporary efforts to reduce the debt have revived interest in such departmental amalgamations as a means of cutting costs. One can only hope that such mergers in the name of economy do not produce some of the ill-assorted bedfellows with which the early Offices were able to contend only because the scale of operations was so small.

During the 1920s and 1930s the expedient of working with omnibus departments broke down under internal pressures created by growth of responsibilities in each sub-area. The new departments that were added consequently doubled the number of potential cabinet posts, and then doubled them again after the Second World War. The expedient then used to keep the cabinet to manageable proportions was, and continues to be, the assignment of more than one portfolio to a minister. Further refinements have led to the use of parliamentary secretaries and ministers without portfolio (but given a junior assignment), thereby creating an inner cabinet and a larger outer cabinet, much in the British tradition of distinguishing the cabinet from the (larger) ministry. Even with such means, and the customary addition of two or more ministers without portfolio, modern cabinets normally number no less than twenty members, creating echoes of Lloyd George's lamentation that one could not govern the country with a Sanhedrin.

One measure to ameliorate the practical problem created by an unwieldy cabinet is to use committees – an expedient which Ontario adopted in a most formal way in the early 1970s. The newly restructured ministries and policy secretariats emerging in response to the recommendations of the Committee on Government Productivity were used as the basis for organizing and chairing the cabinet committees. The composition of each committee reflected the grouping of ministries around the policy secretariats, while presiding over all was the Committee on Planning and Priorities, chaired by the premier.

The increasing burden of operating an over-sized cabinet and its committees has induced a corresponding growth in the staff deemed necessary to service their needs. In this respect, governments of today are building on Whitney's bequest of a central office designed to serve both the personal/political needs of the premier as well as the collective needs of the cabinet. Early recognition of the need to provide such administrative underpinnings for the centre may be accounted for by the pre-eminence of the premier vis-à-vis his colleagues, and the corresponding need to have the means to keep on top of all important administrative matters as well as maintain a grasp of the levers of political power required to perform the roles of party leader and head of government.

At the national level, where central staff organs developed much later, the initial structural response was to meet the collective needs of cabinet first rather than the personal needs of the prime minister. Thus, the Privy Council Office emerged as a power centre primarily as a result of the growing complexity of operating a cabinet and its committees during the Second World War. Only later was there recognition of the first minister's need for staff of his own, the delay undoubtedly resulting from the fact that for years, as his own secretary of state for external affairs, the prime minister had access to some of the wisest senior members of the Ottawa mandarinate. Today, however, the Office of the Prime Minister vies with the Privy Council Office although, at least in theory, the former serves the personal and political needs of the prime minister, while the latter serves the cabinet and its committees.[2]

In Ontario the effort to provide support for the premier has had to be redoubled under postwar pressures from the enormous growth of the bureaucracy and the doubling of the size of the cabinet. Nevertheless, the offices of premier and president of council continue to be combined, as in Whitney's time, rather than divided, as with the Dominion government. In Ottawa's case, separation into two distinct offices has provided no guarantee against interpenetration for, at this highest level where politics and administration meet, the prospect of politicizing the administration is constantly present. Perhaps for this reason, the Ontario practice of combining both functions in one office is simply a fatalistic acceptance of this fact of life. Even so, as one observes the contemporary trend to build up the personal-cum-party side of the premier's office, one might have concern for the premier's ability (even with a deputy premier in place) to cope with the everbroadening span of control.

It is fair to speculate that such growth on the personal/political staff side may be triggered by the growth of administrative infrastructure to support the enlarging needs of the cabinet and its committees. Even more certainly than in the federal case, the right of the premier to rearrange the office to conform with his/her style of leadership and vision of mandate remains unquestioned. However, the struggle to stay on top of both the political and administrative agenda that is reflected in the competitive elaboration of the central service arms dedicated to serving both the personal-cum-political needs of the premier and the collective needs of cabinet may overwhelm the capacity of even the most hardy premier to retain his status as first among equals.[3]

What applies to the premier with particular force finds similar endorsement in the growth of the personal offices of each minister. Up to the Second World War the minister's office was a simple affair, revolving around the minister's secretary. The elaboration of staff support in the minister's office of today is a measure of the expansion of the workload carried by cabinet ministers. However necessary, the development is viewed by some as creating a cadre of temporary political appointees who might block the lines of communication between the minister and his permanent career advisers.[4]

Proliferation of the ABCs

The signs of postwar growth of organizations were not confined to the doubling of the number of departments and the accompanying elaboration of Whitney's initial design for the Office of Premier and Executive Council along with the more elaborate staffing provisions for each minister's office. Beginning with the pioneering ventures of Ontario Hydro and the Municipal Board, increasing resort has been had to non-departmental forms for administering entrepreneurial, regulatory, and allocative functions of government. However, their variations in structural design, particularly those features which provided for special arm's-length relations with the conventional departments, did not begin to attract attention until the 1950s.

In calling attention to this phenomenon in 1957, the provincial auditor started up a hare whose pursuit has since occupied the attention of outside inquisitors and, increasingly, the attention of internal analysts. All this interest has been prompted by the legislature's intermittent but nonetheless pressing concern over an apparently uncontrolled proliferation of non-departmental entities. The government's response to the auditor's report was to set up an independent inquiry, chaired by Walter Gordon, head of a chartered accountancy firm which, like many others, had entered the new field of management consultancy.[5] The Gordon Committee identified eighty-four agencies and made a number of recommendations which were referred in 1960 to a special committee of the legislature on Administrative and Executive Problems, which was renewed during succeeding sessions as the standing Committee on Government Commissions. This oversight committee was vested with the responsibility for invigilating the creation and recommending the 'sun-setting' of the growing galaxy of what now came to be referred to as the ABCs (agencies, boards, and commissions).

This intermittent legislative attention was unsuccessful in stemming the flood. Two decades after the auditor had first drawn attention to the phenomenon, a comprehensive enumeration in 1978 listed nearly seven hundred ABCs. This list was drawn up by the Organization Policy Branch of Management Board in an attempt to classify and establish accountability regimes (based on the degree of arm's-length relationship) for each category. Whether this attempt on the part of the bureaucracy to get a grip on the growth of ABCs accounts for some diminution in their numbers is difficult to say, but in January 1992 the government advertised 'over 510 agencies, boards and commissions' for which citizens could volunteer their candidacy for appointment.[6]

Ontario has not been alone in contending with the growth of ABCs and the problems of their control and accountability. At the federal level, for example, the Lambert Royal Commission on Financial Management and Accountability featured the non-departmental agencies in its final report of 1979. In Australia, at both the state and commonwealth levels, precisely the same concerns were being addressed.[7] In effect, Ontario has participated in an organizational trend which has resulted in the creation of what may appropriately be considered a 'second public service' comprising a confusing mix of non-departmental entities. Vastly outnumbering the central core of departments, the staffing procedures, modes of financing, and lines of accountability of these agencies run the gamut from complete submission to the regimes under which conventional departments operate to virtually complete autonomy. As a practical consequence, making a head count of the public service is an exercise in semantics as one contends with variations in the legal definition of a 'civil servant,' a 'public servant,' or a 'crown employee.'

Of greater concern than the definitional problem are the questions posed for the maintenance of the traditional doctrines of ministerial responsibility and legislative supremacy. Moreover, because of the peculiar mix of administrative and determining powers conferred on many boards and tribunals, there is also concern for the possible diminution of the capacity of the judiciary and law courts to perform their traditional role of preserving rights and ensuring due process. Since many agencies have been vested with the discretion to determine or define 'the public interest,' there is all the more reason to provide assurance that they are accountable.

All of these issues emerged and were addressed in the creation of the several representatives of the ABCs whose successive appearances up to the Second World War have formed part of this history. Growth in their numbers has simply accentuated the need to pay close attention to the accountability issues raised by the conferral of arm's-length relationships on the early exemplars.

The spectacular growth of this second public service is attributable to several factors. The most obvious is the expansion in the use of both the operating corporate business undertakings and the regulatory, deciding tribunals that has accompanied the emergence of new departments to meet new needs. Thus, the corporate agency of which Ontario Hydro remains the outstanding representative has been used for a great variety of enterprises. The corporate board form has been applied to housing development, recreational and industrial parks, research institutes, municipal improvement, telephone development, health insurance, lotteries, educational broadcasting, and waste management.

A comparable expansion of regulatory and deciding tribunals has also occurred, beginning in 1944 with a Labour Relations Board. Agriculture has continued to expand its marketing boards, and financial affairs have come under the expanded regulatory powers of the Securities Commission initiated in Hepburn's day. A selective list of later accretions further demonstrates the extending range and reach of the provincial government: an Energy Board, Telephone Commission, Highway Transport Board, Human Rights Commission, Public Service Labour Relations Tribunal, Health Disciplines Board, and an Environmental Assessment Board.

Further contributions to the lengthening list of ABCs have been made as a result of the notions of participatory democracy that find their most up-to-date expression in the government's advertising for applicants for positions on the boards of these agencies. Most particularly, the extensive use of advisory bodies attached to both departments and many of the ABCs has swollen the second public service. The fact that many of these have been associated with the departments of Agriculture and Health might well be interpreted in the light of this study as a sign of a desire to restore something of that nineteenth-century reliance on the facilitative administrative mode. By this means, it will be recalled, the clients were given a major stake in the provision of relevant services – a stake that gradually disappeared as advancing bureaucratization took over.

This process – here referred to as an internalization of activities – has also contributed to the growth and bewildering variety of forms within the universe of ABCs. Simply put, it has led to the superimposing of one regulatory tribunal upon another. The trend is especially visible where agencies have been vested with discretion to determine rights or define that elusive goal of the public interest. In the case of the marketing boards, the perception that their bias in favour of their client groups might colour their view of the public interest led to the creation of a Food Council in 1962. It was intended to give consumers a voice to balance those of the producers, processors, and distributors. For good measure, the Farm Products Appeal Tribunal was added.

The experience of the Mothers' Allowance Commission and the Minimum Wage Board with discretionary allocative decision-making powers is equally instructive. When they were abolished and their responsibilities assigned to a branch within a department, an additional check was provided by means of a Social Assistance Review Board. However, again emphasizing the internalization of the process, the review board was also set up within the ministry. In somewhat similar fashion, the Workmen's Compensation Board, though remaining a separate agency, has established its own internal Workmen's Compensation Appeal Tribunal. Even the separation of the regulatory and operative functions relating to the liquor trade has not prevented the creation of a third appellate agency, the Commercial Registration Appeal Tribunal, to permit licensees and registrants to appeal decisions of the Liquor Licence Board.

The trend to superimpose regulator upon regulator finds perhaps its best expression in the regulation of Ontario Hydro's rate-setting powers, which Whitney had contemplated assigning to the ORMB in 1911 but then abandoned. The creation of the Ontario Energy Board in 1960 did not immediately affect Hydro, for the board's mandate applied at first only to natural gas. However, in 1973 Hydro was brought under the board's jurisdiction, creating the novel but by no means unique situation where one agent of government regulates another, each with its own policy mandates that need not necessarily coincide.

A complex pattern has now emerged as a result of the introduction of tribunals to review the decisions of other regulatory agencies, or the discretionary determinations of civil servants within a department, or even the decisions taken by an operative corporation such as Ontario Hydro. In this context, the growth in numbers and variety of ABCs might be justified as the outcome of the necessary effort to ensure that offhand administrative justice does not become too casual. However, with increasing complexity, the process tends to draw closer to the potentially more expensive and time-consuming proceedings of the regular courts – the very disadvantages of the conventional judicial system which led to the resort to administrative tribunals in the first place. In any case, the insertion of the privative clause in the enactments for many of these tribunals has not wholly barred the courts from reviewing the reviewers. Thus, in the last analysis, viewing this complex arena of non-departmental agencies and raising the question, 'Who controls the controllers?', one must fall back on the old doggerel

> Big fleas have smaller fleas
> Upon their backs to bite 'em.
> And smaller fleas have lesser fleas
> And so ad infinitum.

The Lengthening of the Hierarchy

Postwar developments that have resulted in growth in the number of departments and the enormous expansion of non-departmental forms have been the sources of a less obvious growth to be found within the several departments. As they responded to the steady but modestly increasing demands placed upon them, the prewar departments managed to retain a structural simplicity by creating dual or even multiple deputy headships for each discrete unit admitted to their respective bailiwicks. There was often little logic in the assemblage of work units thus achieved, but at least the practice appeared to preserve for the respective deputy heads a manageable 'span of control.' There was little evidence of the use of a second tier of officers – the now ubiquitous assistant deputy minister (ADM) – to lighten the burden of coordination and control imposed on the deputy minister. The Department of Agriculture was the first to experiment, though briefly, with the position of ADM. For a longer period the Department of Education also sought to accommodate growth by dividing the responsibilities at the top between a deputy minister concerned with administration and a supervisor of education concerned with policy. This practice was abandoned in the mid-1930s and shortly after the ADM position began to emerge as part of the standard model. Indeed, as each department, both old and new, continued to grow, the internal hierarchy was lengthened even more by the insertion under the ADM level of intermediate tiers of directors, managers, and the like.

Interestingly, one of the contemporary placebos offered by management consultancy experts, as they appraise the resulting complexity of departmental hierarchies, is that of de-layering – in other words, reducing the distance between top management and the frontline official. In that way, it is intended to achieve economies (cutting out the fat in middle management) and to speed up delivery of services and improve access of the public to the decision makers. Paradoxically, the current efforts to economize by cutting down on the number of departments will frustrate the parallel effort to shorten the hierarchical chain. The amalgamation of departments will create bloated versions of the omnibus Offices of old and inevitably the number of 'layers' in the chain of command will multiply. Thus, a reduction in cabinet size simply pushes the problem of an excessive span of control down into the departments, each of which, to solve *its* own span of control problem, will proceed to add new tiers of so-called responsibility centres.

Functional Specialization: Growth of Services for Government

Even de-layering cannot counter the most important source of growth within departments nor, indeed, check the growth in the number of departments as well. The operative phenomenon, virtually non-existent in the period studied here, is the extraordinary postwar increase in staff required to support the enlarged and more specialized activities of the operators within each line department – housekeeping services such as financial, accounting, personnel, communications, accommodation, and the like. Epitomizing the vicious circle syndrome, the introduction of such services into the organization in the name of functional specialization generates an even greater structural complexity that, in turn, calls for more specialist auxiliary services.

This seemingly endless demand for auxiliary and staff services to cope with the 'care and feeding' of the line operators is presumably justified by the greater efficiency and effectiveness to be anticipated from line operators thus freed to focus on the tasks for which their departments were created in the first instance. Whether this claim is justified need not be debated here: the point to be emphasized is the tremendous growth in numbers and the increase in demand for functional specialists as a result of meeting purely housekeeping requirements.

In the evolution of any bureaucracy, as the need is recognized for creating specialized common service units to support line activities, the question arises whether such functions should be provided centrally or whether each department should fend for itself. In general terms and judging from Ontario's experience with its one major common service agency, the Department of Public Works, the response would appear to have favoured centralization as a means of achieving economies of scale. The initial responsibility imposed on Public Works to look after the accommodation needs of the other departments has today been

tremendously expanded, not only by having to cope with the real property services but by the accretion of common services related to the
sophisticated communication and computer technologies of the modern
office. This accumulation of the most important housekeeping responsibilities was acknowledged in 1972 when Public Works was retitled the
Ministry of Government Services.

The growth of one department whose sole raison d'être is to service
the needs of government rather than the public may be taken as simply
an expansion of a traditional task. Unfortunately the growth of the
central agency has in no way inhibited the growth within individual
departments of similar units. Indeed, it can be claimed that the very
presence of a powerful central common service agency encourages,
perhaps even requires, each department to create miniature mirror
images of the several service arms found in the central agency. The
larger user departments may argue that they know their own needs best.
Even the most power-hungry central agency must accept a point when
it is overwhelmed by any attempt to preserve a hands-on approach
towards any but the smallest departments. For the most part, a central
service agency must content itself with establishing and monitoring the
guidelines for the provision of services by departmental units in order
to ensure uniformity and probity of practice. One can perhaps be forgiven for raising the sceptical thought that the common service providers now deemed requisite threaten to outnumber the line personnel
involved in the direct fulfilment of departmental mandates. In any event,
it is clear that growth of the contemporary public service in response to
citizens' demands also begets growth of auxiliary services whose only
claim to legitimacy is to serve the needs of government rather than the
public.

While the Ministry of Government Services and its multitudinous
departmental counterparts are the heirs to the responsibilities of the
former Department of Public Works, for the two most important common services – the provision and management of personnel and of
money – separate administrative arrangements had to be made. Growth
in the numbers of public servants and increasing demand for special
skills was accompanied by greatly expanded governmental budgets – in
both instances creating the need for functionally specialized agencies.
Because people and money constitute the heart of governmental operations, centralized administration of both has been invoked as a means
of ensuring probity, equity, and uniformity in a progressively more
complex and far-flung establishment. The fact that the staffing and
financing of the public service were historically entangled with partisan
political considerations, having little to do with economy or efficiency

and much to do with patronage and graft, also gave saliency to the need for central control and coordination.

The Central Personnel Agency as a Dying Breed

The chapters describing the path to administrative reform indicated that, until after the First World War, providing competent personnel for the public service was very much left to the hazards of party politics. At the senior levels of the early public service, leaving selection essentially to the personal discretion of ministers and cabinet produced what, under the circumstances, was a reputable cadre of officials. The growth of departments and the demand for employees with skills extending beyond the routine handling of paper and records induced a reluctant government to pay heed to the administrative reformers of the day. The upshot was the introduction of a civil service commissioner who established the principles of the merit system which have continued to guide the management of personnel to the present.

However, the attempt to provide at one and the same time a guardian of the merit system as well as a central agency responsible for staffing departments was never fully accomplished. In this respect, Ontario's experience has proven similar to that in other jurisdictions, including that of the federal government. In the latter case, the aspirations of the reformers resulted in the creation of a central agency endowed with more powers than it could properly sustain, with the result that over time it had to devolve many of its responsibilities for personnel administration to departments. Such devolution became even more necessary as the tasks to be assumed under this rubric came to embrace such positive functions as searching for talent, training and development, the maintenance of classification and pay plans, in addition to the original guardian role of 'keeping the rascals out.' Paradoxically, the growth of specialized personnel services makes an even greater call upon the centre to provide standards and guidelines as a defence against departmental initiatives that would destroy the concept of a unified public service.

Although Ontario approached administrative reform with a less centralist bias than the Canadian government, the outcome has been much the same as each faced the same conundrum of trying to preserve a unified civil service in the face of growth in size, complexity, and functional diversification that cry out for decentralization. Curiously, the main ground for the original creation of a central personnel agency, described here as its role of guardian of the merit system, seems to have eroded. The result is that it survives now largely as a legal repository of powers so strenuously fought for since the days of Dr McCutcheon but now delegated to other hands.

In part, this development may be attributed to the emergence of unionized staff and the recognition of their right to bargain collectively. The initial involvement of organized staff in personnel decisions affecting their careers was confined to representation on the original superannuation board. Even in the early post-Second World War period, staff input was of an advisory or consultative nature through a joint council plan modelled on the Whitley Council scheme adopted by the British civil service after the First World War. The advent of collective bargaining in the late 1960s, coupled with a separate Labour Relations Board for public service employees, effectively reduced the historic reliance on the Civil Service Commission to protect the rights of public servants. Theoretically, the commission retains its traditional role of guardian of the merit system which, broadly interpreted, has the effect of imposing limits on the matters which can be dealt with by means of collective negotiating procedures.

Possibly of even more importance than the emergence of collective bargaining to the decline of authority and influence of the central personnel agency has been the recent rise of powerful central agencies to determine, coordinate, and control the government's expenditure budget. What appears to have occurred is that as the tasks associated with the management of the public service evolved in response to growth and increasing functional specialization, the role of an independent central personnel agency has come to be marginalized. Rather, the government as employer has come to be associated with the later arrivals, the central agencies concerned with the expenditure budget.

During the decade of the 1960s an attempt was made to combine the semi-judicial role of guardian of the merit principle with the personnel managerial role in a Department of the Civil Service whose permanent head also served as chairman of the Civil Service Commission. In the major organizational reforms prompted in the early 1970s by the Committee on Government Productivity, the Department of the Civil Service was abandoned, its purely managerial tasks assigned to the new Management Board of Cabinet and an apparent effort made to reaffirm the 'independent' status of the Civil Service Commission by adding outside appointees to its membership. Subsequent developments suggest, however, that the independence of the commission is no longer regarded, even by the staff, as a necessary condition for protection of the merit system and permanent career service. Rather like the proverbial Kilkenny cat, the commission has faded into obscurity and whatever façade of independence was once provided by having external members has been abandoned in favour of a membership drawn entirely from the civil service.

Curiously, the transformation has occurred without altering the statutory base upon which the commission's authority has always relied. It is rather as if the commission, while retaining its outer form, is now required to play host to predators feeding off the statutory powers still residing with it; thus, by delegation, both departmental managers as well as the Human Resources Secretariat of Management Board have pretty well sucked the commission dry of its former managerial responsibilities.[8] Those of its responsibilities once thought to require the attention of an independent quasi-judicial body would now appear to have acquired their own protectors in the shape of employees' unions, appeals tribunals, and grievance procedures linked to agreements achieved through recognition of collective bargaining rights which are far in advance of the paternalistic attitudes of earlier days. Such developments have been very much a part of the administrative history of the contemporary period falling outside the immediate range of this study. Their brief elaboration here is sufficient to indicate how the various elements of the administrative reformers' agenda have been set aside or integrated into the central management concerns of a public service now some ten times the size of its prewar predecessor.

The Ascendancy of Central Financial Management Agencies

The preoccupation of the administrative reformers with developing a permanent career service based on merit tended to concentrate efforts on improving the management of people almost to the exclusion of concern for the productive husbanding of finances. Even the early creation of a Treasury Board as a committee of the Executive Council to deal with governmental financial matters had little impact on the coordination, let alone the control, of the expenditure plans (budget and estimates) and subsequent expenditure practices (the accounts) of departments. Equally immune to control from the centre were the pervasive decentralized procedures for collecting and accounting for governmental revenues. As a result of this tardiness, when the agents of central financial management were at last put in place beginning about the mid-1950s, they had to catch up with the agencies and procedures previously elaborated in the personnel field.

In the process of catching up, it soon became apparent that in addition to the strictly financial management issues, as the Financial Administration Act of 1954 put it, the resuscitated Treasury Board was to concern itself, with 'any matter concerning general administrative policy in the public service' and to make regulations 'for any purpose necessary for the efficient administration of the public service.' Fourteen years later, in 1968, additional powers to establish the terms of employment for crown employees and determine the organization and staff establishments of the departments were harbingers of the new philosophy that control over money subsumed control over personnel. From that point on, the historic functions of the Civil Service Commission came to be embraced by the financial power centre.

The role of that power centre was confirmed in 1971 with the statutory redefinition of the Treasury Board as the Management Board of Cabinet and with a separate minister in charge, vested with authority over both money and people. Twenty years later, reflecting once more the tendency of ongoing functional specialization to beget new organizations, the Treasury Board was re-established. Once again it was associated with the Treasurer's Office but mandated to deal only with the strictly financial management issues which were transferred from the Management Board of Cabinet. The latter agency thus remains the other statutory cabinet committee, under its own minister and retaining the responsibility for approving organization and staff establishment. It is also generally responsible for 'the efficient and effective operation of the public service,' including collective negotiations with employees, representing the government as employer.

This last structural change, it could be said, completes the process of marginalizing the Civil Service Commission. It is an open question whether the power of unionized civil servants and the introduction of their own labour relations board, together with other review procedures such as for classification issues, now provide the counterweight to the centralized and all-powerful executive as employer. What can be said is that all these developments confirm the trend towards the internalization or bureaucratization of all matters connected with the management of the public service. This leaves little room for independent input from outsiders, in particular the elected representatives of the people.

External Accountability

The otherwise gloomy message conveyed by the foregoing prognosis must, of course, be countered by the developments traced earlier as they affect the audit. Admittedly, acceptance of the concept of a genuine post-audit conducted by an independent officer who was clearly designated as a servant of the legislature came belatedly. Nevertheless, the critical importance of this development for the retention of the legislature's capacity to monitor the actions of the executive cannot be over-estimated.

During the long period before the provincial auditor had acquired the thorough-going recognition of his proper status conferred by legislation in 1977, the legislature was not deprived entirely of the capacity to call in question the alleged malpractices of the executive. The traditional right of the Assembly to air grievances before voting supply was used often and effectively. This was especially true before there was any report from the auditor, even of the somewhat nit-picking kind to which James Clancy, the second auditor, was inclined to resort after 1909.

Despite the initial contention of Premier Sandfield Macdonald that a Public Accounts Committee was useless, such a committee was quickly set up and despite dismissive comments about its efficacy made as late as the 1960s, a detailed examination of its reports suggests a much less negative view of its work.[9] Certainly for the administrative historian they comprise one of the most valuable sources of insight into the early workings of the bureaucracy.

That being said, it is also true that the quality of its performance was extremely uneven and, as ever with such committee proceedings, was determined largely by the willingness and ability of opposition spokes-men to exert themselves. Lacking the expertise and guidance of a truly independent auditor, the positive impact of the Public Accounts Com-mittee depended upon individual members. The great transformation that occurred in 1977 effectively provided the independent expertise the committee had long required to enable it to serve the monitoring role so much demanded by the increased volume and complexity of executive transactions. Indeed, as we observe the matters upon which the auditor is authorized to report and thereby bring to the attention of the legisla-ture, concerns are now being expressed that the authority to conduct value for money audits may be jeopardizing the hard-won independence of the auditor by inducing him to trespass on the policy preserves of the executive. If such were to be the case, then we would have come full circle back to the original close association of the audit with the execu-tive branch. Be that as it may, to find in the 1992 auditor's report critical commentary, for example, on the inadequacy of preventive maintenance on the highways of the province, or on the probable risks to the public's safety through insufficient inspection of elevators, or on the way the public trustee handles estates and trusts, suggests that we have come a long way from the feeble strictures on the executive which Charles Sproule dared to venture as first provincial auditor.

Nor have the legislature's efforts to come to grips with the problem of monitoring the complex bureaucratic machine of the present relied only on the reform of the audit function. It is probably not by chance that just two years before the Audit Office was finally given its full regalia of independence another statute was approved in 1975 creating a second 'officer of the legislature,' the provincial ombudsman. Even greater pains were taken to establish the independent status of this office, whose role was to investigate complaints against the administrative decisions and acts of officials of the government of Ontario and its agencies – a procedure in use for at least a century in Scandinavian countries.[10]

The creation of the ombudsman has not exhausted the contemporary repertoire of the legislature's means of seeking to maintain an accountable public service. Throughout the 1960s, in the aftermath of the Gordon Committee Report on the Organization of Government, the structure of standing committees of the legislature was modified so as to provide a more consistent and regular review of the operations of the administrative agencies assigned to each committee. In 1969 the rules of the House were amended to make it possible to refer the estimates for various departments and agencies to the appropriate standing committee, followed in 1971 by the creation of a standing committee on Estimates.[11] Thus, the Estimates Committee now operates alongside the Public Accounts Committee, the latter exercising an ex post facto control, the former conducting the examination of the executive's projected expenditures in a more workmanlike atmosphere than was hitherto possible when estimates were examined only in Committee of the Whole House on supply.

The series of measures taken to supplement the work of the Office of Provincial Auditor are as belated as the steps we have traced in fuller detail to transform the auditor into a genuine counterweight to the overpowering growth in budgets and bureaucracies. The expanded reach of the administrative arm of government, reflected in the multiplication of ABCs, has exacerbated the problems of accountability and control. Their operations raise concerns about the status and capacity of the courts to intervene in the name of preserving 'natural justice.' The discretion accorded many of them to define the public interest for specific clientele groups places even greater burdens on the fragile instruments available to legislators. Of course, the ability of legislatures and courts to perform their proper role of 'keeping civil servants civil' – that is to say, accountable – depends only in part on the institutional arrangements now set in place. In the final analysis, the outcome will depend on the determination, vigilance, and respect for human values possessed by the legislators and the public servants called upon by the electorate to operate within the parliamentary cabinet system inherited by Ontario in 1867.

Notes

Prologue

1 The pages of the *Globe* were used to re-create the picture of the opening-day celebrations and for subsequent developments.

2 For this peculiar illustration of the method of solving the problems of dualism in the pre-confederation Province of Canada, following the riots and fire that led to the abandonment of Montreal in 1848, see J.E. Hodgetts, *Pioneer Public Service: An Administrative History of the United Canadas, 1841–1867* (Toronto: University of Toronto Press 1956), chapter 5, especially 58–62.

3 See Ontario, *Journals of the Legislative Assembly, 1867–68*, where the dates for the Proclamation of Writs reveal the sequence of postponements. The problem was exacerbated by the contemporary mode of stretching out the balloting, the dates for making returns extending from 21 August to 23 September. The Assembly convened on 27 December to elect its Speaker, and the following day heard the speech from the throne.

4 See *Globe*, 27 December 1867, for a full account of the grand opening which, the paper admitted, few could get to see, even though 'properly enough' Toronto's mayor had proclaimed a suspension of business during the afternoon. There was in any case only one gallery.

5 See Frank Yeigh, *Ontario's Parliament Buildings or A Century of Legislation, 1792–1892. A Historical Sketch* (Toronto: The Williamson Book Company, Ltd. 1893), chapter 5, for a detailed account of these and earlier buildings devoted to official governmental business. See also C. Pelham Mulvany, *Toronto Past and Present* (Toronto: W.E. Caiger 1884), 40: 'As long ago as Mrs. Jamieson's time these buildings were considered a mark of the bad taste of Little York. Age has not lent them any dignity.' Eric Arthur's *From Front Street to Queen's Park: The Story of Ontario's Parliament Buildings* (Toronto: McClelland and Stewart 1979) has plans of the old buildings showing where the different departmental offices were located, as well as the library wing and the Legislative Assembly

accommodation. Arthur's reproduction of a report on the state of the buildings in 1880 by Public Works' chief architect, Kivas Tully, reveals interesting details of the cost of maintenance as well as warnings of the fire hazards which in turn set off the call for new buildings in an enactment of 1880 that, after many vicissitudes, culminated in the new Queen's Park Buildings in 1892.

6 See Hodgetts, *Pioneer Public Service*, 55–8 for this expression of administrative dualism in the Province of Canada.

7 See Mulvany, *Toronto Past and Present*, 47.

8 The *Globe* maintained a close watch on these activities, frequently complaining about the delay at the Ottawa end: see issues 2 and 5 August 1867, reporting the imminent sending off of the papers of the Crown Lands Department, the beginning of the staff departures from Ottawa (29 August), and the report of the staff ensconced with Commissioner Richards at his desk (24 September).

9 On the pre-confederation arrangements, see Hodgetts, *Pioneer Public Service*, 39–40, 57. For instance, from a reading of Ryerson's first report after separate provincial status had been granted it would be impossible to detect that there had been any change in status or administrative arrangements. The *Globe* did take note, however, in its issue of 16 October 1867, of Ryerson's arrival in Ottawa to tender his final report under the old regime and that his next report would be made to the Government of Ontario.

10 Thomas Mulvey in his chapter on 'The Provincial Executive Organization' contributed to volume 17 of *Canada and Its Provinces*, edited by Adam Shortt and Arthur G. Doughty (Toronto 1914), estimated that one-eighth of the province's total annual expenditures was for the care of the insane (204).

11 There are several revealing, detailed listings of the staff at headquarters to be found in the *Sessional Papers*, to which attention will later be drawn. However, one must scan the province's *Public Accounts*, looking well beyond the 'Civil Government' heading in order to turn up the not inconsequential numbers in the field, many of whom would be temporary or seasonal employees.

CHAPTER 1: *To Know Thyself: Early Ontario's Administrative Needs*

1 Canada, *Statutes*, 31 Vic., c. 38 (1868) and Ontario, *Statutes*, 31 Vic., c.6 (1868). Inquiries were to be launched whenever the executive deemed such to be in the interest of 'good government of the Province,' or the conduct of any part of the public business, or the administration of justice. Interestingly, the first royal commission to be established under the Dominion enactment was to inquire into the state of the civil service. One wishes that the province had shown a similar interest – for one has to wait for over a century before a comparable grand inquest was commissioned by the executive.

2 An early summation of such research is provided in Joseph Schull's excellent overview of the state of affairs from confederation onwards in *Ontario since*

1867 (Toronto: McClelland and Stewart 1978), especially chapters 1–6. See also Ian M. Drummond's *Progress without Planning: The Economic History of Ontario from Confederation to the Second World War* (Toronto: University of Toronto Press 1987), especially Part I. A sensitive re-creation of this early period that stresses the interplay between the individual, society and the state is G.P. deT. Glazebrook, *Life in Ontario: A Social History* (Toronto: University of Toronto Press 1968).

3 See Morris Zaslow, 'The Ontario Boundary Question,' in Ontario Historical Society, *Profiles of a Province* (Toronto 1967), 107ff.

4 The annual reports of the Bureau of Industries, created in 1882, are invaluable sources of statistics covering much more than the strictly agricultural production figures whose collection was the main assignment of the bureau. Although Archibald Blue, the director of the bureau, frankly admitted the problems of collection which cast doubts on the accuracy of the figures provided, his second annual report for 1883 (*Sessional Papers*, No. 55, 1884) boldly attempts to produce an interesting series of 'Miscellaneous Statistics' reaching back sixty years!

5 Glazebrook, *Life in Ontario,* chapter 5, is especially informative on the province's use of municipal officials to provide the basic law and order services. A broader meaning was attached to the police function in pre-confederation times (98ff) which, following the Baldwin Act of 1849, tended to shift from justices of the peace to elected municipal authorities.

6 The *Journals of the Legislative Assembly* register these opposition concerns, as for example in the administration of liquor licensing laws or to inveigh against the 'centralizing' policy of the government (*Journals*, 1882–3: 98–9, 105; or to demand the restoration of local authorities' power to appoint certain officials, such as registrars of deeds (*Journals*, 1892: 160–1, and *Journals*, 1894: 63).

7 See '1st Annual Report of the Bureau of Industries for 1882,' Ontario, *Sessional Papers*, No. 3, 1883, that contains population returns for 1871 and 1882 (table 21), which appear to have been derived from the decennial Dominion census.

8 A useful quick sketch of the shifting responsibilities for road construction is to be found in a publication of the Department of Provincial Treasurer, *A Conspectus of the Province of Ontario, 1947*, under the heading 'Transportation.' I am particularly indebted to the thorough analysis provided by David Siegel in his doctoral dissertation, 'Provincial-Municipal Relations in Ontario: A Case Study of Roads,' chapters 1 and 2 (University of Toronto 1983).

9 For the pre-confederation roots of this program, see J.E. Hodgetts, *Pioneer Public Service: An Administrative History of the United Canadas, 1841–1867* (Toronto: University of Toronto Press 1956), 120–1, 262–8.

10 A typical instance of the relaxed attitude towards such patronage opportunities is to be found in the 'Report of the Public Accounts Committee for 1882,' *Journals of the Legislative Assembly*, 1882, Appendix 2. Henry Smith (superintendent of

colonization roads) testified 'there was about $6000. voted to that section last year; from the accounts I know that the stores were purchased from Mr. Murray's establishment [the MLA for the area]. I dare say most of them were; I did not know it was a breach of the Independence of Parliament Act for a member to supply goods to the Department; I think the Commissioner [of Crown Lands] knew what was being done.'

11 See Ontario, *Sessional Papers*, No. 43, 1894, for the build-up of the construction responsibilities of Public Works. From the point in 1880 when a move was made to replace the old Government Buildings on Front Street, not a session of the Assembly passed without some contentious debate over cost, choice of architect, or successive supplementaries to cover escalating costs.

12 The retrospective 'Report of the Director of Colonization, 1900,' ibid., No. 29, 1901, has been relied on here and for the next several paragraphs.

13 The second annual report of the Bureau of Industries (1883) lists the population by religion and also shows the number of churches assigned to each denomination. For a later period, Richard Allen in his *The Social Passion: Religion and Social Reform in Canada, 1914–28* (Toronto: University of Toronto Press 1971) provides detailed evidence of the impact of the social gospel movement on public policy. Chapter 1 is especially pertinent here.

14 The statistics in the text are from the second annual report of the Bureau of Industries. On educational developments generally, see Robert M. Stamp, *The Schools of Ontario, 1876–1976* (Toronto: University of Toronto Press 1982).

15 Data from second annual report of the Bureau of Industries.

16 Ontario Agricultural Commission, 'Report of the Commissioners,' *Sessional Papers*, No. 42, 1881: 9. Appendices A to S reproduce the information collected by the various subcommittees ranging from soil and climate, the progress of husbandry, grain, stock, dairying, fruit-growing, bee-keeping, to the proposed functions of a reformed Bureau of Agriculture.

17 For the pre-confederation antecedents of the organized agricultural interests and the means by which government made use of their resources, see Hodgetts, *Pioneer Public Service*, chapter 14.

18 See, for example, Ontario, *Sessional Papers*, No. 43, 1894, 'Return re all persons who, during the years 1871, 1873 and 1892 held office under the Crown and etc ...,' under heading 'Agriculture. Scope of Work.'

19 See 'Report of the Select Committee on Public Health,' in Ontario *Journals of the Legislative Assembly,* 1878, Appendix 2. The quotations and statistics in the text are drawn from this source. A doctoral dissertation for the University of Toronto by Mary Powell tracing the development of public health administration in Ontario has a detailed account of the role played by the medical profession and its early organization in pressing the government to create the Board of Health.

20 A classic administrative history is that of Richard S. Lambert with Paul Pross, *Renewing Nature's Wealth: A Centennial History of the Public Management of*

Lands, Forests and Wildlife in Ontario, 1763–1967 (Ontario. Department of Lands and Forests: Hunter Rose Company 1967).

21 The internal tension between lands (settlers) and forests (lumbermen), as well as the structural dualism of the pre-confederation department are developed in Hodgetts, *Pioneer Public Service*, 128–43 and 56 (structural dualism).

22 A valuable record of the 'Receipts and Expenditures by the Treasurer of Ontario from 1 July 1867 to 31 December 1889' is to be found in *Sessional Papers*, No. 83, 1890. The Dominion subsidy of approximately $1.2 million remained steady throughout this peiod but was equalled or exceeded by revenues from crown lands in 1872, 1873, 1882, and 1887–9. The auctioning off of timber leases accounted for the bulk of this revenue but also for its great variability. See Joseph Schull's brief review of the early policy in *Ontario since 1867*, 58–9.

23 Further reference will be made to these informative inquiries but they may be usefully mentioned here: 'Report of the Royal Commission on the Mineral Resources of Ontario and Means for their Development,' *Sessional Papers*, No. 67, 1889; Ontario Game and Fish Commission, 'Commissioners' Report,' *Sessional Papers*, No. 79, 1892; Royal Commission on Forestry in Ontario, 'Preliminary Report,' *Sessional Papers*, No. 45, 1897–8.

CHAPTER 2: *Early Administrative Modes*

1 This figure of four hundred contrasts markedly with the fifty employees at headquarters referred to in the Prologue.

2 The over-arching coordinating body was the Council of Agriculture and Arts Associations, a statutory continuation of the pre-confederation Board of Agriculture (31 Vic, c.29, 1868). This body disappeared with the formal creation of the Department of Agriculture in 1888. Although the grants to individual associations varied between $500 and $700, there were so many recipients that the total allocation by 1880 was in excess of $100,000 (compared with administrative expense represented by Buckland's salary of $800).

3 See 'Return of all persons etc ...,' *Sessional Papers*, No. 43, 1894, under the heading 'Agriculture. Scope of Work.'

4 Some of the reports reproduced as government documents were veritable illustrated textbooks, like that of the Entomological Society (chartered in 1870) which comprises a major segment of 'Annual Report of the Commissioner of Agriculture and Arts, 1879,' *Sessional Papers*, No. 3, 1880.

5 For Mowat's approach to municipal restructuring, see C.R.W. Biggar, *Sir Oliver Mowat*, 2 vols. (Toronto: Warwick Bros and Rutter 1905), I: 185ff. A succinct account of Mowat's handling of the Municipal Loan Fund is in Schull, *Ontario since 1867*, 67–8. For the broader political implications of Mowat's dealings with the municipalities, see S.J.R. Noel, *Patrons, Clients, Brokers: Ontario Society and Politics, 1791–1896* (Toronto: University of Toronto Press 1990), 243–8.

6 See 'Receipts and Expenditures by Treasurer of Ontario from 1 July to 31 December, 1889,' *Sessional Papers*, No. 83, 1890. Over this twenty or so years Dominion subsidies totalled $25.5 million, crown land revenues $18.5 million. Licences totalled $2.5 million, though they climbed spectacularly from roughly $59,000 in 1868 to over $300,000 in 1889. Law stamp revenues came to about $1.5 million all told.

7 Richard S. Lambert with Paul Pross, *Renewing Nature's Wealth: A Centennial History of the Public Management of Lands, Forests and Wildlife in Ontario, 1763–1964* (Ontario, Department of Lands and Forests: Hunter Rose Company 1967), where the act of 1849 which governed the trade in timber until the end of the century provided for 'wholesome regulations' for granting licences and assessing dues, 'the Act [being] designed both to meet the needs of the industry and to allow government to derive a reasonable revenue' (128ff).

8 The process started with the Liquor Licence Act of 1874 (37 Vic., c.32), while the regulatory mode that was to prevail until 1916 was instituted in 1876 and 1877 (39 Vic., c.26 and 40 Vic., c.18). The legislation authorized the Lieutenant-Governor-in-Council to appoint three 'fit and proper persons' to each local board of licence commissioners as well as inspectors of licences for each city, county, and electoral district, the inspectors to operate under the direction of their respective local boards.

9 See 'Volume of Business Done from 1868 to 1877,' in *Sessional Papers*, No. 71, 1879, under heading 'Provincial Secretary and Registrar-Licence Branch' and 'Treasury Department,' statement of business done in the Criminal Justice Branch.

10 See B.L. Hutchins and A. Harrison, *A History of Factory Legislation*, 3rd ed. (London 1927), where they observe (p. 40) that the factory inspectorate represented the first time a special department of the central government had been set up to administer a single act. K.B. Smellie, *A Hundred Years of English Government* (London: Duckworth 1937), speaking of the 'machinery of administration' in the 1832–70 period, noted (p. 89), 'The industrial revolution compelled the State to create a machinery of administration almost as complex as the new machinery of industry itself.'

11 For a brief but telling contemporary commentary on the myth of the sturdy, self-reliant pioneer, see Alexander Galt's budget message for 1857, quoted in J.E. Hodgetts, *Pioneer Public Service* (Toronto: University of Toronto Press 1956), 269–70, where, after a lengthy recital of the many and varied expenditures that have swollen his budget, he concludes, 'all of which in more populous and wealthy countries are efficiently provided by individual enterprise and private benevolence.'

12 See 'Report, Inspector of Insurance,' *Sessional Papers*, No. 21, 1880, and compare with expanded duties listed in his report in ibid., No. 13, 1894. For a review of Dominion-provincial relations in this arena, see J.A. Corry, *Difficulties*

of Divided Jurisdiction, Appendix 7, Studies Prepared for the Royal Commission
on Dominion-Provincial Relations (Ottawa: King's Printer 1939), chapter 3.

13 See Smith's testimony in 'Report of the Public Accounts Committee,' Appendix
1, *Journals of the Legislative Assembly,* 1879: 54ff.

14 Richard B. Splane, *Social Welfare in Ontario, 1792–1893: A Study of Public
Welfare Administration* (Toronto: University of Toronto Press 1965) contains a
full-scale assessment of Langmuir's contributions. See particularly Langmuir's
'Tenth Report of the Inspector of Asylums, Prisons, etc,' *Sessional Papers,* No.
2, 1878. The illustrations of his varied workload presented in the text are
extracted from his voluminous reports that document the less savoury side of
Ontario society in the 1870s.

15 Workman's report was directed to Langmuir, who then incorporated it into his
own report which, until 1904 and with some variations, went directly to the
lieutenant-governor; the provincial secretary is listed as the 'minister in charge'
only in 1904, and two years later becomes the formal route for submission of the
inspector's reports to the lieutenant-governor. Workman's reports make
wonderful reading, not only for the light they throw on then current medical
approaches to the insane, but also for the acerbic pen, samples of which have
been incorporated from Langmuir's 'Third Annual Report for 1869–70,'
Sessional Papers, No. 6, 1870–1: 89.

16 Langmuir's 'Fifth Annual Report, 1871–2' (*Sessional Papers,* No. 2, 1872–3),
6ff, contains his observations on and recommendations for reforming the system
of distributing grants, which he found to be inequitable and based on illogical
criteria. In his next report (*Sessional Papers,* No. 2, 1874), 127–8, he proceeds to
show how he applied the formula of his own design in allocating the grants, a
scheme then incorporated in the Charity Aid Act of 1874 (37 Vic., c.34).

17 'Seventh Annual Report, 1873,' *Sessional Papers,* No. 2, 1874: 3

18 Ibid. These functions clearly fell within the realm which today would be called
quasi-judicial and were akin to those later conferred on the public trustee who,
like the inspector, enjoyed the legal status of a 'corporation sole.' That status was
conferred on the inspector in 1871 by the Act to establish a Central Prison for
the province (34 Vic., c.7, section 35).

19 Splane in his *Social Welfare in Ontario,* writes of Langmuir: 'It would be difficult to conceive a more felicitous appointment ... If a primary responsibility of
government is to place its programmes under the direction of able administrators, the government of Sandfield Macdonald may be said to have discharged this responsibility in the field of social welfare administration with
extraordinary success' (p. 46). Langmuir's views on his relations with minister
and cabinet were conveyed to an American audience in 1880 (*Sessional Papers,*
No. 8, 1881: 8). Because of the different constitutional arrangements in the
United States, Langmuir is at pains to describe in detail the workings of a

sysem of cabinet government and his own relations with a responsible cabinet minister.

20 See 'First Report of work under the Children's Protection Act, 1893,' *Sessional Papers*, No. 47, 1894; although Kelso's report covered only a six-month period, he gave every sign that he had a firm conception of his role and the means he would use to fulfil it.

21 There is an interesting confirmation of this perception of the value of facts to the regulator in the 'Second Annual Report of the Bureau of Labour for 1901,' *Sessional Papers*, No. 29, 1902: 9.

22 See 'Report of Female Inspector of Factories for July 1st to Dec. 31, 1895,' *Sessional Papers*, No. 29, 1896. Rather like Langmuir's splendid social documentaries, the factory inspectors' reports provide a fascinating insight into working conditions, prevailing attitudes towards children, the impact on the workplace of new technologies, and much more.

23 See 'Report of Chief Inspector of Factories' included in 'Report of Department of Labour,' *Sessional Papers*, No. 10, 1927.

24 Burke's observations are in 'Report of Factory Inspector, 1904,' *Sessional Papers*, No. 8, 1905: 26. In the report for 1907 (*Sessional Papers*, No. 29, 1908: 46), one of Burke's colleagues proffered the comments on appropriate tactics.

25 For a general perspective on this important feature of the administrative state, see J.A. Corry and J.E. Hodgetts, *Democratic Government and Politics*, 3rd ed. rev. (Toronto: University of Toronto Press 1959), chapter 16.

26 On the land surveyors, early architects, and engineers, see Hodgetts, *Pioneer Public Service*, 44ff. A brief account of the associations for architecture, accounting, engineering, and law is to be found in the *Report of the Professional Organizations Committee* (Ministry of the Attorney General, April 1980), Appendix A, 263–71. Schull, *Ontario since 1867*, has brief accounts of the School of Practical Science (p. 73) and the School of Mining (p. 66). On the foresters, see A.P. Pross, 'The Development of Professions in the Public Service: The Foresters in Ontario,' *Canadian Public Administration* 8, no. 3 (1967), 376–404.

27 See '21st Report from the Chairman, Provincial Board of Health,' *Sessional Papers*, No. 36, 1902, where the secretary, Peter Bryce, reviews the history of the board, and its pre-confederation precursors.

28 See 'First Annual Report for 1882,' *Sessional Papers*, No. 13, 1883, in which Edwin Chadwick, founder of the British public health movement, is quoted with approval in respect of the benefit of having laymen (i.e., non-medical professionals) on the regulatory board.

29 See 'Report of the Deputy Registrar General for 1890,' *Sessional Papers*, No. 10, 1892. The encomium to Chadwick is found at p. 52.

30 See '4th Annual Report of the Registrar General,' *Sessional Papers*, No. 6, 1875; ibid., No. 10, 1892, and No. 5, 1893. In the last of these references Dr Bryce

even drafts legislation that would improve the salary of municipal clerks and by enabling them to retain fees for services as divisional registrars provide an inducement for collecting and reporting vital statistics to the centre.

31 See 'Report of the Deputy Registrar General for 1891,' *Sessional Papers*, No. 5, 1893: 10.

32 Commenting on the situation in 1902, Bryce indicated that amendments to legislation in 1896 (undoubtedly inspired by him) had produced improvement in the reporting of divisional registrars (*Sessional Papers*, No. 9, 1904). However, less sanguine was the report of his inspector, Colonel Hamilton, a year later, who could only suggest the need for 'active assistance' by the province, which in his view might include setting a provincial detective on those suspected of breaching the act (*Sessional Papers*, No. 9, 1905: 25). Even as late as 1909 Bryce's successor, Dr Charles Hodgetts, is still harping on the quality of reporting, while calling attention to the consequent delays in processing the data at headquarters for inclusion in reports to the legislature (*Sessional Papers*, No. 19, 1910).

33 See '21st Report from Chairman, Provincial Board of Health,' *Sessional Papers*, No. 36, 1902, where particular reference is made to a report by J.A. Amyot on sewage purification that presaged his appointment in 1904 as provincial analyst.

CHAPTER 3: *Offices as Departmental Building Blocks*

1 Dated 31 March 1847, the letter was addressed to Sir John Harvey, lieutenant-governor of Nova Scotia and is reproduced in Sir Arthur G. Doughty, ed., *The Elgin-Grey Papers, 1846–1852*, 4 vols. (Ottawa: King's Printer 1937), IV: 1356–61. Grey's concern was to keep the number of ministerial political appointments to a minimum in order to provide administrative stability and continuity through the changing passions of colonial partisan politics.

2 Province of Canada, *Statutes*, 1844, 7 Vic., c.65. This enactment of the colonial legislature was thought by the governor to raise sufficient doubts about the competence of the local legislature that he reserved the original bill approved in 1843 in order to have it referred to and ultimately approved by the British authorities in 1844.

3 The references throughout this chapter to the BNA Act have been used in preference to its currently recast form, the Canada Constitution Act of 1982.

4 Ontario never adopted the Dominion mode of providing such flexibility by means of a 'Public Service Re-arrangement and Transfer of Duties Act' (Canada, *Statutes*, 1918, 8 Geo. V., c.6). The implications for legislative control of the executive are dealt with in J.E. Hodgetts, *The Canadian Public Service: A Physiology of Government, 1867–1970* (Toronto: University of Toronto Press 1973), 59ff.

5 For recent demonstrations of the pervasive practice of awarding administrative offices to MLAs, see the *Toronto Star*, 23 February 1972 under the heading

'Keeping an Eye on the Public Purse': of seventy-eight Conservative MLAs, sixty were recipients of additional fees or emoluments – eight had well-paid positions on boards.

6 See 3 Eliz. II, c.30 (1954); also 4-5 Eliz. II, c.21 (1956) for further spelling out of the organization; for the splitting off of a Department of Revenue, see 17 Eliz. II, c.29 (1968).

7 Curiously, this structural transformation was not achieved by a departmental act but by an amendment to the Public Service Act (15 Geo. V., c.10) which in turn was amending the Executive Council Act (*Revised Statutes of Ontario, 1914*, c.14).

8 On the legal foundations of the federal public service and its departments, see Hodgetts, *The Canadian Public Service*, chapter 4.

9 The term deputy minister seems to have evolved in the Province of Canada and appears to have no counterpart either in Britain or in any of its other colonies.

10 The separation permitted by the legislation of 1874 was achieved somewhat back-handedly by stating that the Commissioner of Agriculture and Public Works need not be the same person.

11 The act of 1888 (51 Vic., c.8) was primarily concerned to create a Department of Agriculture with its own ministerial head. Perhaps because of this addition, section 3 of the act amended the Executive Council Act 'so far as the same restricts the Executive Council to six members.' In 1891 the *Globe* (12 March) referred to the appointment of E.H. Bronson as a 'minister without portfolio,' a first for Ontario, although the post had already been adopted by other provinces and the Dominion. The *Globe* approved of a practice which enabled the government to take advantage of the business acumen of a busy man, but the practice itself was not formally recognized until 1910 when the Executive Council Act (10 Edw. VII, c.4) set its stamp of approval on it.

12 The concept of Offices as 'holding companies' for a variety of functions is not unlike the concept of 'ministry,' which was incorporated into the design of Ontario's public service in 1972 on the recommendation of the Committee on Government Productivity. The difference is that the committee's conception was
· based on a logical grouping of complementary functions to be coordinated, whereas the Offices were often marriages of administrative convenience. See Ontario, Committee on Government Productivity, *Report Number Nine* (March 1973), 19–28.

13 The treatment here of the emergence of the Department of Education is indebted to C.B. Sissons, *Egerton Ryerson. His Life and Letters*, 2 vols. (Toronto: Clarke, Irwin and Company 1937 and 1947), II: 532.

14 Ibid., 503.

15 See 'Second Report of the Committee on Public Accounts,' Ontario, *Journals of the Legislative Assembly, 1868–9*, Appendix 4, for recommendation that the treasurer assume control of the disbursements for education. See also Sissons,

Ryerson, II: 563–4. In the 'Public Accounts for the Year 1870–71' (*Sessional Papers*, No. 2, 1871–2), the large accountable sum in Ryerson's name has disappeared.

16 See Sissons, *Ryerson*, II: 598 and generally his chapter 16. Sissons quotes here from one of a series of nine papers prepared by Ryerson for publication in the *Mail* during 1872 when the *Globe* and George Brown were attempting to dislodge Ryerson.

17 The quotations and paraphrasing are taken from Sissons, *Ryerson*, II: 549–51 and chapter 15.

18 See 'Report of Select Committee on Public Accounts,' *Journals of the Legislative Assembly*, 1870–71, Appendix 1, item 13.

19 Sissons, *Ryerson*, II: 616 and 632.

20 Ibid., II: 632, 638. The conclusion is Professor Sissons's, a conclusion with which the opposition would have agreed, although they would have rejected his ultimate endorsation of a politically responsible minister.

21 See coverage of the debate on the education bill in the *Globe*, 22 January 1876. Macdougall was the leading exponent of the view that the bill would subject education to undesirable political pressures, even though he was favourable to bringing expenditures under closer legislative scrutiny.

22 For Meredith's renewal of debate, see *Journals of the Legislative Assembly*, 1882–3: 118 and the *Globe*, 30 January 1883. For Mowat's defence of the original bill, see Sissons, *Ryerson*, II: 641.

23 See Ontario, *Statutes*, 1909, 9 Edw. VII, c.88. In place of the old formulation there now appears the customary provision that there shall be a department of education to be presided over by a minister of education.

CHAPTER 4: *Early Departmental Satellites*

1 See Ontario, *Sessional Papers*, No. 29, 1911, 'Report from Minister of Department of Agriculture for the Year ending Oct. 31, 1910,' 'The Department was legislatively an appendage to the Bureau rather than the Bureau to the Department' (p. 20). When the bureau finally disappeared into a branch in 1918, the minister commented that the bureau had been in place, 'even before the creation of the Department of Agriculture,' *Sessional Papers*, No. 29, 1919: 24.

2 See Ontario, *Journals of the Legislative Assembly*, 1874 (2nd Session), 71–2, for the order-in-council, dated 13 November 1874, which in turn is recommended for approval by a motion of the legislature dated 26 November 1874. The agreement was to be for five years, subject to renewal. Its provisions called for the province to appoint its own agent to handle emigration from Europe but the agent was to be placed under the Dominion's London office.

3 Spence, the senior headquarters official, was listed on the civil government expenditure budget, but his salary and that of a small clerical staff represented

but the tip of the considerable financial involvement – in 1874, close to $160,000. A good part of this sum was devoted to immigration aid societies.

4 See Richard S. Lambert with Paul Pross, *Renewing Nature's Wealth* (Ontario: Hunter Rose Company 1964), 183–4. See also 'Forestry Report for 1889–90,' *Sessional Papers*, No. 16, 1891.

5 See Lambert and Pross, *Renewing Nature's Wealth*, 185; the accolade to Southworth is attributed to Dr B.E. Fernow, who was to become the first dean of a faculty of forestry in the University of Toronto in 1907. For Southworth's assessment of his new role, see his 'Annual Report of the Clerk of Forestry for the Province of Ontario, 1896,' *Sessional Papers*, No. 40, 1896: 5.

6 See 'Report of the Provincial Instructor in Road-Making for 1896,' *Sessional Papers*, No. 24, 1897. The order-in-council was dated 15 April 1896. The tentative nature of this venture is to be found in Campbell's description of his inspection or 'instructional' work, performed on invitation of the municipalities.

7 See 'First Annual Report, Provincial Board of Health,' *Sessional Papers*, No. 13, 1883: xxviii.

8 The two most celebrated cases are *Russell* v. *The Queen* (1882) and *Hodge* v. *The Queen* (1883). For brief elaboration of the litigation surrounding the attempts to regulate the sale and consumption of liquor, see Peter H. Russell, *Leading Constitutional Decisions*, 3rd ed. (Ottawa: Carleton University Press 1982), 41–63.

9 For Whitney's reaction to patronage seekers, see Charles W. Humphries, *'Honest Enough to Be Bold': The Life and Times of Sir James Pliny Whitney* (Toronto: University of Toronto Press 1985), 112–19.

10 Legislation of 1868 (31 Vic., c.19) referred to gold and silver mines and was a re-enactment of Province of Canada legislation in 1864. On this early phase of mining regulation see J.E. Hodgetts, *Pioneer Public Service* (Toronto: University of Toronto Press 1956), 150ff.

11 'Report of the Royal Commission on the Mineral Resources of Ontario and Means for their Development,' *Sessional Papers*, 1889, No. 67: xvi.

12 Ibid., xxi. Section VI of the report (pp. 407–15) develops the detailed prescriptions which were subsequently incorporated in the legislation of 1891 that created the Bureau of Mines (54 Vic., c.8).

13 The importance of Blue to the commission was revealed by the fact that his initial appointment as secretary was elevated to that of assistant commissioner. Nor was this considered necessary because of weakness in the other members, for they included Robert Bell, head of the Dominion's Geological Survey, and W.H. Merritt, an associate of the Royal School of Mines.

14 Whitney's remark was proffered as a response to the Liberal government's efforts to shore up Clergue's enterprises. Asked what would happen if they failed, Premier Ross had responded: 'We can foreclose and then it might be a case of Government ownership.' Whitney's response: 'I think my hon. friend is

prophetic. I think it will be a case of Government ownership.' His remark was indeed prophetic – not for mining but for his own Hydro-Electric Power Commission, that great exemplar of the 'people's power.' H.V. Nelles, in *The Politics of Development* (Toronto: Macmillan of Canada 1974) provides the indispensable treatment of the evolution of resource policy. The Whitney citation is at p. 138.

15 For the pre-confederation operations of the fisheries branch see Hodgetts, *Pioneer Public Service*, 172–5; also Lambert and Pross, *Renewing Nature's Wealth*, 449.

16 See 'Ontario Game and Fish Commission, Commissioners' Report,' *Sessional Papers*, 1892, No. 79. The note of *angst* sounded by the commission is attributable to its chairman, Dr G.A. MacCallum, described as one of a group of 'garrison-sportsmen' capable of acting as the conscience of the province in a domain where rampant individualism had been left to wreak havoc. For this perception see Lambert and Pross, *Renewing Nature's Wealth*, 449–50.

17 'Report of Commissioners,' 143.

18 See 55 Vic., c.10, 1892 and the consolidating statute, 56 Vic., c.49, 1893, where a clearer structural form is provided.

19 See the 'Interim Report,' dated 5 February 1910, appended to 'Final Report of the Ontario Game and Fisheries Commission, 1909–1911,' *Sessional Papers*, 1912, No. 52. Kelly Evans, the commissioner, felt the situation was so desperate that he issued his interim report a full year before the final one.

20 See 48 Vic., c.9, 1885 and 49 Vic., c.45, 1886, where inspectors appointed by local councils are still relied upon as regulators.

21 See 'Commissioners' Report,' 242.

22 The fisheries case is cited as *A.G. Can.* v. *A.G. Ont. et al.* In the Privy Council (1898), A.C. 700. See Bora Laskin, *Canadian Constitutional Law*, 2nd ed. (Toronto: The Carswell Co. 1960), chapter 9.

23 See Georgian Bay Fisheries Commission 1905–1908, 'Report and Recommendations of the Dominion Fisheries Commission appointed to enquire into the Fisheries of Georgian Bay and Adjacent Waters,' esp. pp. 31–2.

24 The involvement of the Parks Commission in the machinations of various companies seeking to exploit the power potential of Niagara Falls is graphically described in Nelles, *The Politics of Development*, 32ff.

25 Nelles has an informative treatment of the public power movement; he makes no reference to the telephone although it was considered a prime candidate for public ownership (ibid., 237ff). Confusion as to which element of the 'state' – local, provincial, or federal – should be the owner resulted in a mixed outcome, Ontario settling for regulation while the western provinces decided upon ownership.

26 Nelles describes the environment which at the time supported 'the construction and operation of a railroad as a public works,' in order to serve the special public purpose of opening up New Ontario (ibid., 110ff). In his study of the T. &

N.O. Railway, Albert Tucker provides many instances of the tight political control maintained over the commissioners. See his *Steam into Wilderness: Ontario Northland Railway, 1902–62* (Toronto: Fitzhenry and Whiteside 1978), *passim*, and esp. p. 25.

CHAPTER 5: *Early Tasks and Administrative Means*

1 See Ontario, *Sessional Papers*, No. 71, 1879, 'Volume of Business Done from 1868 to 1877'; also ibid., No. 43, 1894, 'Return re all persons who ... held office under the Crown etc ...'

2 See ibid., 1879, under heading 'Secretary and Registrar and Registrar General.'

3 See ibid., 1894, under heading 'Provincial Secretary and Registrar Branches.' This estimate was for the year 1884 and had reference only to the Registrar's Branch. Separately listed were the provincial secretary's own branch, the Public Institutions Office, the Insurance Branch, a Divisional Courts Branch and an Inspector of Registry Offices where the incumbent, E.F.B. Johnson, wrote of the volume of his business quadrupling, 306 necessary files having been written in 1892, 'which were copied.'

4 Ibid., under heading 'Business in the Department of the Executive Council and Attorney General.' The next paragraph relies on the same source, as well as the earlier *Sessional Paper*, No. 71, 1879.

5 The *Encyclopedia Britannica* dates the commercial manufacture in the United States of steel pens to 1860, while the fountain pen became popular in the 1880s; the ballpoint pen, though available by the 1890s, awaited the encouragement of the U.S. Quartermaster General's Office in the Second World War, when the advantages of a writing instrument that would not leak at high altitudes and its long-lasting, quick-drying ink made it popular with the military and thereafter led to a rapid expansion in civilian use.

6 See 'Report of the Public Accounts Committee,' *Journals of the Legislative Assembly*, 1897, Appendix 2: 75ff. The members are quizzing the official in charge of the Stationery Stock and trying to pillory him (or his masters) for past excessive purchases of supplies (such as packs of playing cards, boxes of elastic bands, penholders by the gross, thermometers, inkstands, scissors, sponges, letter scales, letter presses, diaries, etc.), some of which had become valueless, much of which could not be sold to the departments because purchased at too high a price by the Queen's Printer who was in charge. For an example of the curious item 'sharpening erasers,' see *Sessional Papers*, No. 16, 1885, 'Public Accounts for the Year ended 31 Dec. 1884' where all of 40 cents is registered for this item.

7 See 'Report of the Public Accounts Committee,' *Journals of the Legislative Assembly*, 1894, Appendix 2: 424ff. The testimony was from David Spence, listed as secretary, Department of Immigration, and his clerk, Alexander Robertson, whom Spence described as a 'kind of foreman' of the writers. Neither

had any control over the number to be appointed, this patronage apparently being enjoyed by the provincial treasurer.

8 Leaving the sessional writers in the working area they had occupied since confederation rather than moving them closer to the legislature they served, now located at Queen's Park, had the effect of leaving Spence in charge, for the Immigration Branch which he headed was also left in the old buildings, presumably because of its proximity to the train station where immigrants had to be met.

9 See 'Report of the Public Accounts Committee,' *Journals of the Legislative Assembly*, 1896, Appendix 1: 43.

10 See 'Public Accounts for the Year ended 31 Dec. 1883,' *Sessional Papers*, No. 15, 1884, which show Attorney General's Office: Typewriter – T. Bengough – $121.50; Secretary and Registrar's Office: same but at cost of $121.65. The supplementary estimates for 1885 and 1886 show additional purchases of typewriters and supplies. An informative history is G. Tilghman Richards, *The History and Development of Typewriters* (London: HMSO, Science Museum 1948). When the Remington Company displayed its machine at the Philadelphia Centennial Exposition of 1876 it attracted much less interest than the Bell telephone, and by 1881 the company had disposed of only 1,200 machines.

11 Blue's request was made to the Public Accounts Committee: see *Journals of the Legislative Assembly*, 1887, Appendix 3: 9. The caligraph for the Attorney General's Office one presumes was to enable the premier and attorney general to sign his name automatically rather than repeatedly by hand.

12 See *Journals of the Legislative Assembly*, 1923: 88–9, 'Answer to a return re number of typewriting machines purchased during fiscal year ending Oct. 31, 1922.'

13 Hilda Martindale, *Women Servants of the State, 1870–1938* (London: George Allen and Unwin 1938), is a definitive study of the British situation, beginning with the state's assumption of the telegraph companies in 1870, where women in some numbers were employed. See also Royal [MacDonnell] Commission on the Civil Service, *Fourth Report* (London: HMSO 1914), chapter 10. The commission endorsed segregation and rejected the equal pay principle on the basis that equal work was not done. Wartime experience did little to modify these attitudes, as the *Final Report* of the Gladstone Committee on Post-War recruitment revealed (London: HMSO 1919).

14 See 'Report of the Ontario Commission on Unemployment,' *Sessional Papers*, No. 55, 1916: 181ff. The chief recommendation of the commission was for a provincial department of labour.

15 See *Journals of the Legislative Assembly*, 1923: 432. The proportion of 30 per cent is based on the only figures that seem to have been made available at the time, dealing with the certification of civil servants as they were transferred from temporary to permanent status – 30 per cent of these being women. Interestingly,

in the 'Report of the Civil Service Commission for the Fiscal Year ending March 31, 1957,' of the total staff of nearly 23,000, approximately 7,500 were females – still around 30 per cent.

16 See 'Public Accounts for the year 1879,' *Sessional Papers*, No. 1, 1880; see also ibid., 1903.

17 See *Journals of the Legislative Assembly*, 1914: 179–80, for reference to the treasurer's findings and the resolution approved by the legislature indicating opposition to government ownership of trunk lines. The *Journals* for 1912 contain the first reference to the Bell Telephone Company, explaining how the case of *Toronto* v. *Bell Telephone Co.*, settled by the Privy Council in 1905, made it impossible for the province to interfere with the company's operations because they were authorized by the Parliament of Canada.

18 See 10 Edw. VII, c.84, 1910, for assignment to the ORMB of sweeping regulatory powers over private telephone companies in the province.

19 See '21st Annual Report of the Provincial Board of Health,' *Sessional Papers*, No. 36, 1903: 28.

20 See Richard S. Lambert with Paul Pross, *Renewing Nature's Wealth* (Ontario: Hunter Rose Company 1967), 234ff.

21 See 'Report of the Public Accounts Committee,' *Journals of the Legislative Assembly*, 1910, Appendix 1: 14–15. For later totals of automobiles owned by the government, see ibid., 1920: 33.

22 Ibid., 1921: 57: a not insubstantial purchase at $1,217.26 each. Not all the field agents enjoyed the benefits of the new mode of transportation, as the all-female group of investigators for the Mothers' Allowance Board were to discover as they pursued their adventurous journeys in remoter parts of the province.

23 An interesting contemporary illustration of the dependency of policy initiatives on the availablity of means to implement them is to be found in the revelation that the vital statistics maintained for so long by the primitive office techniques deployed by the Registrar General's Office only began to be computerized in the 1990s. See *Globe and Mail*, 23 October 1990, 'Soon vital statistics close as computer.' The ten million records accessible only in numbered volumes were to be converted to discs that could be backed up on audio-digital tape held in the space of a shoebox.

CHAPTER 6: *Personnel and Personalities*

1 See *Sessional Papers*, No. 22, 1881, 'Classification of Officers, Chief Clerks, and Clerks required for the Public Service under Section 20, cap.2, 41 Victoria.'

2 See ibid., No. 31, 1869, Treasury Department 'Return re all persons appointed since 1st of July, 1867, with dates, whether temporary or permanent, on salary or fee.' These figures are updated in subsequent *Sessional Papers*, No. 45, 1871–2 and No. 40, 1873 (appointments since 1 Jan 1873), and No. 46, 1874 (numbers

of employees since 1 Jan 1873). See also ibid., No. 11, 1874, containing a running file on appointments along with comparisons with the public service salary costs in the Province of Quebec and the Dominion government.

3 *Sessional Paper*, No. 43, 1894, 'Return re all persons who, during the years 1871, 1873, 1892 held office under the Crown or were employed in or in connection with any Department or Branch of the Public Service, to whom or in respect of whose office or employment any salary or remuneration was paid out of the Consolidated Revenue Fund or any Special Fund.' This return also provides invaluable information on the workload in each agency.

4 See ibid., No. 99, 1894. The total population of the province in 1891 is shown to be 2,114,321, of whom 358,300 (one-sixth) are said to be Catholic. The total appointees for both the inside and outside service came to 1,738. The Catholics in this group numbered 219 which, if the one-sixth proportion was applied, should have been 290. Total salaries, where salaries were paid, were estimated to be $418,000. Applying the one-sixth factor, the Catholics' share of the salary bill ought to have been $69,667 but was in fact $12,000 less than that.

5 For information on Andrew Russell, who had been head of the Surveys Branch before becoming assistant commissioner, see Richard S. Lambert with Paul Pross, *Renewing Nature's Wealth* (Ontario: Hunter Rose Company 1967), 115–18; on Thomas H. Johnson, see ibid., 118–20.

6 See ibid., 163; see also Henry James Morgan, *The Canadian Men and Women of the Time*, 1st ed. (Toronto: William Briggs 1898).

7 For the group of long-lived officials in the department, see 'Report of the Department of Lands and Forests for Year ending 31st October, 1921,' *Sessional Papers*, No. 3, 1921–3. The accompanying accolade to retirees (complete with photographs) is unusual and appears not to have been a practice in other departments. Nor is it common to find such comments as 'their loss will be keenly felt' or they 'take their departure in the knowledge of duty well done,' or 'it is a pleasure to record that each of these officials under the Superannuation Act is provided with an annuity to assist in declining years and to partially compensate for the untiring efforts devoted to the interests of the Crown' (p. 16).

8 For Ryerson's biography, see *Dictionary of Canadian Biography*, Vol. XI (Toronto: University of Toronto Press 1982), 783–93.

9 See Henry James Morgan, *The Canadian Men and Women of the Time*, 2nd ed. (Toronto: William Briggs 1912).

10 An obituary with a photograph of John Millar is to be found in 'Annual Report of the Department of Education for 1905,' *Sessional Papers*, No. 12, 1906. His educational philosophy is summarized as 'character before knowledge.'

11 See Morgan, *Canadian Men and Women*, 1st ed., and *Canadian Who's Who*, (1910).

12 See Morgan, *Canadian Men and Women*, 1st ed.

13 See ibid., both 1st and 2nd eds.

14 For a detailed development of this theme, see J.E. Hodgetts, *Pioneer Public Service* (Toronto: University of Toronto Press 1956), chapter 12.

15 Professor Buckland's contributions, particularly as educator rather than administrator, appear in *Dictionary of Canadian Biography*, Vol. XI, 132–3. Blue's biographical material is to be found in Morgan's 1912 edition as well as in *Canadian Who's Who*. See also Malcolm Urquhart, 'Three Builders of Canada's Statistical System,' *The Canadian Historical Review*, 68 no. 3 (1987), 419–25.

16 See Morgan, *Canadian Men and Women*, 1912 ed.

17 Ibid., 1898 ed.

18 Ibid., 1912 ed.

19 Ibid. Cartwright's salary of $3,000 was higher than his deputy head colleagues but quite in line with the salaries of senior judicial administration personnel.

20 Ibid.

21 Ibid., 1898 ed.

22 Ibid. See also *Dictionary of Canadian Biography*, Vol. XI, for a more detailed account. *The First One Hundred Years* (Office of the Provincial Auditor, August 1986) has a brief account of Cayley, and a review of the work of his successors.

23 Curiously *The First One Hundred Years* contains no reference to Sproule, nor is he featured in Morgan's biographical references. His career trail has been pursued through successive public accounts and the *Sessional Papers.*

24 See Morgan, *Canadian Men and Women*, 1889 ed.

25 Ibid.

26 Ibid., 1912 ed. Mulvey's move was precipitated by the need to fill the vacancy created when Sir Joseph Pope took up the first appointment as undersecretary of state for external affairs. The subsequent struggle between Mulvey and Pope over jurisdictional turf reverberated for some years through the corridors of power in Ottawa. See John Hilliker, *Canada's Department of External Affairs, Volume I. The Early Years, 1909–1946* (Montreal: McGill-Queen's University Press 1990), 44.

27 See Morgan, *Canadian Men and Women*, 1912 ed.; see also Richard B. Splane, *Social Welfare in Ontario, 1792–1893* (Toronto: University of Toronto Press 1965), 46– 51.

28 For details on Armstrong, see Morgan, *Canadian Men and Women*, 1912 ed.

29 The second edition (1936) of *Canadian Who's Who* has more complete biographical details than the first edition (1910).

30 G.M. Rose, *Representative Canadians: A Cyclopaedia of Canadian Biography* (Toronto: Rose Publishing Company 1886).

31 See ibid.; also *Dictionary of Canadian Biography*, Vol. XI: 837–8, where the name is spelled Sidney.

32 See Morgan, *Canadian Men and Women*, 1898 ed.; also Rose, *Representative Canadians.*

33 See Morgan, *Canadian Men and Women*, 1912 ed.; Rose, *Representative Canadians*, and *Canadian Who's Who* (1936).
34 Morgan, *Canadian Men and Women*, 1912 ed.
35 See Peter Oliver, *Public and Private Persons: The Ontario Political Culture, 1914–1934* (Toronto: Clarke Irwin and Company 1975), 255. There is a delightful reference to the senior personnel duly convicted and assembled in the choir of the Kingston Penitentiary of whom Oliver writes: 'Settell [late secretary of Ontario Hydro], Smith, Matthews [respectively minister and deputy minister of the Treasury Department] and the others all had their chance to "open up" at their trials or indeed at any other time. Still, to have belonged ... to that Kingston choir ... would have been an educational experience few provincial politicians would have regarded lightly' (p. 232).

CHAPTER 7: *Organizational Response to the Hands-on Administrative Mode*

1 Perhaps the most forthright exposition of this feature of the scientific management movement's philosophy is to be found in Luther Gulick and L. Urwick, eds., *Papers on the Science of Administration* (New York: Institute of Public Administration 1937).
2 See Roger Graham, *Old Man Ontario: Leslie M. Frost* (Toronto: University of Toronto Press 1990), 94–5, for the make-up of Drew's first cabinet. Drew himself took on the Education portfolio, neither the first nor the last time the premier would opt for this arrangement.
3 The act of 1912 was for the purpose of 'raising Money on the Credit of the Consolidated Revenue Fund of Ontario,' the five million dollars to be available for a wide variety of public works as well as loans to settlers; a minister was to be designated, as was provision for a deputy minister, commissioner, and other staff. It was not until the legislation of 1924 that the administrative organization and separate political direction signalled the adoption of the 'place' basis of administration.
4 For purposes of the Public Service Act, the Game and Fisheries Branch shall 'be deemed a Department and the Deputy Minister shall have and perform the like powers and duties as are conferred or imposed upon a Deputy Minister by that or any other Act in like case' (4 Geo. V., c.46).
5 See *Report of the Royal Commission on the Relations of Labour and Capital in Canada* (Ottawa: Queen's Printer 1889). The experience in the United States with labour bureaus impressed the commission, even though it anticipated the same problems with getting workers to respond to requests for information and the problem for any federal system of overlapping jurisdictions.
6 Both Glockling and Anderson appear in *Canadian Who's Who*, 1912 ed. Glockling was elected president of the Trades and Labour Congress in 1889 and apparently continued to serve as president of the Brotherhood of Bookbinders

and vice-president of the Toronto Labour Temple while serving as secretary to the Bureau of Labour.

7 See *Sessional Papers*, No. 29, 1902: 7.

8 See 'Report of the Ontario Commission on Unemployment,' *Sessional Papers*, No. 55, 1916, especially pp. 41–5.

9 See Ontario, *Journals of the Legislative Assembly*, 1915: 260–1. The relevant legislation was 6 Geo. V., c.35, and 9 Geo. v., c.27.

10 For Riddell's career see *Who's Who in Canada*, 1934–5. His first report as superintendent reveals a powerful new hand at the helm, in marked contrast to the uncoordinated reports previously produced from different agencies. He is also a superb example of the 'intellectuals' who became renowned as the Ottawa mandarinate during the first three decades of the century. See Doug Owram, *The Government Generation: Canadian Intellectuals and the State, 1900–1948* (Toronto: University of Toronto Press 1986).

11 There seems to have been no legislation confirming the early start-up of what was to become one of the largest and most costly of the province's program commitments, Campbell having been appointed by order-in-council as instructor in road making. Thus the subsequent Highways Branch set up in Public Works, unlike most of the other satellites of the period, had no statutory foundation.

12 In his second report as instructor, Campbell inveighs against the 'statute labour or the road-tax system of personal service and commutation [which] though nearly universal among us, is unsound in its principle, unjust in its operation, wasteful in practice, and unsatisfactory in its results' (*Sessional Papers*, No. 59, 1895).

13 In conjunction with the grants program there was also a more long-standing program designed to assist in the buying-out of toll road companies. That this was a slow process is revealed by the series of enactments prompted initially by a legislative committee appointed in 1887 to consider the question of abolishing toll roads: as late as 1919 a Toll Road measure was still being enacted (9 Geo. V., c.58).

14 See *Sessional Papers*, No. 31, 1907: 9.

15 See *Journals of the Legislative Assembly*, 1908: 165.

16 See ibid., 1915: 75 and 1919: 178.

17 Ontario, *Statutes*, 21 Geo. V., c.80, dealing with the Inspection of Public Institutions, specified that the penal and reform institutions were to remain with the Provincial Secretary's Office, all mental institutions were the responsibility of Health. The former earned a department of their own in 1946.

18 An informative account of the circumstances leading to the creation of a department of welfare is provided in Peter Oliver's *G. Howard Ferguson: Ontario Tory* (Toronto: University of Toronto Press 1977), 317–21.

19 Typifying the problem of overlapping jurisdiction, in 1919 legislation was passed that provided for one member of the ORMB to become director of the Bureau of

Municipal Affairs (9 Geo. V., c.25 and c. 48). That the ORMB virtually preempted the role assigned the new bureau was revealed in 1935 when departmental status was finally conferred on the bureau (25 Geo. V., c.16). According to section 8 (1) of Part II, 'The jurisdiction formerly exercised by the Bureau of Municipal Affairs and transferred by ... The Ontario Municipal Board Act of 1932 to the Board, is hereby transferred to the department [of Municipal Affairs].'

20 The initial legislation was 9 Geo. V., c.54 by which the province was authorized to collect funds from the Dominion government to be redirected to the municipalities through housing commissions that were to encourage construction by private contractors.

21 Part II of the omnibus Act for the Reorganization of the Government of Ontario (21 Eliz. II, c.1) for the first time fails to list the Provincial Secretary's Department. Most of its responsibilities appear to have been transferred to the Ministry of Consumer and Corporate Affairs.

22 See 'Report of the Bureau of Colonization for 1909,' *Sessional Papers*, No. 74, 1910.

23 See John T. Saywell, *'Just call me Mitch': The Life of Mitchell F. Hepburn* (Toronto: University of Toronto Press 1991), 172.

24 The 'Report of the Minister of Agriculture for the Year 1918,' *Sessional Papers*, No. 29, 1919, contains an interesting review of the Bureau of Industries up to its transformation into the Statistics and Publication Branch.

25 See 'Report of the Minister of Agriculture for the year ending October 31, 1910,' *Sessional Papers*, No. 28, 1911. This reorganization was in response to a major revision of the Department of Agriculture Act that occurred in 1910 (10 Edw. VII, c.17). Other acts covering the Agricultural Societies (c.18) and Horticultural Societies (c.19) also confirmed the centralizing process now underway.

26 Like the comparable grants for highway construction, provincial legislation was needed to make provision for the Dominion's agricultural aid program (see 2 Geo. V., c.15). The experiment with district representatives was generalized by legislation in 1914 (4 Geo. V., c.20). The name change to agricultural representatives occurred in 1918 (8 Geo. V., c.19).

27 The title was not assistant *to* the deputy minister, be it noted; in any event, with a salary of $2,400 as against the $3,000 paid the deputy, Bailey was clearly intended to be a senior official, not a mere aide.

28 'Report of the Minister of Education for the Year 1906, Part I,' *Sessional Papers*, No. 12, 1907, iii–iv.

29 On Seath, see *Canadian Who's Who* (1910). For an evaluation of his performance, see the excellent treatment in Robert M. Stamp, *The Schools of Ontario, 1876–1976* (Toronto: University of Toronto Press 1982), 106.

30 On Colquhoun and Merchant, see *Canadian Who's Who*, vol. II; 1936–7; in addition, see Stamp, *Schools of Ontario*, who also examines the role of Duncan

McArthur whom Hepburn lured from the History Department of Queen's University to become deputy minister, and six years later minister of education.

31 See Ontario, *Debates of the Legislative Assembly*, 1971: 4810 ff. Opposition leader Robert Nixon, protesting the use of the title 'prime minister,' recalled: 'My dad used to be Premier of Ontario and he said that the biggest change after the election in 1943 was that all stationery that had been printed and embossed "Office of the Premier" was thrown out by the new incumbent and new stationery printed up embossed "Office of the Prime Minister."' The colour also changed from red to blue, he added. The Davis government, aided by a specially commissioned study by Professor Maurice Careless, conceded Nixon's point and formally reverted to the title 'Premier.'

32 In Roger Graham's biography, *Old Man Ontario* (Toronto: University of Toronto Press 1990), there is ample evidence of Frost's commanding style, concealed as it was by an avuncular, folksy presence. An example: 'He was less disposed than Drew to delegate authority to his ministers ... He kept them under a tight rein, often bypassing them altogether to deal directly with their deputies or officials.' (p. 173). Or again, in reassuring the chairman of the newly created Water Resources and Supply Committee that he, Frost, would not be bowing out simply because a Pollution Control Board had been established: 'May I point out that even if the same were assigned to a Government Department ... it would come under my general direction on a policy basis because it is a new and important undertaking which will involve very substantial commitments' (pp. 206ff). Even with Ontario Hydro, where Frost acknowledged that the chairman 'in theory represents only the Commission,' he was nonetheless quite prepared to dictate to Chairman Saunders even the time at which Saunders should take his holidays (pp. 212–13).

33 It is probable that Blake's decision to treat the Office of President of Council as the base of operation for the premier had little to do with notions of providing a strong infrastructure for the head of government and more to do with his abhorrence of the real world of provincial politics in which, if he had retained the portfolio of attorney general, he would have been submerged. This is the strong inference to be drawn from S.J.R. Noel's summation of Blake's brief ten-month tenure before opting (under legislation of his own designing) to take up only his seat in the federal House of Commons: 'Blake had no feel for political life and was generally discomfited by it. "Take the leadership, I beg of you," he once wrote to Alexander Mackenzie ... "for the work outside of the House I have long known myself to be utterly unfit".' See S.J.R. Noel, *Patrons, Clients, Brokers* (Toronto: University of Toronto Press 1990), 230.

34 See *Globe*, 7 February 1872, report of the debate in the legislature on 6 February. Although somewhat confused, there seems to be agreement that 'the addition was constitutional' as long as the holder of the Office of President of Council was not excluded from sitting in the House; there were some proponents

who saw the separate position as an appropriate way of relieving the premier of departmental duties.

35 See *Globe*, 26 February 1878 for the criticism of the two senior officials in the Office of Attorney General and Mowat's defence.

36 The retention of Wallis by Premier Drury is described in Charles M. Johnston, *E.C. Drury: Agrarian Idealist* (Toronto: University of Toronto Press 1986), 81. C.B. Sissons is quoted as expressing concern over his friend Drury's 'want of system' and the consequence that 'his most important cabinet minister would be his private secretary.' Sissons' choice was Hector Mackinnon who had just left the *Globe*, but the latter opted later for the position of federal tariff commissioner. Drury not only stuck with Wallis but upgraded him to the status of deputy minister.

37 See Neil McKenty, *Mitch Hepburn* (Toronto: McClelland and Stewart 1967), 244.

38 See John T. Saywell, *'Just call me Mitch:' The Life of Mitchell F. Hepburn* (Toronto: University of Toronto Press 1991), especially chapters 8 to 10. Walters was relied upon as the hatchet man to implement Hepburn's pre-election promises (threats) to economize through drastic cuts in the bureaucracy.

39 See 'Public Accounts for 1941–42,' *Sessional Papers*, No. 1, 1942. In the 'Department of Prime Minister' there was in the main office R.H. Elmhirst, private secretary at $4,000 and C.J. Foster, general secretary (also civil service commissioner) at $4,000. In the Office of Executive Council, C.F. Bulmer, clerk at $4,500. In the Travel and Publicity Bureau, the director, D.R. Oliver, at $5,200. In the Office of King's Printer, T.E. Bowman at $3,200. And, towering above all, the controller of finance, Chester Walters, at $10,000.

40 See Graham, *Old Man Ontario*, 97. As reported by George Gathercole, one of Walters's associates in the Treasury Department, on his defeat Hepburn remarked to Walters: 'Well, Chester, I guess we're going,' to which Walters was purported to respond: 'No, Mitch, you're going, I'm staying.'

CHAPTER 8: *Twentieth-Century Satellites*

1 See Charles W. Humphries, *'Honest Enough to Be Bold': The Life and Times of Sir James Pliny Whitney* (Toronto: University of Toronto Press 1985), 141.

2 See W.R. Plewman, *Adam Beck and the Ontario Hydro* (Toronto: Ryerson Press 1947), 48–9. Plewman makes later reference (p. 448) to an Allan Dymond, chief law clerk in the Office of Attorney General, who did the actual drafting of the Hydro statute.

3 See *Sessional Papers*, No. 85, 1913; No. 53, 1914; and No. 65, 1916 for the interim and final reports of the Commission to Inquire into Workmen's Compensation. Sir William was appointed by order-in-council on 30 June 1910,

with instructions to prepare a model bill. See *Journals of the Legislative Assembly,* 1910: 154.

4 'Annual Report of the Ontario Railway and Municipal Board to Dec. 31, 1906', *Sessional Papers,* No. 9, 1907; quotations are from pp. 3, 4.

5 On this debate, see John Willis, 'Section 96 of the B.N.A. Act,' *Canadian Bar Review* 18 (1936), 116–36; also F.R. Scott, 'Administrative Law, 1923–47', *Canadian Bar Review* 26 (1948), 268–85.

6 Premier Whitney is quoted by Humphries, in *Honest Enough to Be Bold,* as taking this view of the commission's status: 'The Government will be so close to the work which may have to be done that the Commission must practically [be] a Committee of the Cabinet with certain statutory powers' (p. 155).

7 See Merrill Denison, *The People's Power: The History of Ontario Hydro* (Toronto: McClelland and Stewart 1960), 54; reliance has been placed on Plewman's *Adam Beck* for the details of Beck's successful effort to preserve and enhance the autonomy of Hydro.

8 See Peter Oliver, *G. Howard Ferguson: Ontario Tory* (Toronto: University of Toronto Press 1977), 152. Although opposed to public ownership as a general principle, as Oliver concludes, 'He was willing to admit, however, that "each situation must be dealt with upon its merits", and his knowledge of Ontario conditions and needs led him to an abiding commitment to the Hydro as an instrument which served Ontario well both internally and in its external affairs.'

9 See 'Report of the Public Accounts Committee,' *Journals of the Legislative Assembly,* 1911, Appendix 1; ibid., 1913, especially pp. 23–5; and ibid., 1916, where the first hundred pages of proceedings carry the Clancy-Beck exchange. In this instance the committee seems to have sided with Auditor Clancy, whereas in the accounts committee's proceedings for 1915 Clancy contended with a much more hostile reception, particularly from Ferguson, over the auditor's power to prepare statements for any member of the legislature which had not been vetted by the treasurer (see ibid., 1915: 68ff).

10 'Final Report of Royal Commission on Laws Relating to the Liability of Employers,' *Sessional Papers,* No. 53, 1914: 7. A second volume of proceedings contains the session with P. Tecumseh Sherman at pp. 188–208.

11 Interestingly, the chairman of the WCB in a speech delivered in 1923 to the Building Association of Hamilton, summarizing a decade's achievements, used this quotation from Meredith as the opening text, treating it almost like Holy Writ. Reproduced in Appendix to 'Report of Workmen's Compensation Board for 1923.'

12 'Report for 1915 of the Workmen's Compensation Board, Ontario,' including also report for 1914 (Toronto: A.T. Wilgress, King's Printer 1916), 6.

13 See Roscoe Pound, *Administrative Law: Its Growth Procedure Significance* (Pittsburgh: University of Pittsburgh Press 1942), 22. For a less critical view, see James M. Landis, *The Administrative Process* (New Haven: Yale University Press 1938).

CHAPTER 9: *Expanding the Universe of Satellites*

1 For the circumstances surrounding enactment of the mining act of 1906, see Scott
   Young and Astrid Young, *Silent Frank Cochrane: The North's First Great
   Politician* (Toronto: Macmillan of Canada 1973), chapter 3.
2 'Eighteenth Annual Report of the Bureau of Mines, 1919,' *Sessional Papers*, No.
   4, 1910: 46.
3 See E.C. Drury, *Farmer Premier: The Memoirs of E.C. Drury* (Toronto:
   McClelland and Stewart 1966), 108. But see also Peter Oliver, *G. Howard
   Ferguson* (Toronto: University of Toronto Press 1977), 216 for indication of the
   Hearst government's prior interest in social legislation.
4 See 'First Annual Report of the Minimum Wage Board, 1921,' *Sessional Papers*,
   No. 73, 1922, which gives a good account of the circumstances leading up to its
   creation.
5 See 'Fifth Annual Report for 1925,' *Sessional Papers*, No. 38, 1926: 35. For the
   wage orders issued in its second year, see ibid., No. 89, 1923, where the board
   defends itself against a charge of being 'aloof and academic' by calling attention
   to its practice of widespread consultation.
6 See John Saywell, *'Just call me Mitch'* (Toronto: University of Toronto Press
   1991), 189–91, for the reaction to the notion of industrial codes and the
   consequent cautious approval forced on Labour Minister Roebuck.
7 In its first report the commission took unusual pains to describe how it went
   about setting up its organization: see 'Annual Report of the Mothers'
   Allowances Commission of the Province of Ontario for the Year Ending Oct. 31,
   1921,' *Sessional Papers*, No. 89, 1922. Apparently the commission's control
   over its own staff subsequently yielded to patronage considerations to which
   Elizabeth Shortt, the wife of the redoubtable civil service reformer Adam Shortt,
   took such exception that she resigned as vice-chairman of the commission (see
   Oliver, *Ferguson*, 360).
8 Charles M. Johnston, *E.C. Drury: Agrarian Idealist* (Toronto: University of
   Toronto Press 1986), 152.
9 See 'Second Annual Report of the Mothers' Allowances Commission for the
   Year 1921–2,' *Sessional Papers*, No. 98, 1923, also report for 1927, which also
   covered 1926, ibid., No. 44, 1928.
10 For Ferguson's views, see Oliver, *Ferguson*, 217–8: 'the Government has no
    control over the Workmen's Compensation Board ... We have no more right to
    interfere than we have in the affairs of the ordinary Court of Justice.'
11 On the political importance of the regulation of the liquor trade, see Peter Oliver,
    Public and Private Persons: The Ontario Political Culture (Toronto: Clarke
    Irwin & Company 1975), chapter 4; Margaret Prang, *N.W. Rowell: Ontario
    Nationalist* (Toronto: University of Toronto Press 1975), chapter 9; and Johnston,
    E.C. Drury, 154ff.

12 Peter Oliver in his thorough study of Ferguson cites several examples of Ferguson's adroit evasion of responsibility for agencies like the WCB or Ontario Hydro. 'When flooded with complaints about lax enforcement of the OTA,' writes Oliver, 'he [Ferguson] would point out that "you apparently have the impression ... that the Ontario Government is expected to police the Province and look after law enforcement in every locality. This of course is an erroneous idea"' (p. 218).

13 On Ferguson's skilful promotion of his liquor bill, see ibid., 278–80. As Oliver reports, 'On 2 December 1927, the province's annual financial statement revealed that Ontario had achieved its first surplus in years. Two million dollars in liquor revenue had made the difference.'

14 See Saywell, *'Just call me Mitch,'* 174–6, for indications that in the regulation of the liquor trade *plus ca change ...*

15 See *Journals of the Legislative Assembly,* 1915: 235–6.

16 For the apparent uncontroversial nature of the marketing board legislation, see Saywell, *'Just call me Mitch,'* 292. Indicative of the jurisdictional problems arising out of these new ventures in regulating markets, the province's legislation for the Livestock Board incorporated 'by reference' the terms already set out in Dominion legislation, as a method of achieving uniformity across the country. The constitutional issues are usefully described in J.A. Corry, *Difficulties of Divided Jurisdiction,* and L.M. Gouin and Brooke Claxton, *Legislative Expedients and Devices adopted by the Dominion and the Provinces,* Studies Prepared for the Royal Commission on Dominion-Provincial Relations, *Appendix 1* (Ottawa: King's Printer 1939).

17 See Royal Commission on Milk, *Report of the Ontario Royal Commission on Milk, 1947* (Toronto: King's Printer 1947), x–xi, and in the detailed notations at pp. 4ff.

CHAPTER 10: *Regulation and Reform of the Public Service*

1 See J.E. Hodgetts, *Pioneer Public Service* (Toronto: Univeristy of Toronto Press 1956), 108ff. for the colonial struggle over the civil list.

2 For a brief account of British practices, see J.E. Hodgetts, 'Unifying the British Civil Service: Some Trends and Problems,' *Canadian Journal of Economics and Political Science* (14 February 1948), 1–19.

3 See *Journals of the Legislative Assembly,* 1874, 1st Session, 81.

4 Ibid., 2nd Session, 106–7. Cameron sought to top Mowat's amendment by a further amendment of his own which seems not to have succeeded, despite what one would argue today was a more accurate statement of the constitutional position than was Mowat's: 'the Public Accounts Committee is the channel through which ... this House can obtain full information as to the proper or improper expenditure of the public money, and that it is the duty of the advisers of His Excellency, the Lieutenant Governor to the House, to lay before the Committee the fullest information touching every item of the expenditure of public money.'

5 Pursuant to this requirement, the government prepared a detailed classification, with numbers of persons in each category, published in *Sessional Papers*, No. 22, 1881.

6 The *Globe* covered these debates quite fully, the debate on first reading on 7 February being more extended than on the bill's subsequent appearances on the 14 and 26 February.

7 For comparable developments at the federal level, see J.E. Hodgetts, *The Canadian Public Service: A Physiology of Government, 1867–1970* (Toronto: University of Toronto Press 1973), 50–1.

8 C.R.W. Biggar, *Sir Oliver Mowat*, 2 vols. (Toronto: Warwick Bros and Rutter 1905), II: 727.

9 A good sample is to be found in the proceedings of the Public Accounts Committee, *Journals of the Legislative Assembly*, 1896, Appendix 1, and also for 1897–8, where the expenditures in connection with supplying various public institutions are probed for hours on end.

10 A Royal Commission on the Working of Municipal Institutions in 1888–9; a Commission on Municipal Taxation in 1893, and a Commission on Payment of Fees to Officials in 1895 all explored this question, as did the Ontario Public Service Commission (not to be confused with the Civil Service Commissioner) in 1922.

11 See 'Report of the Public Accounts Committee,' *Journals of the Legislative Assembly*, 1922, Appendix 2. See particularly pp. 32ff, where charges of T.H. Lennox against Attorney General Raney for employing thugs and criminals in the enforcement of the OTA are aired.

12 See *Journals of the Legislative Assembly*, 1899: 283.

13 Ibid., 1906: 96, 211, where returns requested were 'not brought down'; however, some figures on game wardens and fisheries overseers were presented (p. 195), as were figures for officials dismissed in East and West Nipissing (p. 123), even though in the latter case an obvious complete housecleaning had occurred.

14 Ibid., 1912: 257.

15 Ibid., 1913: 367; 1914: 66–7; 1916: 19; 1917: 66.

16 Ibid., 1912: 258.

17 *Globe*, 12 March 1914.

18 References here and throughout to the developments at the federal level depend on J.E. Hodgetts, William McCloskey, Reginald Whitaker, V. Seymour Wilson, *The Biography of an Institution. The Civil Service Commission of Canada, 1908–1967* (Montreal: McGill-Queen's University Press 1972).

19 For the material on Shortt's involvement I have relied on the Shortt Papers in Queen's University Archives.

20 Wrong's four pieces were carried in the *Globe* on 9, 11, 12 and 13 February 1918. The first piece concentrated on patronage in the civil service; the second,

on patronage as applied to government contracts (a system that 'terrorizes business' and adds an estimated 20% to the cost of public works); the third piece dealt with the reforms that were necessary, observing that unlike the Canadian Pacific Railway, for example, where 'there is an eternal shifting and changing based upon the test of efficiency' a 'Government cannot have the ready test of the capacity of its servants which is furnished by the balance sheet of a business house, and since this is wanting, there is always need for more careful selection'; the fourth piece helped explain Wrong's other venture, the creation of a public watchdog over any reformed system; for such, public 'support and watchfulness will be required finally to kill this thing.'

21 See *Globe*, 7 March 1917, where Carter's speech is reproduced under the by now familiar heading, 'Government Balks at Patronage Reforms.'

22 The evolution from commissioner to commission in the various provinces is briefly recounted in J.E. Hodgetts and O.P. Dwivedi, *Provincial Governments as Employers: A Survey of Public Personnel Administration in Canada's Provinces* (Montreal: McGill-Queen's University Press 1974), 17ff.

23 *Globe*, 28 February 1918.

24 Ibid., in the same debate defending the differences between the government's measure and the federal legislation.

25 Ibid., 16 April 1919. Hearst's remarks were reported under the heading 'Civil Service Reform Asked: Proudfoot and Dewart clash with Premier Hearst.'

26 Ibid., 12 March 1920. Ferguson was attacking Dewart but clearly intended his 'instructive' remarks to register with the neophyte Premier Drury.

27 Whitney's comment was made during the debate on Rowell's motion for reform, as reported in the *Globe*, 2 April 1912. Hearst was speaking against Dr McQueen's motion for civil service reform (what the *Globe*, reporting the debate on 12 March 1914, referred to as 'an old friend').

28 This distinction is reminiscent of that provided by a leading member of Tammany Hall who, in the context of machine politics in the United States, was prone to speak of 'honest' and 'dishonest' graft.

29 *Globe*, 28 January 1921.

30 See *Journals of the Legislative Assembly*, 1921: 37. The notion itself carries overtones of the populist precepts being promoted by J.J. Morrison whom Howard Ferguson, in the same debate, characterized in his attack on the 'group system of government' as the 'Master of Ontario Administration.'

31 *Globe*, 2 February 1921. After registering his approval of Dr McCutcheon, Drury continued: 'This Government ... can look back and say it has been actuated by one notion in making appointments, and that has been the motive of getting the right man for the right place. We have appointed no one because of previous party connection.' See also *Journals of the Legislative Assembly*, 1922: 263 and 1923: 45.

CHAPTER 11: *Implementing the Administrative Reform Agenda*

1 A brief account of J.M. McCutcheon's career is in *topical*, December 1978, commemorating sixty years of the Civil Service Commission. See also biographical details provided at time of his appointment in the short-lived *Civil Service Bulletin*, December 1918.

2 For assessment of the impact of the scientific management movement on federal civil service reform, see J.E. Hodgetts, William McCloskey, Reginald Whitaker, V. Seymour Wilson, *The Biography of an Institution: The Civil Service Commission of Canada, 1908–1967* (Montreal: McGill-Queen's University Press 1972), especially chapter 4. For developments in the United States, a typical treatment is to be found in O. Glenn Stahl, *Public Personnel Administration* (New York: Harper and Row 1962), a fifth edition of a classic study first produced in 1936 by William E. Mosher and J. Donald Kingsley.

3 On the extensive reliance of most provinces on the consultancy expertise in the United States, see J.E. Hodgetts and O.P. Dwivedi, *Provincial Governments as Employers: A Survey of Public Personnel Administration in Canada's Provinces* (Montreal: McGill-Queen's University Press 1974), 125–35.

4 See 'First Annual Report of the Civil Service Commissioner for Ontario,' *Sessional Papers*, No. 72, 1919.

5 'Second Annual Report ... for Year ending Oct. 31, 1919,' ibid., No. 65, 1920.

6 A recollection of his son, Dr J.W. McCutcheon, in a letter to the author, 7 March 1984: 'After Mitch Hepburn became premier, my father read in the morning paper that he had been fired the previous day.'

7 *Sessional Papers*, No. 91, 1922 (emphasis added).

8 'Fifth Annual Report ... for the Year ending Oct. 31, 1922,' ibid., No. 91, 1923. Addressed to Premier Drury, this was the last the public were to see of the commissioner's reports until the thirtieth report for the year ending 31 March 1947.

9 Fourth Annual Report ...for the Year ending Oct. 31, 1921, ibid. (emphasis added). In his previous report for the year ending 31 Oct. 1920, McCutcheon had made the same observation in defending the need for a pension plan: 'It is now generally conceded that the payment of wages does not discharge an employer's full responsibility toward his workmen. In addition, he must provide suitable working conditions, safeguard their lives and health, and generally interest himself in their welfare.' I am indebted to J.W. McCutcheon (letter of 7 March 1984) for this reference to his father's contribution in Stratford: as organizer of a committee 'which convinced the railway to put its tracks on the other side of the Avon river,' he may be said to have preserved the park where the Shakespeare festival is now held.

10 See *Journals of the Legislative Assembly*, 1880, p. 104. Introduced as Bill 104 by Provincial Secretary Hardy, it received only a first reading before its withdrawal.

11 See Charles M. Johnston, *E.C. Drury, Agrarian Idealist* (Toronto: University of Toronto Press 1986), 128–9.

12 See E.C. Drury, *Farmer Premier, The Memoirs of E.C. Drury* (Toronto: McClelland and Stewart 1966), 112. Drury's recollection may have been somewhat faded for he spoke of working on the measure in the fall of 1921, for legislative approval the next session. There were indeed amendments in both the 1921 and 1922 sessions, but the original pension act was approved in 1920.

13 Extensive use of temporary assistance is recorded in the early reports, many of these temporaries seemingly becoming permanent fixtures by virtue of annual renewals. All of this help, classified as clerk/stenographer, involved only female employees – verification of the impact of the typewriter on employment opportunities for women.

14 See Public Service Superannuation Board, '1st Report for Year ending Oct. 31, 1921,' *Sessional Papers*, No. 79, 1922. Also '2nd Report,' ibid., No. 88, 1923.

15 The pre-confederation Public Service Act for the Province of Canada upon which Ontario's 1878 enactment was based had much the same classification plan, with officers separated from clerks who in turn were divided into four classes. For the first time provision was made for deputy heads.

16 For a brief account of the approach to position classification, see Stahl, *Public Personnel Administration*, chapter 9.

17 See Hodgetts and Dwivedi, *Provincial Governments as Employers*, 129, as reported in an unpublished paper by J.S. Stephen, an officer with the Civil Service Commission, 'The Merit Principle in Classification.'

18 A flavour of the bitter debate over installation of the plan is conveyed in R. MacGregor Dawson, *The Civil Service of Canada* (London: Oxford University Press 1929), 95. Dawson's generally hostile treatment of the work of the outside experts was based on his higher regard for the simplicity of the British classification and more immediately, as he recalled to the author, by unfortunate encounters while doing his doctoral research in Ottawa with the dogmatism of the consultants.

19 See Hodgetts and Dwivedi, *Provincial Governments as Employers*, 129–32.

20 Taylor Cole, *The Canadian Bureaucracy* (Durham, NC: Duke University Press 1949), 195.

21 See Royal Commission on Government Organization, *Report 3, Personnel Management*, chapter 4, 143–4. 'The merit system in many of its current practices, frustrates the attainment of the principle; in its name many absurd procedures are tolerated; the system has become an end in itself.'

22 The legislation of 1947 (11 Geo. VI, c.89) which provided for a three-member commission, placed restrictions on the hitherto free-wheeling use of infinitely renewable 'temporary' appointments by limiting their extension to one year, non-renewable.

23 See Neil McKenty, *Mitch Hepburn*. (Toronto: McClelland and Stewart 1967), 49.

24 John Saywell's *'Just call me Mitch'* (Toronto: University of Toronto Press 1990) has a lively account of the vigorous housecleaning undertaken in the early months of Hepburn's regime. See especially pp. 170–5 and footnote references there to the personal files of the premier.

25 For the dismissals during Hepburn's first year in office, see *Journals of the Legislative Assembly*, 1935. At p. 44: Question: How many civil servants dismissed or resigned since the Hepburn government took over and on whose recommendation? Answer: 1,330; on recommendation of the responsible minister. See also pp. 67–73 (JPs and crown attorneys); p. 87 (Liquor Commission employees); p. 102 (district medical officers of health); p. 103 (Department of Labour); p. 235 (Ontario Hydro). Also brought down on 9 April was the report of a committee on dismissals from government service of ex-servicemen. Many other specific requests received no reply, but the government did respond to queries about the competence of new deputy ministers as well as a question about the number of relatives of cabinet ministers taken on (only two, so it was claimed – the brother-in-law of the attorney general as the latter's private secretary, and the son of the minister of lands and forests as his secretary).

26 As a personal footnote, the author recalls receiving a request to address the Ontario Young Liberals Association on the subject of civil service reform, the invitation coming from C.J. Foster, who was listed on the executive of the association while actively employed as civil service commissioner.

27 See *Journals of the Legislative Assembly*, 1944: 14.

28 An order-in-council dated 25 January 1944 is cited in the commissioner's '28th Report for the Year ending March 31, 1945' as the authority to conduct such continuing examinations for clerk typists and the like. As a commentary on the difficulties of recruiting under wartime conditions, the commissioner reported: 'Because there were more vacancies than applicants it has not been possible to build up any eligibility lists, although numerous examinations were given.'

29 See *Journals of the Legislative Assembly*, 1955–6: 128–9. In the calendar year 1955, 3,728 candidates were recruited in this manner.

CHAPTER 12: *Financial Management and Public Service Accountability*

1 See F.F. Schindeler, *Responsible Government in Ontario* (Toronto: University of Toronto Press 1969), especially chapter 8.

2 This distinction between internal and external control of the public purse parallels the framework used for my analysis of developments in the the Province of Canada. These were carried forward into the new Dominion and were influential in guiding Ontario's lawmakers. See J.E. Hodgetts, *Pioneer Public Service* (Toronto: University of Toronto Press 1956), chapter 7.

3 An up-to-date assessment of the somewhat kaleidoscopic situation precipitated by changes in government following the long unbroken rule of the Conservative

party is to be found in G. White, ed., *The Government and Politics of Ontario*, 4th ed. (Toronto: Nelson, Canada 1990), especially articles by R.A. Loretto and M. McElwain.

4 See 'Report of the Royal Commission on the Financial Position of the Province of Ontario,' *Sessional Papers*, No. 4, 1900: 12.

5 This procedure, characterized today as 'vote netting' (i.e., the legislature appropriating money only for the operating costs not covered by the revenues collected), was a significant heritage from the pre-confederation period and remained to plague the new Dominion as well as Ontario because the Post Office and Customs and Inland Revenue – the 'revenue departments' inherited by the Dominion – continued this practice for some years. See Hodgetts, *Pioneer Public Service*, 99–100.

6 'Report of the Public Accounts Committee,' *Journals of the Legislative Assembly*, 1888, Appendix 2, testimony of S.C. Wood, 54ff.

7 'Report of the Royal Commission on the Financial Position of the Province,' 5, where the commission concluded that 'The tendency of each improvement of system has been to centralize financial control and responsibility more immediately in the Treasurer and his department.'

8 'Report of the Public Accounts Committee,' *Journals of the Legislative Assembly*, 1889, Appendix 1: 56–7.

9 See Auditor Sproule's testimony to the Public Accounts Committee, *Journals of the Legislative Assembly*, 1888, Appendix 2: 10, and ibid., 1902, Appendix 3: 15.

10 See *Journals of the Legislative Assembly*, 1903: 142. Ford was transferred in October 1902 from the Attorney General's Office where he had been private secretary to the minister.

11 Quoted in the lively and informative commemorative history of *Office of the Provincial Auditor: The First Hundred Years* (published by Office of Provincial Auditor August 1986), 12.

12 'Report of the Public Accounts Committee,' *Journals of the Legislative Assembly*, 1930, Appendix 2: 30–1.

13 Ontario Committee on Taxation, *Report: Vol. III, The Provincial Revenue System* (Toronto: Queen's Printer 1967), chapter 25.

14 'Second Report of the Public Accounts Committee,' *Journals of the Legislative Assembly*, 1878, Appendix 1: 73.

15 *The First Hundred Years*, 17, quoting a seasoned employee's recollections.

16 'Return re copies of Orders re Office of Provincial Auditor,' *Sessional Papers*, No. 18, 1869.

17 See 'Report of the Public Accounts Committee,' *Journals of the Legislative Assembly*, 1870–71, Appendix No. 1, Evidence of William Cayley in Appendix B.

18 See 'Report of the Public Accounts Committee,' ibid., 1888, Appendix 2: 10ff.

19 See his remarks before Public Accounts Committee in ibid., 57.

20 Ibid., 59. According to *Sessional Paper*, No. 43, 1894, detailing business transacted: in 1873, 3,400 cheques were issued as against 17,000 in 1892.
21 Ontario, Committee on Government Productivity, Interim Report Number One, 'A Progress Report and Interim Recommendations to the Executive Council,' 15 December 1970: 17.
22 See *The First Hundred Years*, 11, 13.
23 See '2nd Report of the Public Accounts Committee, Jan. 22, 1869,' *Journals of the Legislative Assembly*, 1868–9, Appendix 4; also ibid., 1870–71, Appendix 1.
24 Ibid., 1892, Appendix 1: 25.
25 Ibid.: 26.
26 *Globe*, 11 March 1909 for an editorial voicing the opposition's suspicions.
27 'Report of the Public Accounts Committee,' *Journals of the Legislative Assembly*, 1915, Appendix 1: 77.
28 14 Geo. VI, c.5. See ibid., 1949, Appendix 1. The whole of this report represents an important contribution from the Public Accounts Committee after a number of years when it was rather inactive.
29 21 Eliz. II, c.3. Only by reading this act in conjunction with an act to amend the Audit Act (20 Eliz. II [1st Session] 1971, c.54) can one infer that a transfer has been made, in that the auditor is directed to supervise the preparation of the public accounts for 1970–1 but not beyond, when the treasurer is to take over.
30 Quoted in *The First Hundred Years*, 19.
31 25-26 Eliz. II, c.61.

Epilogue: Beyond the Formative Years

1 See Committee on Government Productivity, 'Report Number Nine,' dated March 1973 but presented October 1972, dealing with 'The Ministry Concept.' For analysis of the proposals by the executive officer of the committee, see J.D. Fleck, 'Restructuring the Government of Ontario,' *Canadian Public Administration* 16, no. 1 (Spring 1973), 55–68. For critical analysis see, in the same issue, comments of J.R. Mallory, and in ibid., 18, no. 2 (Summer 1975), K. Bryden, 'Executive and Legislature in Ontario: A Case Study of Governmental Reform,' 189–216.
2 An early view of the Privy Council Office is provided by Arnold Heeney, 'Cabinet Government in Canada: Some Recent Developments in the Machinery of the Central Executive' *Canadian Journal of Economics and Political Science*, 12 (1946), 282ff. For a view some twenty-five years later by a successor incumbent secretary, see Gordon Robertson, 'The Changing Role of the Privy Council Office,' *Canadian Public Administration* 14, no. 4 (Winter 1971), 487–508. An early assessment of the emergence of the Office of Prime Minister is to be found in Thomas D'Aquino, 'The Prime Minister's Office: Catalyst or

Cabal? Aspects of the Development of the Office in Canada and Some Thoughts
about its Future,' *Canadian Public Administration* 7, no. 1 (Spring 1974), 55–79.
3 The classic account of the operation of the cabinet is F. F. Schindeler,
Responsible Government in Ontario (Toronto: University of Toronto Press 1969),
chapter 3. A recent updated assessment is to be found in Edward E. Stewart,
Cabinet Government in Ontario: A View from the Inside (The Edward Dunlop
Lectures, published by the Institute for Research in Public Policy, Halifax 1989).
As secretary to the cabinet and clerk of the Executive Council, Stewart
exemplified the historical combination of the two roles and observes in his first
lecture that 'the growth of Cabinet and the creation of new or revised Cabinet
posts is a story in its own right and tracing the evolution of Cabinet organization
in Ontario, in some ways, parallels the growth and development of the Province
itself' (p. 9). For a first-rate analysis of the role of the prime minister in shaping
the changes to the central offices that serve his/her varied needs, see Peter
Aucoin, 'Organizational Change in the Machinery of Canadian Government:
From Rational Management to Brokerage Politics,' *Canadian Journal of Politics*
19, no. 1 (March 1986), 3–27.
4 Opposition criticism of the expansion of ministerial offices produced the
following statistics, as reported in the *Globe and Mail*, 20 April 1993. In the
Premier's Office, a staff of fifty-three, up from thirty-seven in the predecessor's office. An estimated 312 political assistants were working in
twenty-seven ministerial offices, for a combined salary budget of over $15
million.
5 See Ontario, Committee on the Organization of Government in Ontario, *Report*
(Toronto 1959).
6 This internal report was prompted by the recommendations of the Committee on
Government Productivity which in its 'Report Number Nine' dealt with
'Agencies.' The advertisement for candidates for vacancies on the boards of the
ABCs appeared in the Toronto press and noted that information was available in
public libraries throughout the province.
7 See Canada, Royal Commission on Financial Management and Accountability,
Final Report (Ottawa: March 1979), 'Part IV. Crown Agencies,' and Australia,
Royal Commission on Autralian Government Administration, *Report* (Canberra:
Australian Government Publishing Service 1976), 81–95.
8 For convincing evidence to support the prognosis in the text, see 'Managing
Human Resources in the Ontario Public Service,' March 1986, a review
commissioned by the Honourable Elinor Caplan, chairman, Management Board
of Cabinet (known as the Moher Report after its chairman, W.P. Moher, manager
of executive development and organization, Imperial Oil Limited). While paying
lip service to the principle of an independent commission as a protector of the
merit system, the recommendations call for further dilution of the Civil Service
Commission's responsibilities in the cause of enabling deputy ministers and

senior managers to 'take the lead in developing human resource strategies and policies and practices.'

9 See Sandfield Macdonald's comments in the *Globe*, 11 January 1868. For later negative assessment, see *The First Hundred Years*, 19: 'Although Ontario had a Public Accounts Committee since 1868, it did not start to function with any degree of force or independence until the 1960's.'

10 The evolution of the idea of the ombudsman in Canada and abroad is described by one of its strongest proponents, Donald C. Rowat, *The Ombudsman Plan: The Worldwide Spread of an Idea*, 2nd ed. (Lanham, Maryland: University Press of America 1986).

11 For these changes, see *Journals of the Legislative Assembly*, 1960: 58–63; 1968–9: 218–19; 1971: 10–12.

Index

accountable warrants, 51

Accounts. *See* Public Accounts

administrative discretion, 36–7, 50–1, 143–5, 158–9, 186, 238–9

administrative mode, 24–43 *passim*, 73, 110, 151–2; enabling (facilitative), 10, 19, 25–8, 35, 110, 129; hands-on (operative), 10, 17–18, 22–3, 42–3, 110–39 *passim*; regulatory, 29–42

administrative reform: legal authority for, 168–75; movement, 176–83 *passim*; and prohibition, 176, 183; in Dominion, 179–82; and scientific management, 191–2; platform, 192–7, 214, 244

advisory councils, 239

agencies (ABCs), 56–7, 140–3, 146, 154, 237–41, 249

Agricultural College, 17–19, 26, 89, 98, 104

Agricultural Development Board, Ontario, 165

agricultural marketing boards, 20, 129, 165–7

agricultural representatives, 129

Agriculture, Board of, 19, 47, 96; commissioner of, 6, 18–19, 48–9; enabling administrative mode in, 25–7; Department of, 26–7, 48, 83, 126–30, 231, 241; centralization in, 27, 83, 111, 127–9; employees in, 89, 91, 98, 107; satellites of, 126–7. *See also* Bureau of Agriculture

agriculture, societies and associations in, 26, 128–9

Amusement Tax, 218

Anderson, John, 116

appeal tribunals, 239–40

appropriations, 219–21

Armstrong, J.S.P., 138

Armstrong, S.A., 102, 108

Arthur Young and Company, 191, 205

assistant deputy minister, 129–30, 241

Attorney General, Office of, 6, 9, 13, 46, 73–5, 80; employees in, 87, 91–2, 98–100, 107; connected with Executive Council, 90, 98–100, 135–6

audit: Act (1886), 220, 223–5; Act (1906), 228; Act (1909), 226–7; Act (1950), 228; Act (1977), 225, 229–30, 248; as regulatory instrument, 29; of Hydro, 149–50; of revenues, 217–19; versus comptrol, 221–30. *See also* Provincial Auditor, Office of

Australia, 37, 238

automobile, impact on administration, 60–1, 81, 83, 118–20

Christie, Robert, 102
Citizenship Branch, 126
Civil List, 169
civil servants. *See* public servants
civil service. *See* Public Service Act;
   administrative reform; merit system;
   patronage; spoils system
Civil Service Assembly of the United
   States and Canada, 179, 191, 202
Civil Service Association (Ontario),
   187, 194, 197, 209
Civil Service Commission: proposals
   for, 176–88; Dominion, 183–4, 205,
   207; decline of, as central personnel
   agency, 210–13, 244–7
civil service commissioner, 79, 85, 137;
   created for Ontario, 178–88; versus
   commission, 179, 183–4, 186–7, 210,
   212–13
Civil Service Research Centre, 181
Clancy, James, 149–50, 225–7, 229, 248
classification plan, 86–7, 172, 192,
   201–9
Clergue, Francis H., 69
clientele organization, 117, 126–30,
   164–7, 239–40
Cochrane, Frank, 66, 69, 113, 155
Cody, Henry J., 117
collective bargaining, 196, 245–7
colonization, 126–7; and roads, 14, 118,
   127, 217. *See also* immigration
Colquhoun, A.H.U., 107, 133
commissioner of agriculture and public
   works, 6, 47–8, 58, 95. *See also*
   Agriculture; Public Works
commissioner of Crown lands. *See*
   Crown lands; Lands, Mines and
   Forests
commissioner of public works. *See*
   Public Works
commissions of inquiry, 11–12. *See*
   also royal commissions

Committee on Government Productivity, Ontario, 223–4, 229–30, 234–5,
   245
Committee on Organization of Government in Ontario, 209, 237–8, 249
Committee on Public Accounts. *See*
   public accounts
Committee (Smith) on Taxation, 219
comptrol, 219–24. *See also* audit,
   expenditure management
corporation, public, 62, 71–2, 146–7,
   150, 163–5, 239
Correctional Services, Departmnent of,
   233
Cotnam, Harvey, 220–1, 228–9
Council of Public Instruction, 17, 50–8;
   reintroduced, 131–2
counting machine, 78
courts. *See* justice, administration of
Crooks, Adam, 53, 59
Crown lands: commissioner of, 6–7,
   21–2, 111; as source of revenue, 22,
   30, 216–7; employees in, 88, 91–4,
   107; Department of, 112–15. *See also*
   Lands, Mines and Forests
Crozier, J.A.G., 94
Cudney, R.J., 125–6

defalcations, 100–1, 216, 218, 223–4
DeLury, A.T. 117
departments: legal basis for, 44–8;
   integration of, 110–30 *passim*;
   postwar growth of, 223–41. *See also*
   individual titles
deputy minister: as assistant commissioner, 47, 61; emergence of, 54–5,
   87, 96, 100, 111; double-barrelled,
   112–14, 116, 122, 130–4, 241
Dewart, H.H., 184, 186–7, 200
Drew, George, 112, 125, 127, 138, 212
Drury, E.C.: on financial scandal, 109;
   on pensions, 109, 197–8; and welfare

THE ONTARIO HISTORICAL STUDIES SERIES

Peter Oliver, G. *Howard Ferguson: Ontario Tory* (1977)

J.M.S. Careless, ed., *The Pre-Confederation Premiers: Ontario Government Leaders, 1841–1867* (1980)

Charles W. Humphries, *'Honest Enough to be Bold': The Life and Times of Sir James Pliny Whitney* (1985)

Charles M. Johnston, *E.C. Drury: Agrarian Idealist* (1986)

A.K. McDougall, *John P. Robarts: His Life and Government* (1986)

Roger Graham, *Old Man Ontario: Leslie M. Frost* (1990)

John T. Saywell, *'Just call me Mitch': The Life of Mitchell F. Hepburn* (1991)

A. Margaret Evans, *Sir Oliver Mowat* (1992)

Joseph Schull, *Ontario since 1867* (McClelland and Stewart 1978)

Joseph Schull, *L'Ontario depuis 1867* (McClelland and Stewart 1987)

Olga B. Bishop, Barbara I. Irwin, Clara G. Miller, eds., *Bibliography of Ontario History, 1867–1976: Cultural, Economic, Political, Social*, 2 volumes (1980)

Christopher Armstrong, *The Politics of Federalism: Ontario's Relations with the Federal Government, 1867–1942* (1981)

David Gagan, *Hopeful Travellers: Families, Land and Social Change in Mid-Victorian Peel County, Canada West* (1981)

Robert M. Stamp, *The Schools of Ontario, 1876–1976* (1982)

R. Louis Gentilcore and C. Grant Head, *Ontario's History in Maps* (1984)

K.J. Rea, *The Prosperous Years: The Economic History of Ontario, 1939–1975* (1985)

Ian M. Drummond, *Progress without Planning: The Economic History of Ontario from Confederation to the Second World War* (1987)

John Webster Grant, *A Profusion of Spires: Religion in Nineteenth-Century Ontario* (1988)

Susan E. Houston and Alison Prentice, *Schooling and Scholars in Nineteenth-Century Ontario* (1988)

Ann Saddlemyer, ed., *Early Stages: Theatre in Ontario, 1800–1914* (1990)

W.J. Keith, *Literary Images of Ontario* (1992)

Cornelius Jaenen, ed., *Les Franco-Ontariens* (Les Presses de l'Université d'Ottawa 1993)

Douglas McCalla, *Planting the Province: The Economic History of Upper Canada, 1784–1870* (1993)

R.D. Gidney and W.P.J. Millar, *Professional Gentlemen: The Professions in Nineteenth-Century Ontario* (1994)

A.B. McKillop, *Matters of Mind: The University in Ontario, 1791–1951* (1994)

Edward S. Rogers and Donald B. Smith, eds., *Aboriginal Ontario: Historical Perspectives on the First Nations* (Dundurn 1994)

James Struthers, *The Limits of Affluence: Welfare in Ontario, 1920–1970* (1994)

J.E. Hodgetts, *From Arm's Length to Hands-On: The Formative Years of Ontario's Public Service, 1867–1940* (1995)